THE LIFE AND WITNESS OF DAVID

THE LIFE
AND WITNESS
OF DAVID

Larry R. Helyer

CASCADE *Books* • Eugene, Oregon

THE LIFE AND WITNESS OF DAVID

Copyright © 2020 Author Name. All rights reserved. Except for brief quotations in critical publications or reviews, no part of this book may be reproduced in any manner without prior written permission from the publisher. Write: Permissions, Wipf and Stock Publishers, 199 W. 8th Ave., Suite 3, Eugene, OR 97401.

Cascade Books
An Imprint of Wipf and Stock Publishers
199 W. 8th Ave., Suite 3
Eugene, OR 97401

www.wipfandstock.com

PAPERBACK ISBN: 978-1-5326-9132-4
HARDCOVER ISBN: 978-1-5326-9133-1
EBOOK ISBN: 978-1-5326-9134-8

Cataloguing-in-Publication data:

Names: Last, First. | other names in same manner

Title: Book title : book subtitle / Author Name.

Description: Eugene, OR: Cascade Books, 2020 | Includes bibliographical references.

Identifiers: ISBN 978-1-5326-9132-4 (paperback) | ISBN 978-1-5326-9133-1 (hardcover) | ISBN 978-1-5326-9134-8 (ebook)

Subjects: LCSH: subject | subject | subject | subject

Classification: BS580.D3 H45 2020 (print) | BS580.D3 (ebook)

Manufactured in the U.S.A.   DECEMBER 7, 2020

To my dear sister Linda, who not only shares
a family history but also a like precious faith.

And in memory of my aunt Nan Wilson,
who made the stories of David come alive.

1 Samuel 1 to 1 Kings 2 is one of the most astounding pieces of narrative
that has come down to us from the ancient world.

—ROBERT ALTER, *THE DAVID STORY*

Something crucial in human history begins with the biblical figure of
King David. He is the original alpha male, the kind of man whose virile
ambition always drives him to the head of the pack.
He is the first superstar.

—JONATHAN KIRSCH,
KING DAVID: THE REAL LIFE OF THE MAN WHO RULED ISRAEL

The David story immerses us in a reality that embraces the entire range
of humanness, stretching from the deep interior of our souls to the
farthest reach of our imaginations. No other biblical story has this range
to it, showing the many dimensions of height, depth, breadth, and length
of human experience as a person comes alive before God—aware of God,
responsive to God.

—EUGENE H. PETERSON, *LEAP OVER A WALL*

CONTENTS

PREFACE

MY FIRST INTRODUCTION TO the life of David took place in a small Sunday school class in Kent, Oregon. My aunt Nan was a gifted Bible teacher who brought to life the stories of David. One of the assignments she gave us third, fourth, and fifth graders was to make a biblical scroll containing illustrated episodes of David's life. So, I took a broom handle from which I cut two sticks and scotch-taped a roll of paper several feet long to my improvised scroll handles. I then sectioned the paper into various episodes of David's life. Each episode consisted of a drawing accompanied by Scripture illustrating the story. Included were David's encounter with a lion and bear while shepherding his father's sheep, his slaying of the Philistine giant Goliath, his covenant with Jonathan, his opportunity to kill Saul in the desert, among others. David was my hero, and I imagined myself carrying out similar exploits.

These childhood impressions were fleshed out as I grew older, especially when I studied Bible as an undergraduate and in graduate school. Archaeology, cultural backgrounds, Hebrew language, hermeneutics (the art of interpretation), history, and theology added nuance and perspective to the stories I had loved as a child. Then, in 1968–69 came the opportunity of a lifetime—a State Department grant in Middle Eastern Studies at the American Institute of Holy Land Studies in Jerusalem, Israel. My wife and I spent a wonderful year studying the Bible in the land of the Bible—a truly transformational experience that deepened our love for Scripture and our desire to share its truths with others. We visited sites where David was born, roamed, and reigned—exhilarating stuff!

Ten years in the pastorate helped me close the gap between the then and the now and to relate Scripture to the lives of parishioners who desired to hear God's Word and discern his will for their lives. Then followed thirty rewarding years teaching the Bible to undergraduates at Taylor University in Upland, Indiana. In my opinion, I had the best job in the world!

Now in retirement in Mount Juliet, Tennessee, another serendipity—the opportunity to teach Bible classes to eager, adult learners at Providence UMC. I join David in thanksgiving: "The boundary lines have fallen for me in pleasant places; surely I have a delightful inheritance" (Ps 16:6).

So, why have I devoted the last couple of years to the life and witness of David? The short answer is because he "still speaks, even though he is dead" (Heb 11:4). In sacred Scripture we have an inspired record of a man who literally changed his world, a man who also wrote songs inspired by the Holy Spirit that have communicated God's Word to literally the entire world. The witness of David remains timely and transformative. Those who have ears to hear will certainly hear God's voice speak to them, in whatever circumstances they find themselves, as they read the story about the man and read the songs written by the man—a man after God's own heart.

The quest to retell the life of David has been personally rewarding. Many new details and insights have emerged and enriched my theological understanding of redemptive history. I invite the reader to share in the fruit of my labors. "I will praise you, LORD, with all my heart; I will tell of all your wonderful deeds" (Ps 9:1).

ACKNOWLEDGMENTS

WHILE IT IS TRUE that "of making many books there is no end" (Eccl 12:12), it is also true that the writing of books is a communal effort. Many mentors, parishioners, and former students have contributed to the writing of this book. First, I wish to pay tribute to my very first Bible teacher, my aunt Nan. What a blessing to have had such an inspirational teacher at a formative stage in my life. Her memory is indeed a blessing!

Another very significant person was my dear mother, who in her own right was a very capable Bible teacher in our Sunday school and Vacation Bible School programs. She saw to it that I didn't play hooky and completed my Sunday school lessons. Studying the life of David, I have come to realize the significant role DNA played in shaping my teaching career—I inherited genes from both my parents that have served me well. May their memory be blessed!

After college and seminary, I pastored two churches, one in Oregon and the other in California. Many hours went into sermon preparation and mid-week Bible studies. The feedback and encouragement from those dear saints meant more to me than they will ever know. And the long hours pondering the text paid dividends later during a thirty-year teaching career in the biblical studies department at Taylor University.

Which brings me to one of the most valuable resources I've been privileged to tap into—the inquiring minds of motivated undergraduate students taking my classes in biblical literature. The genius of the Jewish Yeshiva educational model features dialogue and dispute between two students who study Talmud and Torah together, putting into practice the principle of Proverbs 27:17: "As iron sharpens iron, so one person sharpens another." Over the years, I've had many students who sharpened my understanding of Scripture with provocative questions and profound observations. A heartfelt thanks to each and every one! They too are of blessed memory.

My beloved wife has read and edited drafts of this, my eighth book. Her corrections and suggestions have greatly improved the wording, spelling, and content. "She speaks with wisdom, and faithful instruction is on her tongue" (Prov 31:26).

Finally, another shout-out to the Cascade Books team for their congeniality and expertise. Thanks, Rodney Clapp, for your editorial oversight. I appreciate the niche you folks fill in the publishing world. Many blessings in this age and the age to come!

LIST OF ABBREVIATIONS

Biblical Texts and Versions

ESV	English Standard Version
HCSB	Holman Christian Standard Bible
KJV	King James Version
LXX	Septuagint
MT	Masoretic Text of the Hebrew Bible/Old Testament
NASB	New American Standard Bible
NET	New English Translation
NJPS	Tanakh. The Holy Scripture: The New JPS translation
NRSV	New Revised Standard Version of the Bible
NT	New Testament
OT	Old Testament
REB	Revised English Bible
TNIV	The New International Version
Vg	Vulgate

Other Ancient Texts

ANET *Ancient Near Eastern Texts Relating to the Old Testament.* 3rd ed., with suppl. Edited by J. B. Pritchard. Princeton: Princeton University Press, 1969.

Ant.	Josephus, *Antiquities of the Jews*
b.	Babylonian Talmud
Haer.	Irenaeus, *Adversus haereses* (*Against Heresies*)
Hist. eccl.	Eusebius, *Ecclesiastical History*
J. W.	Josephus, *Jewish War*
m.	Mishnah
Tg.	Targum
Sir	Sirach
Yoma	*Yoma*

Secondary Sources

AB	Anchor Bible
ABD	*The Anchor Bible Dictionary.* 6 vols. Edited by David Noel Freedman. New York: Doubleday, 1992.
BAR	*Biblical Archaeology Review*
BASOR	*Bulletin of the American Society of Oriental Studies*
BEB	*Baker Encyclopedia of the Bible.* 2 vols. Edited by Walter A. Elwell. Grand Rapids: Baker, 1988.
BSac	*Bibliotheca Sacra*
DSB	Daily Study Bible
EBC	Expositors Bible Commentary
IDB	*The Interpreter's Dictionary of the Bible.* 4 vols. Edited by G. A. Buttrick. Nashville: Abingdon, 1962.
IEJ	*Israel Exploration Journal*
ISBE	*International Standard Bible Encyclopedia.* 4 vols. Edited by G. Bromiley. Grand Rapids: Eerdmans, 1979–88.
JETS	*Journal of the Evangelical Theological Society*
JSOT	*Journal for the Study of the Old Testament*
NIVAC	New International Version Application Commentary
NIDB	*New Interpreter's Dictionary of the Bible.* 5 vols. Edited by Katharine Doob Sakenfeld et al. Nashville: Abingdon, 2006–2009.

TNIVSB   *The New International Version Study Bible*. Edited by Kenneth L. Barker et al. Grand Rapids: Zondervan, 2006.

TNTC   Tyndale New Testament Commentaries

TOTC   Tyndale Old Testament Commentaries

WJT   *Westminster Journal of Theology*

ZPEB   *Zondervan Pictorial Encyclopedia of the Bible*. 5 vols. Edited by Merrill C. Tenney. Grand Rapids: Zondervan, 1975.

1

CLIMBING INTO DAVID'S FAMILY TREE

It's good to know where you come from. It makes you what you are
today. It's DNA, it's in your blood.

—ALEXANDER MCQUEEN

To FULLY APPRECIATE AND understand a superstar personality, one must investigate his or her roots. Ancestry and family history play important roles in shaping us, even if we are quite oblivious to their influence. Heredity silently but powerfully influences who we are. Though unaware of it at the time, David was destined for greatness. Not because he was born into an aristocratic and wealthy family like Alexander the Great; he was not. Nor was his father one of the movers and shakers of his day—he wasn't even on the radar of the powers that be at the time. In fact, we learn that when David went out to confront Goliath, neither King Saul nor his commander, Abner, even knew who David's father was.[1]

JESSE'S GENEALOGY

So, who was David's father? Jesse was an Ephrathite landowner who lived near the village of Bethlehem and, like his neighbors, owned sheep.[2] But

1. 1 Sam 17:55–58.

2. The Bible seems to identify Ephrathah and Bethlehem (Gen 35:19; Ruth 4:11). Ephrathah is probably a clan name, and Bethlehem a village within the clan territory.

Jesse also descended from one of the most powerful tribes in the ancient federation of Israel, the tribe of Judah. In fact, one of Jesse's direct ancestors, Nashon, served as a distinguished Judahite civil and military leader, being the first to offer contributions for the newly installed tabernacle.[3]

Caleb ben Jephunneh

Also found in the family tree was a certain Caleb ben (son of) Jephunneh,[4] a man with remarkable faith and courage.[5] His complete trust in the Yahweh's promises and power is narrated in the story of the twelve spies sent to spy out the land of Canaan and report back their findings to the people of Israel.[6] Caleb and the celebrated Joshua were the only two spies to urge the people to proceed with the invasion. When the majority report emphasized the formidable opposition they faced, Caleb "silenced the people before Moses and said, 'We should go up and take possession of the land, for we can certainly do it'" (Num 13:30). But the people were disheartened and rebelled. They refused to believe that Yahweh could or would enable them to conquer the Canaanite inhabitants.

Caleb and Joshua tried valiantly to dissuade them from their refusal: "Do not be afraid of the people of the land, because we will devour them. Their protection is gone, but the LORD is with us. Do not be afraid of them" (Num 14:9). Their impassioned plea fell on deaf ears: "But the whole assembly talked about stoning them" (Num 14:10). Caleb's courageous confidence re-echoes in young David's challenge to the Philistine champion Goliath: "This day the LORD will deliver you into my hands, and I'll strike you down

---

The Ephrathah clan is named after a woman, an unusual occurrence that testifies to her status and influence in the clan (1 Sam 17:12; Ruth 1:2). See Lucker, "Ephrathah," 557-58.

3. Num 2:3; 1 Chr 2:10; Num 7:12.

4. Num 13:6.

5. Whether Caleb ben Jephunneh (Num 32:12; Josh 14:6) is the same person as Caleb of Hezron (1 Chr 2:18) is debated because the former is identified as a Kenizzite. Some suggest that this non-Israelite clan (cf. Gen 15:19) was absorbed into and eventually reckoned as belonging to Judah. On the other hand, it may be that Kenizzite is a gentilic of Kenaz (i.e., a tribal designation), in which case one could argue that Caleb ben Jephunneh descended from Caleb of Hezron. For further discussion on the complexities of sorting out the identity of the two Calebs, see Fretz and Panitz, "Caleb," 808–10; and Hasel, "Caleb," 573–74.

6. Yahweh is the personal name of the God of Israel and in most English translations is rendered as LORD in small caps. In this book, I will use Yahweh except when quoting from the English Bible, where LORD is used. The name Yahweh probably means something like the self-existent one. See Exod 3:14.

and cut off your head" (1 Sam 17:46). Another interesting connection is the fact that both Caleb and David were threatened with stoning by their dispirited kinsmen following devastating setbacks.[7]

The stories of Caleb ben Jephunneh don't end with the aborted invasion of Canaan. Yahweh promised Caleb and Joshua that because of their faith they would live to enter the Promised Land. That promise was kept. Remarkably, at age eighty-five, Caleb led the attack on the dreaded Anakites (giants) of Hebron and drove them out. He then enlarged his inheritance by taking the city of Debir lying south of Hebron.[8]

Oral traditions were an essential aspect of life among middle eastern peoples (they still are among traditional, non-westernized families). The exploits of their ancestor Caleb were almost certainly recited and celebrated among the clans and families of Judah. I can easily imagine Jesse regaling his sons around the fire with the heroic deeds of Caleb ben Jephunneh, consciously and subconsciously influencing their thinking and behavior.

In fact, David probably imitated the fearless warrior Caleb while tending the family sheep in the Wilderness of Judah. Recall how young David described his exploits to Saul: "When a lion or bear came and carried off a sheep from the flock, I went after it, struck it and rescued the sheep from its mouth. When it turned on me, I seized it by its hair, struck it and killed it" (1 Sam 17:34–35). In short, young David acted the part of the mighty warrior Caleb from the tribe of Judah.

Judah the Patriarch

But there is more to David's ancestry than that; in fact, a lot more. Climbing higher into David's ancestral tree reveals more surprises. Today, the unraveling of the genetic code and its DNA sequences has opened a new day in genealogy. Each somatic cell of our bodies contains the total genetic information unique to us, enabling the tracing of one's ancestry into the mists of antiquity. I recently submitted a saliva sample to the genographic project of *National Geographic*. The results traced my regional ancestry back five-hundred to ten-thousand years ago, with about 72 percent of my DNA coming from northwestern Europe. If David's DNA could be analyzed, I think a surprising fact would come to light. He inherited some Canaanite DNA. The basis for this conjecture lies in a story, recorded in Genesis 38,

---

7. 1 Sam 3:6.

8. The actual capture of Debir is attributed to Caleb's nephew, Othniel, who also received as a reward Caleb's daughter, Aksah, in marriage (Josh 15:13–19; Judg 1:11–15).

involving Judah, the grand patriarch of this proud tribe. As they say, we all have skeletons in our family closet, and Judah certainly had his share.

As it turns out, Judah disgraced himself in his treatment of his youngest brother, Joseph, the darling of his father Jacob. It was Judah who urged his brothers to sell Joseph to slave traders going to Egypt rather than kill him.[9] To his credit, he later acknowledged his guilt to Joseph.[10] Later, Judah went a step further and offered to take Benjamin's place when Grand Vizier Joseph's missing silver cup turned up in Benjamin's sack—secretly planted by Joseph's servants at his orders.[11] Worth noting in this narrative is the leading role Judah played as spokesperson for the brothers, even though he was not the firstborn.[12] More than that, he took responsibility for the welfare of the youngest son, Benjamin.

Judah's actions foreshadowed greatness. Indeed, Jacob's deathbed blessing prophesied the future preeminence of the tribe of Judah, resonating with messianic overtones.[13] The patriarch prophesied the coming of a great descendent of Judah who will possess the scepter and ruler's staff and to whom the nations will be obedient.[14] One hears in these words a preview of the grand throne room scene in the book of Revelation featuring "the Lion of the tribe of Judah, the root of David" (Rev 5:5). Enigmatically, the prophecy further proclaims, "he will wash his garments in wine" (Gen 49:11), in my view, a veiled reference to the blood of "the Lamb of God, who takes away the sin of the world!" (John 1:29).[15]

Not long after this dramatic (and traumatic!) episode, another skeleton comes to light. Contrary to custom, Judah separates from his brothers and stays at Adullam with Hirah, the Canaanite.[16] Deviating even further from patriarchal preferences, he marries a Canaanite woman, the daughter of

9. Gen 37:26–27.

10. Gen 42.

11. Joseph shrewdly framed Benjamin to see what his brothers would do when, once again, a favored son was faced with lifetime servitude in Egypt—just like Joseph himself had experienced when these same brothers callously turned their backs on him. I borrowed the anachronistic title Grand Vizier from Ottoman times in order to describe Joseph's high office. Prime Minister would also be appropriate (cf. Gen 41:41–43).

12. Gen 43:3; 44:18–34.

13. Gen 49:8–10.

14. Gen 49:10.

15. See Rev 5:6; 7:14; 19:13. Note that the Lion of Revelation 5 is paradoxically also "a Lamb looking as if it had been slain" (Rev 5:6).

16. Adullam was known for its cave and great rock, which apparently served as a stronghold. David will make use of it as a hideout after his escape from Saul and perhaps as a stronghold during a war against the Philistines (1 Sam 22:1; 2 Sam 23:13; 1 Chr 11:15; Mic 1:15).

Shua. Intermarriage with Canaanites was something abhorred by the family of Abraham and Isaac.[17] Then, compounding his transgressions, Judah fathers two sons, Perez and Zerah, through his Canaanite daughter-in-law, Tamar.[18]

The Tamar episode is not one of the highlights in the life of the patriarch. Judah fails at a number of points to be a bearer of the Abrahamic blessing to all peoples. In fact, Tamar the Canaanite demonstrates more integrity than Judah, a fact he forthrightly acknowledges.[19] Whether Tamar believed in the God of the patriarchs is not stated. I think she did. If so, she was a forerunner of two other Gentile women, the Canaanite Rahab and the Moabitess Ruth, who cast their lot with the God of Israel. As it turns out, all three of these Gentile women are in the direct line of Jesus the Messiah.[20]

Truly, there is a wideness in God's mercy, and throughout the OT we encounter Gentiles who by faith are incorporated into the people of God, anticipations of the great influx of Gentiles in the post-Pentecost era of redemptive history.[21] The upshot of Judah's involvement with Tamar is that Perez is a direct ancestor of David. That Tamar was not discretely deleted from Judah's family tree is reflected in a blessing uttered over Boaz and his new bride, Ruth: "Through the offspring the LORD gives you by this young woman, may your family be like that of Perez, whom Tamar bore to Judah" (Ruth 4:12).

Achan the Zerahite

Another embarrassment crops up in an ancestor named Achan from the Zerahite clan of Judah (Zerah was the brother of Perez). This man succumbed to the lure of loot in the aftermath of the sack of Jericho.[22] Against explicit orders not to take any of the things devoted to Yahweh's treasury, Achan stole "a beautiful robe from Babylonia, two hundred shekels of silver and a bar of gold weighing fifty shekels" (Josh 7:21). The result was an unexpected setback in the attack on Ai. Once the culprit was discovered, Achan

17. Gen 24:3; 26:34-35; 28:1, 8.

18. The later Mosaic Law prohibited a man from having sex with his daughter-in-law, even after her husband had died (Lev 18:15). The penalty for both parties was death (Lev 20:12).

19. Gen 38:26.

20. Matt 1:3-5.

21. On the theological significance of the Tamar story, see Matthewson, "Genesis 38."

22. Josh 7.

and his immediate family paid the ultimate price, being stoned to death at a place called Achor.[23] Achan's failure at Jericho replays in King David's lure of lust in his shameful adultery with Bathsheba and his prideful attempt to number the people of Israel. We will revisit these moral meltdowns in some detail later.

Hur

On the positive side, there were two Judahite ancestors who stood tall and stood out among their peers. One was named Hur. This man experienced some of the most dramatic events in the birth of the nation. His status is evidenced by the fact that he served as a close adviser and associate to Moses.[24] The most noteworthy episode involving Hur was an Amalekite surprise attack upon the Hebrews during their encampment in the Sinai wilderness. Aaron and Hur stood alongside Moses and upheld his hands in intercession to Yahweh for the people of Israel so that they could repel the attack.[25] Moses had such confidence in his leadership ability he appointed him and Aaron as judges during his absence on Mount Sinai.[26] Hur's stalwart spirituality left a lasting legacy and resurfaces in the spiritual ardor of King David.[27]

Bezalel ben Uri

Another outstanding Judahite, a grandson of Hur, was a man of extraordinary artistic ability. His name was Bezalel and his claim to fame lay in his exquisite fashioning of the furniture, utensils, vessels, and tapestries of the Tent of Meeting during the wilderness wanderings.[28] If doubts be entertained about how he could have possibly acquired the requisite skills, one needs to remember that the Hebrews had only recently escaped from Egypt. Bezalel probably received his training as an apprentice and craftsman in Egypt, one of the great cultural centers of the ancient world. In fact,

23. Josh 7:26.

24. Later Jewish tradition says Hur married Miriam, Moses' sister (Josephus, *Ant.* iii.2.4 [54]).

25. Exod 17:8–13.

26. Exod 24:14.

27. 2 Sam 6:13–16.

28. Exod 31:1–11.

the Tutankhamun exhibit features decorative pieces that probably resemble furniture in the wilderness tabernacle.[29]

My point is this: creative genius is something inherited as part of the genetic code—of course inherent ability must be developed through instruction and diligent practice. It thus comes as no surprise that David's artistic side displays itself in multiple ways. He was both a gifted musician and songwriter as well as a craftsman of musical instruments. We later learn that much of the temple hymnody was the product of his literary and musical genius. The legacy of David was extraordinary, and we will devote an entire chapter summarizing his many contributions to the heritage of Israel.

Jabez

One more Judahite merits honorable mention. Named Jabez by his mother, an unusual though not unprecedented occurrence in a strongly patriarchal culture, his name sounds similar to the Hebrew word for pain and was chosen because Jabez' birth was very painful. This, however, is not why the Chronicler singles this man out for special praise. It was Jabez' character that set him apart from his peers: "Jabez was more honorable than his brothers" (1 Chr 4:9). Not only was he an honorable man, he was not afraid to ask great things of God, including personal blessing, safety, and freedom from pain: "Oh, that you would bless me and enlarge my territory! Let your hand be with me, and keep me from harm so that I will be free from pain" (1 Chr 4:10).

Although the request is daring, the response is extraordinary: "And God granted his request" (1 Chr 4:10). One hears in the bold requests of Jabez many similar requests rising from the prayers of David too numerous to list. Though not without his flaws, David was an honorable man who cried out for great things from the true and living God. His story may have inspired the Baptist missionary William Carey to utter this famous exhortation: "Expect great things from God. Attempt great things for God."

Enough has been said to illustrate my point about the powerful influence of heredity. Episodes in the PBS series *Finding Your Roots* with Dr. Henry Louis Gates Jr. illustrate this in amazing ways. In David we see a man like Caleb, a warrior and leader who inspired other men to follow and serve him—even die for him. We also see a man possessed of the Holy Spirit, the same Spirit that enabled Hur to be a spiritual leader and Bezalel

---

29. In this regard, the Ark of the Covenant could plausibly be patterned after some of the chests found in the Tomb of Tutankhamun. I highly recommend seeing this marvelous exhibition.

to be a master craftsman. In David, the sovereign God chose a man with "designer genes" to accomplish great things and prepare the way for even greater things.

The Historicity of King David

Before we delve into the story of David, however, an important question must be addressed: Are the narratives about David historical? Many modern scholars are skeptical and will dismiss my retelling of David's life as naïve, simplistic, and uncritical because I accept at face value the Hebrew narratives as handed down in sacred Scripture. Detractors counter with this challenge: prove that the David of Scripture really existed. Others, less skeptical, shake their heads and fault my reading as tone deaf to the multi-faceted layers and competing viewpoints present in the received text, oblivious to the need to read against the grain and to employ a hermeneutic of suspicion, that is, to assume that those with vested interests and commitments are telling the story and slant it to suit their agendas. In their view, I have presented as factual what is in reality an idealized, often partisan, and sometimes legendary account of a person whose historical reality, if not questionable, is, at the very least, considerably less than what I've portrayed in this book. A full reply would require another book, but I must at least justify my approach.

Methodology

At the outset, I address the question of method. How does one read and interpret the Bible? That raises an all-important question concerning the nature of the biblical text. No one can be completely neutral in this regard.[30] There are basically three options:

- Accept the traditional, historic position of the Christian church, which confesses the divine inspiration and authority of Scripture.

- Reject the confessional stance and treat the Bible as no different than any other piece of ancient literature.

- Attempt "to have your cake and eat it too" by qualifying the concepts of inspiration and authority in order to accommodate Scripture to the standards of a modern educated mentality, a position admittedly far

---

30. "All scholars approach their work as whole persons, with beliefs and convictions of various sorts in place. Objectivity is never absolute." Provan et al., *Biblical History of Israel*, 106.

short of the creedal approach adopted by the historic Christian church whether ancient, medieval, or modern.[31]

My methodological starting point lies in a commitment to Jesus Christ as Lord and his final authority in all matters of faith and practice.[32] Consequently, I accept his verdict on the authority of Scripture. This of course begs another question, namely, can we trust the Gospel traditions as reliable witnesses to what Jesus actually said and did? Once again, this requires a lengthy response in defense of the trustworthiness of the Gospels. I point the reader to the work of New Testament scholars Craig Blomberg and Craig Keener for arguments in support of the reliability of the Gospel tradition.[33] All parties in the debate agree that according to the Gospel tradition *as we have it*, Jesus accepted the inspiration and authority of the Old Testament.[34] We can go a step further and demonstrate that he sanctioned the authority of further revelation in what the church later designated the New Testament.[35] Therefore, to reject the witness of Christ to the authority of both Testaments fails to read the text from its divinely intended perspective and purpose.

If it be objected that adopting the traditional approach to Scripture abandons reason and amounts to a dogmatic imposition on the text, I respond by saying that the text itself claims to be divine revelation.[36] Thus to reject the clear witness of Scripture to its origin and authority necessarily imposes an alternative and alien interpretive framework on the text. In such an approach, the autonomous reader now stands over the text rather than

31. The Enlightenment, an eighteenth-century movement that sought to elevate human reason as the primary authority and source of knowledge, was a watershed in the rise of modernity. A primary objective was to "liberate" the Bible from the creedal claims and constraints of the institutional church. This is not to say that everything bequeathed to modernity by the Enlightenment should be rejected, far from it. Nonetheless, the rejection of divine revelation as a valid source of knowledge is antithetical to a sound method of interpreting Holy Scripture and results in a greatly eviscerated gospel.

32. "There is but one only rule and article in divinity. He that knoweth not well the same is no divine: namely, upright faith and confidence in Christ. Out of his article all the others do flow and issue forth, and without this article the others are nothing." Luther, *Table Talk*, 60.

33. Blomberg, *Jesus and the Gospels*; and Keener, *Christobiography*.

34. Matt 4:3-4, 7, 10; 5:17-19; Mark 12:24; Luke 24:25-27; John 10:35.

35. John 14:26; 15:26; 16:12-15; 2 Pet 3:16.

36. See 2 Tim 3:16-17; 2 Pet 1:20-21. "A Biblical Theology of the New Testament which deserves this name must suit the biblical text hermeneutically, i.e., it must attempt to interpret the Old and New Testament tradition as it wants to be interpreted. For this reason, it cannot read these texts only from a critical distance as historical sources but must, at the same time, take them seriously as testimonies of faith which belong to the Holy Scripture of Early Christianity." Stuhlmacher, *How to Do Biblical Theology*, 1.

under it and reads against the grain, that is, contrary to the way the text itself
wants to be read.[37]

Intention

That the biblical text wants to be read as an historical account could hardly
be made clearer by the author/editor of First Chronicles:

> As for the events of King David's reign, from beginning to end,
> they are written in the records of Samuel the seer, the records
> of Nathan the prophet and the records of Gad the seer, together
> with the details of his reign and power, and the circumstances
> that surrounded him and Israel and the kingdoms of all the
> other lands. (1 Chr 29:29)

If it be objected that Chronicles is a late, post-exilic account of Israel's history, one should note that in the exilic books of First and Second Kings, we
have reference to "the annals of Solomon" (1 Kgs 11:41), "the annals of the
kings of Israel" (1 Kgs 14:19), and "the annals of the kings of Judah" (1 Kgs
14:29). But the books of Samuel also witness to written sources upon which
the author/editor drew. David's lament for Saul and Jonathan is said to be
written in "the Book of Jashar" (2 Sam 1:18). Samuel wrote down the duties
of kingship "on a scroll and deposited it before the LORD" (1 Sam 10:25). In
Second Samuel, we have summary lists of David's victories, David's government officials and mighty men, and a census with a grand total of fighting
men.

In brief, there are sufficient reasons to affirm that the events recorded
in Scripture about David and his reign are not literary inventions, but rather,
have a basis in historical fact documented by state archives and prophetic
records. This is not to say that literary artistry and conventions were not also
creatively employed.[38] The narrator knows how to tell a good story in ways

---

37. A moment's reflection makes clear that a "neutral" or unbelieving stance also
employs a circular argument. One simply must begin somewhere! See further Childs,
Biblical Theology, 12. Nor should we think that reason must be abandoned if we accept
the testimony of Scripture to itself. In fact, reason plays a significant role in the interpretive process. The only stipulation is that reason must follow the lead of faith. With
Anselm (1033–1103), I adopt the posture of "faith seeking understanding." Even earlier,
Augustine (354–430) said "believe that you may understand." In other words, Christian
faith does not demand that we sacrifice reason on the altar of faith; it demands that
reason serve and deepen our faith. In the words of the Apostle Paul, "present your
bodies a living sacrifice, holy, acceptable unto God which is your *reasonable* service"
(Rom 12:1 KJV).

38. "In all biblical narrative and in a good deal of biblical poetry as well, the domain

that appeal to his readers and listeners—real history can be really engaging history!

A qualification is necessary. These books are obviously not intended as a history of Israel; they are focused on rise and fall of the House of Saul and the eventual triumph of the House of David. Nonetheless, this fascinating story unfolds against the backdrop of a real history; namely, Israel's history during the Levantine Iron Age.

The books of Samuel narrate the story of an extraordinary person, the key player in leading Israel through a major transition in their national history. At the beginning of David's story, Israel is just emerging from a tribal federation and evolving into a rudimentary form of monarchy under the House of Saul. By the end of David's story, Israel sits astride the Levant as a major regional power headed by a strong central government.

Canonical Considerations

But far more is going on than that. Just as clearly, the books of Samuel witness to an important, even critical connection to what went before. The events recorded bear an unmistakable relationship to the foundational documents of Israel; namely, the Torah of Moses. David's story continues and in part fulfills the promises to the patriarchs. Looked at from the perspective of the entire Christian Bible, the books of Samuel take their place in a grand meta-narrative of redemptive history, anticipating what will come later. As I will repeatedly point out, David's story plays a vital role in the continuing NT witness of God's master plan culminating in a new creation and a new Jerusalem.

In the final analysis, only an overarching theological purpose can do justice to the books of Samuel.[39] In this literary masterpiece, David son of Jesse plays a crucial role in bringing about God's ultimate purpose: to re-establish his kingdom on earth. David's story thus moves us closer to the fulfillment of the prayer Jesus taught his disciples: "Your kingdom come, your will be done, on earth as it is in heaven" (Matt 6:10). *The link between David and Christ is a master key to understanding the unfolding message of Scripture.* "This is the genealogy of Jesus, the Messiah *the son of David*, the son of Abraham" (Matt 1:1).

in which literary invention and religious imagination are joined is history *for all these narratives, with the exception of Job and possibly Jonah, purport to be true accounts of things that have occurred in historical time.*" Alter, "Introduction to the Old Testament," 17. Emphasis mine.

39. See further Bergen, *1, 2 Samuel*, 55.

The reader may still have a nagging question. Is the story factual? Did the events narrated actually occur as stated, or is this a fictional and romanticized version of what really happened?[40] The short answer is that artifactual and literary evidence does exist supporting the essential historicity of the biblical narratives about David.

For the record, I want the reader to know that "as interesting as these discussions are, the biblical texts are not fundamentally dependent on external verification to establish their historical worth."[41] In the final analysis, the Spirit of God witnesses to the truthfulness of the Word of God. "When he, the Spirit of truth comes, he will guide you into all the truth" (John 16:13). In the words of the Apostle Paul, "We have not received the spirit of the world but the Spirit who is from God, that we may understand what God has freely given us" (1 Cor 2:12). King David's testimony stands sure: "the word of the Lord is right and true . . . " (Ps 33:4).

But I also want the reader to know that my case by no means rests solely on the internal witness of the Spirit. Facts matter and faith founded on fiction is foolish. Therefore, for the reader who wishes to examine and weigh the corroborating evidence, I provide documentation in the rest of this chapter. I think it speaks for itself. For the reader who is not interested in pursuing this further, skip to the next chapter to continue the story of a superstar.

EVIDENCE FOR THE HISTORICITY OF DAVID
THE TALE OF THE TEXT: LITERARY EVIDENCE

Three texts have either been discovered or reconstructed from previously existing texts appearing to refer to the House of David as an historical entity on the stage of middle eastern history in the Iron Age.

Tel Dan Inscription

The star witness is the Tel Dan Inscription. This remarkable discovery, like many in archaeological digs, was serendipitous. As the excavation team at Tel Dan was closing up operations after the 1993 season, one of the staff members, Gila Cook, happened to catch a glimpse of a piece of slab peeking out of the debris. Because of the angle of the early morning sunlight,

40. As argued by Davies, *In Search*; Finkelstein and Silberman, *Bible Unearthed*; and Lemche, "David's Rise."

41. Provan et al., *Biblical History of Israel*, 260.

she detected what appeared to be writing on the surface. This attracted her attention and she gathered other staff members to examine it. The lead excavator, Abraham Biran, was astounded. Before him was an Aramaic inscription. After the inscription was carefully studied, Biran released a restoration and translation.[42]

In his opinion, now corroborated by other epigraphic specialists, the slab was part of a memorial or victory stela authorized by Hazael, king of Aram.[43] As Biran reconstructs the text, Hazael boasts of killing "[Jeho]ram son of [Ahab] king of Israel and [Ahaz]iah son of [Jehoram kin]g of Beth-David."[44] The level from which the fragment was found dates to the eighth century BC, but the inscription itself, on epigraphical grounds, dates to the ninth century. The discrepancy is explained by the fact that the stela was actually found in secondary use, that is, reused in later construction.

A majority of ANE scholars now acknowledge that this inscription constitutes an early (perhaps the earliest) non-biblical reference to the Davidic dynasty. Despite a few naysayers, the fragment counts as empirical evidence for the historicity of the biblical David. To be sure, this does not validate the biblical account of David's recorded exploits, but it does caution against an outright dismissal of his historicity and relegation to mythology.

Mesha Stela

A second but contested occurrence of "House of David" has been proposed by André Lemaire. He reconstructed line 31 of the famous Mesha Stela as follows: "And the *House of David* inhabited Horonaim." The Mesha stela (also called the Moabite Stone), dating to about 840 BC, celebrates a Moabite king's victory over Israel and Judah.[45] If Lemaire's reading is correct, it would predate the Tel Dan Stela and thus be the earliest reference to David outside the Hebrew Bible.

42. Biran and Naveh, "Tel Dan Inscription," 1–18.

43. Hazael crops up in a number of biblical passages: 1 Kgs 19:15, 17; 2 Kgs 8:9–15, 28–29; 9:14–15; 10:32; 12:17–18; 13:3, 22, 25; Amos 1:4.

44. The brackets are restorations of missing or eligible letters.

45. See 2 Kgs 3:4. The Mesha Stela was discovered in 1868 by Frederick Augustus Klein at Dhiban, Jordan (ancient Dibon). The inscription, written in Moabite, a language closely related to Hebrew, is the longest Iron Age inscription found in the Levant. The text parallels an episode in 2 Kgs 3:4–8 and mentions the House of Omri. Lemaire reconstructed line 31 as "House of David," but others prefer to read it as "Balak," a king of Ammon also mentioned in the Bible and who sought to undermine and defeat the Hebrews during their sojourn in Ammonite territory prior to the invasion of Canaan (Num 22–24).

Shishak Inscription

A third possible occurrence of "House of David" has been proposed by Kenneth Kitchen based upon his new reading of the Shishak Inscription (Shoshenq I).[46] He believes that there is a reference to "the highlands of David," where the context points to areas around the vicinity of Jerusalem. If Kitchen's reading stands, this would indeed be the earliest extra-biblical reference to David since the inscription dates to only about fifty years after David's death. Since Kitchen's reading is disputed, I include it as a *possible* reference to David.

In light of the above, I conclude that sufficient evidence exists for holding to a *probable* reference to David in extra-biblical material. As of yet, there is none for King Solomon. But one must take into account that there are only four references from the ninth through the seventh centuries BC indisputably referring to an Israelite or Judahite king. The lack of any extra-biblical reference to Solomon may well lie in the geo-political circumstances at the time of the united kingdom. The great river valley kingdoms of Egypt and Assyria-Babylonia were in a period of relative decline and thus did not interfere with Israel. Whereas they had commercial ties with Israel, they did not seek to dominate "the land between" and consequently there are no victory stelae or annalistic accounts of conquest. In other words, the four references to kings of Israel or Judah appear in records or inscriptions that refer to military conquest. These include Shalmanezer's black obelisk (ninth century), Sargon's inscription (eighth century), Sennacherib's prism (early seventh century), and Nebuchadnezzar's chronicle (early sixth century).

I take this a step further: the Israelite and Judahite kingdoms that all ANE historians agree did exist did not suddenly appear on the scene.[47] The foundations and basic infrastructure had already been laid in the days of David and Solomon. In other words, the history of the united kingdom was *not invented* by literary geniuses but was a *necessary historical precursor* to

46. See 1 Kgs 11:40; 14:25; 2 Chr 12:2–12. According to Egyptian records, Shishak successfully campaigned in both Judah and Israel. Shishak recorded his conquests on the walls of the temple of Amun in Thebes. See Kitchen, "How We Know When Solomon Ruled"; and Rainey and Notley, *Sacred Bridge*, 170–71.

47. As argued in the revisionist history of Finkelstein and Silberman who adhere to a "low chronology," that is, they date material previously ascribed to the Solomonic age (10th cent. BC) to the time of Ahab (9th cent. BC). Thus, in their version of Israel's history, there was no central government with the necessary infrastructure to support it until the time of the House of Omri. Furthermore, they endorse the minimalist view of biblical history by accepting the biblical version *only if corroborated* by extra-biblical sources and certified archaeological evidence. In their view, the Bible doesn't qualify as a valid historical source for reconstructing Israel's history. Finkelstein and Silberman, *Bible Unearthed*, 180–86.

the undisputed post-united kingdom era of Israel and Judah. The minimalist and revisionist historians have a blind spot in this regard.[48]

THE TALE OF THE TELL:
ARTIFACTUAL/ARCHITECTURAL EVIDENCE

The next question is whether inscriptional evidence can be supported by architectural and material evidence on the ground. Here again, recent archaeological work is beginning to throw welcome light on a formerly dark corner. Prior to 1993, it was not uncommon to hear archaeologists and historians discount the biblical version of David's kingdom because there was a dearth of artifactual evidence dating to the tenth century BC. Despite the old adage that "absence of evidence is not evidence of absence," many demurred and either discounted or dismissed the scriptural narratives. That approach, however, has been challenged as new excavations in the new millennium are unearthing verifiable material evidence of a Judahite kingdom displaying the trappings of a well-organized central government.

Three primary pieces of material evidence have bolstered the case for the essential historicity of the David narratives.

City of David

The first comes from the most excavated site in all Israel and probably the entire Middle East, namely, the ancient site of Jerusalem. Most archaeologists assumed that the southern ridge, just south of the Temple Mount and east of the Old City of Jerusalem, had yielded up all that could be extracted until Eilat Mazar returned to the Ophel ridge in 2005–2008 and began a new, long term excavation.[49] Her persistence paid off. She uncovered a substantial public building, labeled the Large Stone Structure, sitting atop the ridge above the so-called Stepped Stone Structure known for some years from prior excavations. The latter dated from the Middle Bronze Age and

48. A blind spot created by their commitment to a so-called "scientific approach" that does not "blindly" rely on biblical testimony, but instead employs empirical evidence as the control on what can or can't be accepted as factual in the biblical accounts. Provan, Long, and Longman carefully analyze their faulty assumptions and methodology in *Biblical History of Israel*.

49. "Since most expected that no substantial remains were left at the top of the hill, my proposal of renewing excavations at the location in search of King David's palace did not initially receive the support of my colleagues or of benefactors." Mazar, *Preliminary Report*, 13.

served to shore up the eastern slope on which the ancient city perched. It appears to have been incorporated into Iron Age Jerusalem and may be what First Kings calls "the Millo."[50]

Eilat sparked both excitement and controversy when she publicly announced that in her opinion the monumental building was none other than David's palace![51] Of course, this astonishing claim was met with outright denial or extreme skepticism from so-called minimalists and revisionists. Nonetheless, a number of well-respected archaeologists have supported her claim.

Kirbet Qeiyafa

Joseph Garfinkle, Saar Ganor, and Michael Hasel set off an explosion of their own with their claim that a site known as Khirbet Qeiyafa, located on the western edge of the Judean Shephelah and dated to the late eleventh and early tenth century BC, witnesses to the presence of a central government in Judah.[52] Furthermore, it was a Judean city, not a Canaanite or Philistine city, and provides material evidence for a legitimate Judean kingdom on the scale implied by the biblical narratives in Second Samuel. Particularly significant are the large number of jar handles with finger imprints, indicative of governmental regulation of commodities like oil and wine.[53] As noted by Garfinkle, the Iron Age IIA pottery assemblages from Qeiyafa correspond to those unearthed by Mazar on the Ophel, thus dating both sites to the time of the united kingdom.

Once again, minimalists and revisionists assailed the validity of the findings and proposed alternate interpretations of the evidence.[54] The excavators of Khirbet Qeiyafa have answered their critics and, while it is premature to declare complete validation, a number of leading archaeologists accept their basic conclusions.[55]

---

50. This is translated "the terraces" in the TNIV; "the supporting terraces" in HCSB; and transliterated "the Millo" in the ESV, NAB, NRSV, and REB (1 Kgs 9:15).

51. See Mazar, "Did I Find King David's Palace?" 16–27, 70.

52. See Garfinkle et al., *In the Footsteps*.

53. "The Qeiyafa storage jars clearly indicate early administration and centralisation, which are unknown in Iron Age I sites, but well established in the Iron Age IIA–B." Garfinkle and Kang, "Relative and Absolute Chronology," 11.

54. See, e.g., Finkelstein and Fantalkin, "Khirbet Qeiyafa," 38–63.

55. Predictably, those with maximalist views have generally agreed with Mazar and those with minimalist leanings have disagreed.

Tel 'Eton

Tel 'Eton, a third site further south in the Shephelah, has just recently provided more evidence for the scope of the Davidic kingdom. Displaying typical Hebrew architecture, cultural features (lack of pig bones), and pottery from the early tenth century BC, Tel 'Eton apparently served as an important city on the southern frontier of Judah, not far from Hebron. The excavators identify Tel Eton with biblical Eglon, an identification now widely accepted.[56]

In Garfinkle's reconstruction of the earliest phase of Iron Age IIA (or transitional Iron Age I-IIA), the relatively small number of sites evidencing a central government structure demonstrates the initial stages of what would later develop in Iron Age IIA and IIB.[57] In other words, facts on the ground are now beginning to confirm what the biblical text implies about the earliest phase of the united kingdom.

Garfinkle has drawn attention to the need to reassess earlier surface surveys taken in the regions of Judah and Samaria. For various reasons, these surveys failed to detect Iron Age IIA remains, which are now coming to light by excavation. There is every reason to believe that new excavations will further augment the evidence.

METHODOLOGICAL LIMITATIONS OF ARCHAEOLOGY

Another important factor, a game changer, must be taken into account. Archaeologist Erez Ben-Yosef has recently questioned the assumption that "archaeology is the key to revealing the reality of the biblical period."[58] His studies of mixed nomadic/sedentary societies in the Arabah (south of the Dead Sea) highlighted a methodological flaw: "Archaeologists have focused too much on stone architecture, assuming that if a people hadn't any, they could not possibly establish a kingdom of any substance."[59] In fact, says Ben-Yosef, "we now have convincing evidence for a strong and centralized biblical-era nomadic kingdom—the biblical Edom . . ."[60] Because semi-nomadic

---

56. Josh 10:3, 5, 23, 34, 36–37; 15:39.

57. Katz and Faust, "Chronology of the Iron Age IIA," 103–27.

58. Ben-Yosef, "Architectural Views," 63. The limitations of archaeology were already addressed in the 1970s by Yamauchi, *Stones and the Scripture*, and updated in Yamauchi and Wiseman, *Archaeology and the Bible*. More recently, see Hoffmeier and Millard, *Future of Bibliccal Archaeology*.

59. Ben-Yosef, "Architectural Views," 54.

60. Ben-Yosef, "Architectural Views," 54.

societies leave behind scant or no architectural features, modern scientific field methods are incapable of detecting them.

CONCLUSION

In short, we have a clear illustration that absence of evidence (architectural) is not evidence of absence (centralized government). Ben-Yosef argues that a semi-nomadic/sedentary population existed in the Judean highlands, the Kingdom of Judah, which was, like ancient Edom, quite capable of developing a sophisticated, centralized government *just like the biblical record depicts*. It's high time to reinstate the Old Testament as an essential and valid source for reconstructing the history of ancient Israel.[61]

The bottom line is this: the Davidic Kingdom described in Second Samuel was not a figment of exilic and post-exilic fantasies, it is rooted in reality. The way the text wants to be read is essentially the way it was. Philip Davies and Neil Lemche's mythical world of King David and his mighty men exists only in their imagination.

61. For approaches that take seriously the biblical record as a valid source for reconstructing the history of Israel, see Bright, *History of Israel*; Garfinkel et al., *In the Footsteps*; Kaiser and Wegner, *History of Israel*; Merrill, *Kingdom of Priests*; and Provan et al., *Biblical History of Israel*.

2

ROMANCE IN A BARLEY FIELD

Taken as a whole, the story of Ruth . . . was written to give us encouragement and hope that all the perplexing turns in our lives are going
somewhere good. They do not lead off a cliff. In all the setbacks of our
lives as believers, God is plotting for our joy.

—JOHN PIPER

Tragic Turn of Events

DAVID'S EXTENDED FAMILY HISTORY begins with his great grandfather and
his great grandmother in a barley field. That intriguing statement requires
unpacking. The charming book of Ruth, set in the time of the tribal federation and the charismatically appointed judges, narrates the story of a woman
named Naomi and the troubles that befell her. Her name means "pleasant"
but her life gradually turned very unpleasant: "'Don't call me Naomi," she
told them. "Call me Mara, because the Almighty has made my life very
bitter'" (Ruth 1:20). She and her husband, Elimelek, lived in Bethlehem. A
severe famine forced them to migrate eastward across the Jordan Valley to
the tableland of Moab known as the Medeba Plateau (Josh 13:9).

Why would they move there? Moab is even farther removed from the
Mediterranean and closer to the great Arabian Desert, and thus seemingly
the recipient of even less rainfall. The answer lies in the unique topographic

and climatological features characterizing the region. Even though farther
from the sea, the highlands of Moab may still receive more rainfall, in a
given year, than the hill country of Judah, which is what happened in this
story.[1]

Naomi's plight, however, only deepens in Moab when both her husband and then her two married sons die without heirs, leaving her a desti-
tute widow with two Moabite daughters-in-law who are also widows. Living
in a foreign land, Naomi has no hope for the future.[2] She decides to return to
her homeland and live out her days of poverty among her kinfolk in Bethlehem. She is accompanied by Ruth, one of her remarkable daughters-in-law
and the heroine of the story, after whom the book is named and whose name
means "friend" or "companion." Naomi, in fact, had urged both daughters-
in-law to stay in their homeland. From Naomi's point of view, their fate
would certainly be better in Moab than to accompany her to Judah where
they had few or no prospects for anything but abject poverty.[3] Naomi even
lodges "the bitter complaint that the cause of her calamity is none other
than Yahweh himself, who has stretched out his hand against her" (Ruth
1:20–21).[4] In this complaint we hear echoes of Job, Jonah, and Jeremiah.[5]

1. The explanation goes something like this. Air parcels that rise will expand and
cool leading to condensation and precipitation. Conversely, air parcels that sink will
contract and warm. This is called adiabatic cooling and warming. The degree change is
5.6 degree Fahrenheit per one-thousand feet of elevation change. Since moist air from
the Mediterranean rises to cross the central mountain ridge of Israel (ca. 3,000 feet or
ca. 16 degrees Fahrenheit of cooling), during the rainy season, the air condenses and
falls as precipitation. Once it crests the ridge, it plunges down into the Jordan Rift Valley
some four-thousand feet, where it both warms and extracts any available moisture. As it
crosses the Dead Sea, it picks up more moisture by evaporation and then cools as it rises
once again up to the Medeba Plateau (ca. 3,000 feet), where it produces precipitation.
Long term records show a high degree of variability in rainfall amounts even in villages
not far from one another. In short, the story in Ruth accords with observable weather
patterns. See also Baly, *Geography*, 69–76.

2. Phyllis Trible captures the plight of Naomi this way: "From wife to widow, from
mother to no-mother, this female is stripped of all identity. The security of husband and
children, which a male-dominated culture affords its women, is hers no longer. The defini-
tion of worth, by which it values the female, applies to her no more. The blessings of old
age, which it gives through progeny, are there no longer. Stranger in a foreign land, this
woman is a victim of death—and of life." Trible, "Human Comedy," 167–68.

3. Kalas, *Faith*, 88–89.

4. Bush, *Ruth*, 86. Curtis James observes that "the collapse of Naomi's world did not
happen in a day but was spread out over years of heartache and tragedy . . . Naomi's grief
was a long time coming, the buildup of years of major disappointments, setbacks, and
losses retold by the biblical narrator as cold facts in five short verses, without so much
as a sigh or a tear." Bush, *Ruth*, 37.

5. Helyer, *Life and Witness*, 76–77.

Custis James goes further and adds, "I think Naomi actually out-Jobed Job. Both tragically lose their families and the life they worked to build. But Job is not alone. He still has his wife and a community to surround him (such as they are). Job is not an immigrant and he is not a woman."[6]

Given Naomi's accusation against Yahweh, Ruth's decision to cast her lot with Naomi and Yahweh is all the more remarkable (Ruth 1:16–18). Ruth's commitment is further heightened by the fact that, as a Moabitess, Israel was not only a foreign country, it was sometimes a hostile country.[7] Custis James highlights the importance of Ruth's decision:

> [T]his is one moment in biblical history that has never been given the earthshaking significance it deserves . . . What causes this scene literally to rock the entire book and ranks it among the most dramatic moments in all of biblical history is not (as we have supposed) the tender display of Ruth's deep devotion to her mother-in-law, but the collision that takes place between the weight of evidence Naomi has mounted against God and the radical choice Ruth makes . . . [It] will alter the course of Israel's history and advance the redemptive purposes of God.[8]

A New Beginning in a Barley Field

So, owning neither property nor possessing any substantial source of income, Naomi and Ruth at least found lodging in Naomi's ancestral hometown, probably with relatives. I'm assuming Elimelek sold his property rights to a third party when he migrated to Moab. This money enabled him to make a fresh start in Moab. Naomi, as his widow, apparently was still entitled to the usufruct (produce) of the ancestral inheritance, *if it could be redeemed.* That is the major obstacle to be resolved in the story.[9] The time of her return to the village of Bethlehem, "the house of bread" (Ruth 1:22), at the beginning of barley harvest (March–April), already foreshadows a reversal of fortune. In order to "put bread on the table" in the "house of bread" (Ruth 1:20–21), Ruth volunteers to glean in the barley fields. And it is in the barley fields where the God of Jacob begins to turn Naomi's bitterness and emptiness into great joy and fullness.

---

6. James, *Ruth*, 44.

7. Num 22–25; Deut 23:3–6; Judg 3:12–14.

8. James, *Ruth*, 45.

9. Bush, *Ruth*, 243

Having grown up on the Medeba Plateau, a region well-suited to growing barley and wheat, Ruth no doubt had spent many hours during harvest time binding grain into sheaves so they could be transported by cart to the threshing floors. There, with the aid of heavy sledges pulled by donkeys or oxen over the sheaves, the precious kernels were knocked out of their husks.[10]

In ancient Israel, harvest time was also the occasion for a communal safety net, that is, a custom whereby the indigent were permitted to glean the edges of the grain fields and what was left behind after the harvesters.[11] This practice enabled them to acquire just enough grain to make bread and survive. Ruth readily volunteers for this backbreaking but life-saving work. Not knowing anyone or anything about the area, "she found herself working in a field belonging to Boaz, who was from the clan of Elimelek" (Ruth 2:3).

This was not an accident. Similar to the story of Esther, the God of Jacob is behind the scenes orchestrating the redemption of bitter Naomi.[12] Right on cue, the hero of the story, Boaz the kinsman, shows up at the field. It's tempting to embellish the story a bit by describing Boaz as galloping into the field on a white horse! His character is reflected in the reverential greeting of the workers: "The Lord bless you!" (Ruth 2:4). Indeed, the Lord is about to do precisely that.

Boaz immediately spots a young woman unknown to him. This may strike the modern western reader as a bit contrived, especially since the field had a number of women workers.[13] Such is not the case. Villagers in a middle eastern culture are acutely aware of who is who. A stranger is detected immediately. Inquiring of the overseer, Boaz is informed not only about her

---

10. The present author grew up in the wheat and barley country of north central Oregon, up on the Columbia River Plateau. In fact, the ranch I lived on was almost exactly the same elevation as Bethlehem and received about the same annual rainfall. Of course, we used combines that could harvest a hundred acres a day. Today, in the fields surrounding Bethlehem, one still sees a few plots of land that are harvested in the traditional manner; but for the most part, combines have replaced the old ways.

11. Lev 19:9–10; 23:22; Deut 24:19.

12. Bush captures the theological significance of what happens this way: "The labelling of Ruth's meeting with Boaz as 'chance' is nothing more than the author's way of saying that no human intent was involved. For Ruth and Boaz, it was an accident, but not for God. The tenor of the whole story makes it clear that the narrator sees God's hand throughout. In fact, the very secularism of his expression here is his way of stressing that conviction. It is a kind of underplaying for effect. By calling this meeting an accident, the writer enables himself subtly to point out that even the 'accidental' is directed by God." Bush, *Ruth*, 106.

13. Farm labor in biblical times was gender determined and still is in traditional cultures. I have observed this in parts of the West Bank (Palestinian Authority), and while touring the Cappadocia area in Turkey. Women put the grain in shocks and the men operate the threshing machinery.

identity but also about her devotion to Naomi and her diligent labor. As it turns out, Boaz already knows a little about this young woman whom he had not yet met in person. Village news travels fast!

One is tempted to read into this story romantic notions of love at first sight. That may infer too much, but it's not as if this never happened in biblical times because it did.[14] What we can say is that Boaz was impressed with Ruth as "a woman of noble character" (Ruth 3:1) and perhaps entertained the idea that she would make an excellent wife. Be that as it may, he takes immediate steps to ensure her safety and essentially puts feet on his prayer for her: "May you be richly rewarded by the Lord, the God of Israel, under whose wings you have come to take refuge" (Ruth 2:12). In effect, Boaz becomes the Yahweh's wings and, as we learn, will also cover her with his cloak, that is, marry her.

A DARING PROPOSAL

In modern culture, it's fashionable for male suitors to go to extraordinary lengths and spend extravagant amounts of money in order to propose to their intended. In biblical times, marriages were arranged between the respective family heads spelling out such essential matters as the bride price and dowry. The delightful story of how Boaz and Ruth got engaged departs somewhat from the cultural norm.

Here's how it came about. When Ruth returned from her first full day of gleaning, she brought back an unusually large amount of grain, owing to Boaz's extremely generous permission for gleaning granted to Ruth.[15] In fact, "the amount Ruth lugged home belongs in the *Guinness Book of Records*. After gleaning and winnowing, she has accumulated an *ephah* of barley . . . *approximately twenty-nine pounds* of grain . . . *fifteen* times what Boaz's harvesters were pocketing as a fair day's wage."[16]

When Ruth tells Naomi in whose field she gleaned, Naomi immediately sizes up the situation and sets the stage for Ruth's marriage to Boaz.[17] Stereotypes of Jewish mothers spring to mind, but this isn't just a Jewish stereotype—it's a universal motherly concern for unmarried daughters.

So how is it that Naomi senses redemption in the "happenstance" that Boaz deliberately shelters Ruth? That involves two intertwined social customs quite foreign to modern conventions. The first relates to the loss of

14. Gen 29:17–18; 1 Sam 18:20.

15. Ruth 2:15–16.

16. James, *Ruth*, 112.

17. Naomi "becomes a full-scale matchmaker." Kalas, *Faith*, 93.

ancestral property through poverty and the provision for its redemption.[18] The second is called levirate marriage and provides for widows whose husbands die without male heirs. An exception against marrying one's sister-in-law is granted for a brother of the deceased to marry the widow and father a male heir who continues the deceased brother's property rights. Strictly speaking, the levirate marriage provisions mention only brothers of the deceased. In the case of Boaz, he is a relative but not a brother of Mahlon. For that reason, we should probably describe what happens in Ruth as a "levirate-type responsibility."[19] These customs serve both as a safety net for widows and keeps the patrimony (property) in the clan.

Further explanation is required. In patriarchal societies, women are found in only one of four possible houses.

- They live in their father's house until married, or, if unmarried, they remain there.

- Once married, they belong to their husband and live in his house. In fact, they belong to their husband as movable property or chattel. This runs quite against the grain of modernity! If widowed or divorced, they may return to their father's house, if this is possible, with at least the hope of remarriage.

- If a return to their father's house is not possible, they might become a household servant in the house of a relative or neighbor.[20]

- In worst case scenario, they might be forced to live in a house of ill repute and resort to prostitution in order to avoid starvation.

The notion of an independent woman living on her own simply wasn't an option since she could possess neither property nor income. In Naomi's case, the only support available comes from kinfolks and neighbors who, out of the goodness of their hearts, provide basic sustenance. She has no means of redeeming the property of her husband, Elimelek. Boaz, a blood relative of Elimelek, is her ticket out of poverty and the continual shame of having to depend upon others to survive.[21] If Boaz redeems Elimelek's patrimony, the crops it produces serve as Naomi's social security, and by marrying Ruth, any son issuing from that marriage inherits the patrimony and preserves the name of Elimelek in the clan of Ephrathah. And that is

18. Lev 25:23–28.
19. See Lev 18:16; Deut 25:5–10; and Bush, *Ruth*, 227.
20. See Lev 25:39.
21. See Lev 25:35.

precisely what happens. But let's enjoy the story about how it actually came about.

Naomi puts in play a stratagem. The key move is that Boaz must marry Ruth. But how can that be achieved, given that Boaz was probably not an eligible bachelor? Presumably, he already has a wife and family and is considerably older than Ruth. That is where the institution of levirate marriage comes into play. Naomi knows that Boaz is a kinsman and that under the stipulations of levirate marriage or something akin to it, he could, if he so chose, exercise the option of marrying Ruth and raising up a male heir who would eventually inherit the patrimony of Elimelek. Boaz would then have to be willing to assume the cost of such a purchase with the full understanding that Elimelek's patrimony would pass on to his son by Ruth and not to his son or sons by a prior wife or wives. To be sure, we are never told in the story whether Boaz was married or a widower, but, given cultural norms, we may safely assume it was one or other. Since some men of wealth and status could afford more than one wife, such as Jacob (Gen 29), Gideon (Judg 8:29), and Elkanah (1 Sam 1:2), we can't rule out the possibility that he had more than one wife.

A NIGHT ON THE THRESHING FLOOR

We come now to the most fascinating part of the story. After the harvest season is over, Naomi devises "a daring plan."[22] She instructs Ruth to personally request Boaz to assume the responsibility of kinsman redeemer and marry her. That's asking a lot! Two hurdles must be overcome. Fulfilling the request entails redeeming Elimelek's property, with the understanding that should Ruth bear a son, the property will belong to this son and his heirs. And Ruth is a foreigner—a Moabitess at that. Would Boaz step up and fulfill the responsibility of a kinsman redeemer? Naomi is counting on it, given his preferential treatment toward Ruth during the harvest season.

Let's frankly admit that Naomi's plan carries unmistakable sexual overtones and a direct appeal to male ego. The plan involves surreptitiously going down to the threshing floor after hours and sleeping at the feet of Boaz. One can be sure that a Hollywood version of this would receive an R rating! Some modern interpreters assume the same. Such is hardly the case, as a straightforward reading of the narrative demonstrates. Both Ruth and Boaz are exemplary persons and act in exemplary ways.[23] In short, even

---

22. Bush, *Ruth*, 243.

23. Bush, *Ruth*, 153.

though the narrative employs terminology that in certain contexts implies sexual intercourse, nothing of the sort occurred at the threshing floor.

It's important to digress for a moment. The scene for Ruth's proposal is set at a threshing floor. Most modern readers are quite unfamiliar with the background. Threshing floors were relatively level places at the top of a hill or on ground open to the prevailing westerly winds. After the threshing sledge has been dragged repeatedly over the sheaves, most of the grain has been dislodged from its husks. What we have at this point is a pile of chaff (stalks and husks) mixed in with the kernels of grain.

The winnowing phase of harvesting involves the laborious work of tossing forkfuls of chaff into the breeze in order to blow the chaff away, allowing the kernels to fall back onto the threshing floor. Psalm 1 metaphorically employs this imagery: "Not so the wicked! They are like chaff that the wind blows away" (Ps 1:4). Winnowers systematically work their way around the threshing floor so that eventually you wind up with a pile of grain that can be gathered up into baskets or sacks and transported home for grinding into flour for bread, roasting as a sort of fast-food snack, and feeding livestock. Whereas barley bread was consumed, the highest quality and preferred bread was made from wheat.[24]

Back to the story. Ruth continued to glean throughout the wheat harvest running into May and June. Perhaps the daring proposal took place at the end of May or first part of June. And so, in the middle of the night, Boaz was startled and awoke to find a woman lying at his feet. In response to Boaz's enquiry as to her identity, Ruth cut right to the chase. She identified herself as Boaz's servant and asked him to marry her—that is what the idiom "spread the corner of your garment over me" means (Ruth 3:9). Boaz doesn't hesitate—this woman had touched his heart. And he was probably flattered that Ruth chose him rather than a younger man as a possible husband! He assured her, "I will do for you all you ask" (Ruth 3:11).

A Day in Court

There is a snag in the proposal. Boaz informs Ruth there is a nearer kinsman. I think Naomi was already aware of this relative; but she intuitively knew that Boaz would be a much better match for Ruth. Her instincts are confirmed by the way the nearer relative is referred to in the narrative. The Hebrew expression used is literally "so and so" (Ruth 4:1). The TNIV, NIV,

---

24. Judg 7:13–13; Exod 29:2; 34:22; Deut 32:14; Ps 81:16; Ezek 27:17. As a side note, the soft white winter wheat that we raised on our ranch in Kent, Oregon, was primarily exported to Asian markets where it was highly prized for making noodles.

ESV, and NRSV completely disguise this vague, sometimes uncompliment-ary, designation by rendering the Hebrew "my friend." The HCSB has it quite wrong: "Boaz called him by name," something he definitely did not do! The JSB nails it with its more literal rendering: "Come over and sit down here, So-and-so!" The fact that he is never named in the story is very telling and, when push comes to shove, So-and-so backs out of his obligation and punts the ball to Boaz. I suspect Naomi was quite sure this would be the case.

Once again displaying his integrity, Boaz elects to follow the tradi-tional custom and offer the nearer relative an opportunity to step up to the plate and perform the role of kinsman redeemer. We fast forward from the threshing floor to the plaza area just inside the Bethlehem city gate. Here is where the equivalent of city hall was located and where criminal cases and civil matters such as property transfers were adjudicated.[25] Boaz convenes a quorum of ten men to witness the proceedings.[26] He then directly addresses the nearer kinsman ("So-and-so") and informs him that Naomi "is selling the piece of land that belonged to our relative Elimelek" (Ruth 4:3). The translation "selling" is problematic, and I follow those scholars who think it probably means something like "transferring," that is, she is transferring her right to repurchase Elimelek's land to a near kinsman.[27]

At first, So-and-so readily agrees to redeem the property, but quickly declines the offer once marrying Ruth is understood to be part of the deal. He publicly explains his refusal solely in economic terms: "I might endan-ger my own estate . . . I cannot do it" (Ruth 4:6).[28] He defers to Boaz and symbolically signals his decision by taking off his sandal and handing it to Boaz. Boaz then affirms before the witnesses that he will both purchase the property and marry the widow Ruth. It is noteworthy that Boaz explicitly states his primary motivation: "to maintain the name of the dead with his property, so that his name will not disappear from among his family or from his hometown" (Ruth 4:30).[29] This speech reinforces Naomi's high regard for Boaz, a man who shows "kindness to the living and the dead" (Ruth 2:20).

25. Whereas most commentators assume that the proceedings were entirely oral in nature, we can't rule out the possibility that a written record was also made. See Hess, "Reading and Writing," 1–9.

26. In order to conduct a synagogue prayer service, ten adult males must be present, called a minyan. *B. Kethub.* 2b cites a rabbinic tradition that this requirement is based on the text from Ruth.

27. "Here so many ambiguities, uncertainties, and unknowns confront us that any final solution to the problems involved will doubtless permanently escape us." Bush, *Ruth*, 211–15.

28. "[H]is words clearly express concern only for his own patrimony and interests; they show no concern for Ruth and the line of Elimelech at all." Bush, *Ruth*, 246.

29. Bush, *Ruth*, 247.

The courtroom scene concludes with the village elders and people pronouncing the transaction official: "we are witnesses" (Ruth 4:11). This is followed by an extraordinary, threefold communal blessing upon the new couple:

- May "the woman coming into your home" follow in the footsteps of the matriarchs Rachel and Leah who together "built up the house of Israel" (Ruth 4:11).

- May Boaz attain a position of standing and fame in Bethlehem.

- May the family of Boaz through "this young woman" (the Moabitess) be on par with that of Perez the son of the tribal patriarch Judah through Tamar (the Canaanite) (Ruth 4:13).

Remarkable! Even though a Moabite, she is acknowledged as worthy of taking her place among the leading matriarchal figures of Israel's storied past, without the least hint of bias or discrimination. Clearly, her steadfast devotion to Naomi, her faith in Yahweh, and her noble character won over the goodwill of all the Bethlehemites.[30] She is now one of the family, a member of the Ephrathite clan.[31] In this story, both Boaz and Ruth display *chesed*, a rich Hebrew word conveying the notions of steadfast loyalty, faithfulness, kindness, love, and mercy.[32] How fitting that two such individuals should find each other and become man and wife.

A Day of Rejoicing

That brings us to the much anticipated and delightful finale. Despite the fact that Ruth had been childless for ten years, shortly after her marriage to Boaz, she conceives and gives birth to a son. One is reminded of the matriarchal struggles to provide an heir during the patriarchal period.[33] The birth of Obed sets off a time of celebration and joy.[34] It also brings the story of Naomi full circle. She whose life had been turned to bitterness and emptiness now celebrates a remarkable change in circumstances—a sweet and

---

30. See, e.g., Ruth 1:16; 2:11, 17; 3:1, 11; 4:15.

31. "Bethlehemites scoop the young foreigner into the family circle." James, *Ruth*, 194.

32. Ruth 2:20 (Boaz) and 3:10 (Ruth).

33. Gen 11:30; 15:2–4; 16:1; 17:17; 18:10; 21:1; 25:21; 29:11; 30:1.

34. "In the end, the whole town erupts in celebration as Boaz grasps his kinsman's sandal and announces his determination to fulfill his obligation as Elimelech's kinsman-redeemer." James, *Ruth*, 194.

full life, amply provided for by a kinsman redeemer and a grandson who continues the line of Elimelek.

This son is fittingly named Obed, meaning "servant." In Hebrew culture the term '*eved* ("slave" or "servant") doesn't always connote servile circumstances, as English readers might imagine, but rather, the high honor of serving the Lord God of Israel. For example, the prophets of Yahweh were also called "servants of Yahweh," and yet they were held in highest esteem. Obed lovingly serves his grandmother by providing for her well-being. The benefits, however, are mutual: "the child Naomi holds in her arms . . . learned deep lessons about God at the knee of this female Job."[35] In short, Ruth's son continues to do what she herself had faithfully done in caring for Naomi. The village women get it right: "your daughter-in-law is better to you than seven sons" (Ruth 4:15).[36]

THE GENES OF GENEALOGICAL GREATNESS

The narrative concludes with an abbreviated version of David's genealogy beginning with Judah's son, Perez, and tracing it down to Jesse, David's father. Viewed in terms of the overarching story of redemptive history in the Bible, a crucial moment in the unfolding of the Kingdom of God arrives when David takes his place on the stage of history. The reader of the NT knows, of course, that David son of Jesse is an ancestor of Jesus, the greater Son of David and true King of Israel,[37] indeed, the King of Kings and Lord of Lords.[38]

The stage is set. Given his ancestral DNA, we shouldn't be surprised to learn that David altered the course of Israel's history, indeed, of the entire Middle East during the Iron Age.[39] I don't mean to imply that heredity is the sole determining factor accounting for the amazing career of David. Scripture points to something far transcending genes at work. That "something extra" becomes clear in the story that now beckons us.

35. James, *Ruth*, 205.

36. The village women function much like a chorus in Greek dramas, pointing to the heroic period in the Iron Age as the cultural and historical backdrop of the book of Ruth.

37. Matt 1:1, 4–6, 17.

38. Matt 28:18; Rev 19:16. "By concluding with this 'coda,' . . . the book is brought into relationship with the Bible's main theme of redemptive history." Bush, *Ruth*, 268.

39. An archaeological term used to designate the period of approximately 1200 BC to 586 BC. David is generally dated to ca. 1,000 BC, or, more specifically, Iron Age IIA.

3

PRECURSORS TO THE RISE OF DAVID

In those days Israel had no king; everyone did as they saw fit.

—JUDGES 21:25

THE BOOK OF JUDGES concludes with an alarming statement. Two interrelated problems coexist: lack of unified leadership and lack of spiritual commitment to the Sinai Covenant. The root problem is the failure to observe the Law of Moses with its primary demand for absolute loyalty to Yahweh: "You shall have no other gods before me" (Exod 20:3). This fundamental spiritual failure spawned national disunity. The book of Judges repetitiously reminds the reader, "They forsook the LORD, the God of their ancestors, who had brought them out of Egypt. They followed and worshiped various gods of the peoples around them" (Judg 2:12). In accordance with the curses of the Sinai Covenant, whenever Israel went astray, they suffered the consequences of disobedience.[1] These disciplinary measures included a wide range of natural disasters and warfare, the latter coming for the most part from the indigenous peoples of Canaan and Transjordan who oppressed and usurped rule over Israel. When the Israelites repented, "the LORD raised up judges, who saved them out of the hands of these raiders" (Judg 2:16).

Like the cycles of a washing machine, Israel's history during the era of the judges falls into a recurring sequence: apostasy, oppression, repentance,

1. Lev 27:14–46; Deut 28:15–68. On the nature of the Sinai Covenant as a suzerainty treaty, see Helyer, *Yesterday*, 138–45.

and deliverance.[2] And so, over the course of more than three-hundred years,[3] we have a record of twelve judges (thirteen if we include Abimelek) whom the Lord raised up to deliver the Israelites from their oppressors. The judges are a mixed bag of "The Good, the Bad and the Ugly."[4] For example, Samson, the last judge recounted in the book of Judges, is portrayed as a morally flawed champion who in his suicide inflicts more casualties on the enemy than during his lifetime. At the conclusion of Judges, one senses that something must change—how much longer can this depressing cycle continue? Note especially that the Samson stories unfold against the backdrop of a Philistine oppression. Though mentioned in Judges earlier, by the time of Samson, this ethnic group constitutes the most serious challenge to Israel's control over the land of Canaan.[5] The Philistine threat dominates the background of the early chapters of First Samuel to which we now turn.

CRISIS AND TRANSITION

The first ten chapters of First Samuel cover a period of crisis and major transition in Israel's history. In this section, we have snapshots of the last two judges who ruled over the tribal federation, the priests Eli and Samuel. Eli's judgeship was a disaster. He allowed his two sons Hophni and Phineas to abuse their priestly prerogatives and commit gross immorality in the tabernacle itself. An unnamed prophet denounces Eli and prophesies that his two sons "will both die on the same day" (1 Sam 2:34). Eli's tenure as judge ends shortly thereafter with a devastating defeat at the hands of the Philistines. After receiving the news of his sons' death and the capture of the ark, he falls backwards from his chair and breaks his neck. The wife of Eli's son Phineas gives birth to a son on the same day and bestows upon him a name that sadly summarizes the state of affairs: "She named the boy Ichabod ["no glory"], saying, 'the Glory has departed from Israel'" (1 Sam 4:21).

Following Eli's death, the people of Israel turned to Samuel, given the widespread acknowledgment "that Samuel was attested as a prophet of the LORD" (1 Sam 3:20). There are striking similarities between Samson and Samuel. Both were born to mothers who had been barren and both were

2. "The dreary cycle of rebellion-retribution-repentance-restoration-rebellion is repeated over and over again throughout the book of Judges, which in many respects rehearses the darkest days of Israel's long history." Youngblood, *1 & 2 Samuel*, 325.

3. See Judg 11:26.

4. Taken from the featured song and name of the 1967 movie starring Clint Eastwood. In my opinion, the title describes rather well the movie!

5. Judg 3:31; 10:7.

dedicated as Nazarites.[6] As "the Spirit of the LORD began to stir" young Samson (Judg 13:25), so the LORD "revealed himself to Samuel [while still a boy] through his word" (1 Sam 3:21). Both prophets led Israel against the Philistines, though with very different approaches and results. Samson "led Israel twenty years" (Judg 16:31) and "Samuel continued as Israel's leader all the days of his life" (1 Sam 7:15).

Unfortunately, the end of Samuel's career mirrored that of his foster father, Eli. In his old age, Samuel "appointed his sons [Joel and Abijah] as Israel's leaders" (8:1), who "turned aside after dishonest gain and accepted bribes and perverted justice" (8:3). What ensued brought about one of the most significant shifts in Israel's history—the transition from tribal federation to monarchy. In short, the elders of Israel rejected Samuel's sons as leaders and clamor for a king: "Now appoint a king to lead us, such as all the other nations have" (8:5).

TRIBAL FEDERATION

The demand for a king requires further discussion concerning the geopolitical background of this seismic shift in government. During the period of the judges, Israel functioned as a federation of twelve tribes owing exclusive allegiance to Yahweh and bound to his covenant laws delivered at Mount Sinai. In principle, the king of Israel was Yahweh alone. His rule was administered through tribal elders and a priesthood who provided national leadership, decided civil and criminal cases, conducted worship at the central sanctuary in Shiloh, and passed along the inherited traditions to the next generation. Being a patriarchal culture, most local and family matters were settled by clan and family heads, all of whom were men. The judges were temporary leaders raised up by the Spirit of Yahweh in times of national emergency. Though Gideon was asked to be king—and at times acted like one—he never accepted the title. Abimelek, Gideon's son, aspired to be king and was even crowned as such at Shechem, but his reign was only regional and short-lived.[7]

In principle, the federation should have worked; in reality, it failed to provide cohesive, unified leadership. The tribes lacked a sense of unity and each tended to fend for itself. Careful reading of the story in Judges illustrates the point: most crises were met by the tribes immediately impacted. If there was no direct threat, tribes opted out. In spite of this lack of full tribal participation, they managed to survive. This dramatically changed with the

6. Judg 13; 1 Sam 1:1–20.

7. See Judg 8:22–35; 9:1–57.

rise of the Philistine threat. Now for the first time, an ethnic group bent on dominating the entire land of Canaan enters the picture. Optional participation was no longer viable. Only if the tribes were all in could they realistically survive the crisis. The tribal elders sized up the dilemma in terms of how best to confront the Philistine aggression. Their answer was based on the observation that all the neighboring countries governed through kings. Politically this amounts to a concentration of power in the hands of a few, typically a strong leader with the resources to govern, including a strong military.

Shift to Central Government

Samuel reluctantly gave in to their demand, though not without warning them of the downside of kingship.[8] In short, central government costs money—lots of it.[9] Of course, in an agrarian society, taxes are not primarily monetary, but in kind. The central government confiscates a tenth of the produce of the land and drafts young men to serve in the military. Women too are commandeered to serve in the king's ever-expanding household and court. We'll have occasion to see how this plays out during the Davidic monarchy. In the days of Saul, the expenses of central government were quite modest in comparison to the extravagant government spending during the golden age of King Solomon.

Philistine Threat

The Philistine threat was the single most pressing issue facing the tribal elders. As the stories of Saul's reign unfold, it quickly becomes apparent how precarious things were. Philistine garrisons were located up on the central ridge not far from the capital of Saul's fledgling kingdom at Gibeah. A quick perusal of the geography of Canaan makes clear that the key to controlling the land of Canaan lies in controlling the central ridge dominating the east-west and north-south routes. Saul's primary task was to push the Philistines off the central ridge back down to their narrow coastal enclave. In

---

8. 1 Sam 8:10–18.

9. It goes without saying that the government of the United States of America is the most expensive in human history. This should not be taken as a censorious comment. The size of our population, the enormous amount of income generated by our economy, and the ever-increasing expectations and expenses of the federal government must be taken into account. Needless to say, strong disagreements over the size of the pie and how it should be sliced remain a constant feature of American political debate.

this endeavor, Saul achieves partial success; complete success was a major achievement of King David. But more on that later.

First, who were the Philistines? They were a leading tribe in a federation of Greek peoples, called the Sea Peoples by the Egyptians, driven from their homeland by invaders in the twelfth and thirteenth centuries BC. Many of the displaced Sea Peoples migrated from the Aegean to the eastern Mediterranean, including the narrow coastal strip of Canaan.[10] In other words, following the biblical chronology, the Philistines arrived after the Hebrews' settlement in the central highlands. They, too, settled down and adopted many of the customs and deities of the indigenous Canaanites and even of the Egyptians who nominally controlled portions of the region. They did, however, preserve many of their ancestral traditions harking back to the Heroic Age of Greek history depicted in Homer's account of the Trojan War in the *Iliad*. They were, in short, a formidable foe.

The struggle for the control of Canaan between the Hebrews and the Philistines lies in the background of the stories in Judges and the early chapters of First Samuel. The stakes are high in which the winner basically takes all.[11] Prior to the rise of David, the Philistines held the upper hand because they possessed significant advantages over against their Hebrew rivals.

The military ethos of the Philistines grew out of a culture that glorified war. The Homeric epic, the *Iliad*, illuminates this mindset. Young Philistine boys aspired to be warriors and excel in warfare. Very early on, they were schooled in the martial arts and military tactics.[12] The Philistines relied on a professional army led by trained officers. It was quite different for the Hebrews. They were a pastoral, agrarian society. Though having a history that involved periodic warfare, the focus was not on war and glory in battle, but on tending flocks, cultivating olives and vines, raising barley and wheat, and living peaceably with one's neighbors. In times of crisis, citizens were

10. See Romey, "Ancient DNA."

11. It is one of the ironies of history that this ancient conflict over the land of Canaan has *mutatis mutandis* reemerged in the current impasse between the Israelis and Palestinians. The word "Palestine" is the Latin translation of the term "Philistine." The Romans designated the region comprising what is today Israel and the Palestinian Authority as the province of Palestine. In 1923, the British mandatory government reverted back to this name as the official designation for the region. Adding to the irony, some Palestinians carry Philistine DNA (as do, no doubt, a few Israelis!). The current struggle, like its ancient counterpart, threatens to be a zero-sum game. The as-yet unanswered question is whether a two-state solution can resolve the conflict. Historical precedent would suggest that such an outcome is unlikely, but I continue to be hopeful.

12. As reflected in Saul's attempt to deter David from taking on the Philistine champion Goliath: "You are not able to go out against this Philistine and fight him; you are little more than a boy, and he has been a warrior from his youth" (1 Sam 17:33).

called up to serve in the militia, but none of the officers had received formal military training.

When it comes to weaponry, the disparity was even more pronounced. The Philistines possessed state-of-the-art weapons made of iron, not bronze, and incorporated chariots into their army.[13] By contrast, the Hebrews were citizen foot soldiers and possessed only farm implements like "plow points, mattocks, axes and sickles" for weapons (1 Sam 13:20). In one engagement, only Saul and his son Jonathan had swords and spears.[14] Furthermore, the Hebrews lacked the technology to produce iron weapons, being entirely dependent upon the Philistines even for their iron-pointed farm implements. The technological advantage heavily favored the Philistines.

A third significant advantage grew out of their consolidated political and military structure. The Philistines early on formed an alliance of five cities that ruled over Philistia, a sort of Philistine pentapolis. Each city-state elected a strong leader (Heb. *seren*, ruler) and in times of war the cities joined forces under the direction of a commander in chief. They could mobilize for war quickly and in general presented a united front. This contrasts sharply with the tribal federation and the initial phases of monarchy under Saul. One senses that when "Saul gathered all Israel" (1 Sam 28:4), this hardly represented a levy of all eligible males from the tribes.

GAME-CHANGER

David addressed this disparity and transformed his little kingdom into a formidable military power. How he did it will be spelled out in more detail later. The point is that at the end of Samuel's career, the situation confronting the tribal federation was desperate and explains why the tribal elders radically altered their form of government. In their view, it was the only hope for national survival as an independent people. A start was made under the leadership of Saul, but it was David who accelerated the process and guided the fledgling monarchy to unprecedented heights of power.

We should not, however, attribute David's remarkable achievement solely to a charismatic, gifted leader. The Hebrews did in fact possess a

13. Cast iron and bronze are comparable in durability and ability to hold an edge. Cast iron, however, is easier to produce because it only requires one raw material. Bronze is an alloy of copper and tin and thus one needs access to both sources, a circumstance usually requiring trade with neighbors. Steel is definitely superior to both cast iron and copper, but the technology to produce it did not develop until the Roman era. War chariots intimidate and overwhelm foot soldiers, which can decisively change the outcome of a battle.

14. 1 Sam 13:19–22.

decisive advantage, a game-changer really, that in the end accounts for David's stunning success—let's call it the Yahweh factor. The God of Israel purposed to establish through David a secure and strong kingdom. All the historical, psychological, and sociological factors to which one might appeal for explanation fall under God's sovereign control. *Israel rose to prominence under David because this was part of God's plan for redemptive history.* This will be further developed as we follow the amazing career of David.

4

DAVID ENTERS THE STORY

But you, Bethlehem Ephrathah, though you are small among the clans
of Judah, out of you will come for me one who will be ruler over Israel
whose origins are from of old, from ancient times.

—MICAH 5:2

RISE AND FALL OF THE HOUSE OF SAUL

THE STORY OF SAUL, the first king of Israel, reads like a Greek tragedy by
Aeschylus, Euripides, or Sophocles. Beginning as a most unlikely and self-
effacing candidate to head up the fledgling monarchy, he ends up falling
on his sword (literally) on the heights of Mount Gilboa.[1] Just as the Greek
tragedies induced grown men to weep, so too the life of Saul elicits a sense
of deep sadness. It could have been and should have been so much better. Saul's career illustrates Lord Acton's adage, "Power tends to corrupt and
absolute power corrupts absolutely."[2] The full story requires a book length
study. Here I only touch on his career as a necessary foil to set the stage for
the appearance of our hero, David son of Jesse.

1. See 1 Sam 9:21; 10:16, 20–22, 27; 31:1–4.

2. The rest of the quote goes like this: "Great men are almost always bad men, even
when they exercise influence and not authority: still more when you superadd the ten-
dency or the certainty of corruption by authority."

As indicated in the previous chapter, Saul's primary task was to repel the Philistine attempt to dominate the land of Canaan. To this end he made a noteworthy start. Assisted by his courageous and noble son, Jonathan, the Hebrews were divinely enabled to drive the Philistine forces off the central ridge back down to their coastal enclave.[3] The Philistine region consisted of a confederated pentapolis ruled over by the rulers of Gaza, Ashdod, and Ashkelon, located along the Mediterranean coastline, and the inland cities of Gath and Ekron.[4]

Unfortunately, Saul's defense of the Hebrew hill country against a massive Philistine incursion involved a major transgression. Samuel had issued strict orders to wait seven days for his arrival to offer sacrifice *before engaging the enemy*. The set time passed, but no Samuel. Because Saul's troops "were quaking with fear" and "began to scatter" (1 Sam 13:8), he "offered up the burnt offering" (13:9).[5] Strictly speaking, the law of Moses separated the civil powers of the king from the cultic duties of the priesthood. Pagan kingship made no such distinction. Acting like a king "such as all the other nations have" (8:5, 19), Saul was caught red-handed. "Just as he finished making the offering, Samuel arrived . . . " (13:10). Talk about bad timing!

Samuel demanded an explanation. Saul's attempt to justify his actions revealed his limited trust in Yahweh: "So I *felt compelled* to offer the burnt offering" (13:11). That in a nutshell points to Saul's fundamental flaw—he trusts in his own devices more than the LORD God of Israel. That failure eventually proves fatal (1 Sam 28, 31). Many years later, the prophet Isaiah warned Ahaz, king of Judah: "If you do not stand firm in your faith, you will not stand at all" (Isa 7:9b). He, too, failed the test. Samuel's remorseful reproach, "You have not kept the command the LORD your God gave you" (13:13), would have been an apt epitaph on Saul's tomb. The House of Saul would not long endure. But, in the same breath, Samuel offers hope for the nation. "[T]he LORD has sought out a man after his own heart and appointed him ruler of his people . . . " (13:14).

In the short run, the Lord grants a stunning victory over the Philistines, due in no small measure to the courage of Jonathan (1 Sam 14:1–46).

---

3. 1 Sam 13–14.

4. Josh 13:3; Judg 3:3; 1 Sam 6:4, 16, 18. Readers will have doubtless heard about and seen TV coverage of the modern Palestinian city of Gaza and surrounding area known as the Gaza Strip. The other ancient Philistine cities are today located in the State of Israel.

5. "This does not imply that he did so personally. Gilgal boasted a sacred shrine where priests would have been in attendance, and it is recorded that Ahijah was in Saul's entourage (14:3)." Mackay, *1–2 Samuel*, 144.

Following that, Saul delivers punishing blows to the immediate neighbors (14:47–48). Saul's successes suggest that all is well after all.

Yahweh offers Saul a second chance to demonstrate his trust and obedience. Has he learned from his failure? Alas, he fails again and for the same basic reason—he doesn't completely obey a direct, divine order.[6] Samuel's resounding condemnation means that Saul has reached the point of no return: "Because you have rejected the word of the LORD, he has rejected you as king" (15:23b). There will be no third strike—he's out! "The Lord has torn the kingdom from you today and has given it to one of your neighbors—to one better than you. He who is the Glory of Israel does not lie or change his mind . . . " (15:28–29). And that one who is better is waiting in the wings about to step out on the stage of history.

DAVID'S STORY BEGINS IN BETHLEHEM

"Oh, little town of Bethlehem, how still we see thee lie."[7] The words of the Christmas carol are remarkably appropriate for what next happens. The Lord commissions Samuel to go to the sleepy hamlet of Bethlehem and anoint a new king. He may have been somewhat surprised that the new king should reside in Bethlehem and belong to the relatively insignificant family of Jesse, though he shouldn't have been. After all, Samuel was well aware that the celebrated Gideon came from the weakest clan in Manasseh and the least of his family[8] and Saul, whom Samuel himself anointed as the first king, was from the smallest tribe of Benjamin and from the least of all the clans of Benjamin.[9] In hindsight, of course, we smile and say, "How completely appropriate!" Recall that Jesse's grandfather was the noble Boaz and his grandmother was none other than the Moabite convert, Ruth—individuals of deep faith and sterling character. Jesse carried on the family tradition of being a faithful servant of Yahweh, just like his father Obed (whose name means "servant"). This was the family that shaped the man after God's own heart. We should hasten to add David would not be the last or even greatest king to claim Bethlehem as his birthplace. Just as Micah

6. 1 Sam 15:1–3, 9.

7. I write these lines on the anniversary of Phillips Brooks' death in 1893. He wrote the lyrics for the beloved Christmas carol, "O Little Town of Bethlehem" and was reckoned to be one of the finest preachers of his day.

8. Judg 6:15.

9. 1 Sam 9:21. The Apostle Paul summarizes how God works out his kingdom purposes: "God chose the lowly things of this world, and the despised things—and the things that are not—to nullify the things that are, so that no one may boast before him" (1 Cor 1:28–29).

foresaw that "the ruler over Israel . . . whose origins are from of old, from ancient times" sprang from Bethlehem (Mic 5:2), so too Matthew identified this Bethlehemite as "Jesus the Messiah, the son of David, the son of Abraham" (Matt 1:1; 2:1–6).

When Samuel showed up unannounced in Bethlehem, the elders trembled. They feared collective punishment for some unknown transgression.[10] The elders' fear mirrored an atmosphere of fear pervading all Israel at the time. Israelites were fearful about the state of the nation. They had good reason to be afraid. Although Samuel's final rejection of Saul was probably not publicly witnessed, word probably leaked out. What the people knew was that Samuel had no more contact with Saul and that alone was deeply disturbing.[11] They were also painfully aware that the Philistine threat was far from resolved. Unbeknown to them, fear also hung like a burial shroud over Saul. The sacred historian tersely observes: "Now the Spirit of the Lord had departed from Saul, and an evil spirit from the LORD tormented him" (1 Sam 16:14). As a result, Saul struggled with bouts of deep depression.[12] His attendants suggested music therapy, so he authorized a search for a skillful lyre player.[13] Immediately, the name of David surfaced and so, as a court musician, David first gained access to the king himself. The irony of the appointment reminds us of the Exodus story in which Moses, the Hebrew slave, brought up and raised in Pharaoh's household, became the deliverer from Egyptian bondage.[14] Similarly, prior to David's appointment in Saul's court, a divine appointment of greater magnitude and importance unfolded in the little town of Bethlehem.

David's Private Anointing as King

Much to the elders' relief, Samuel indicated he had come in peace and wished to offer a communal sacrifice to which the elders were invited on the precondition of their prior consecration. To this restricted group, a special

10. "Perhaps the elders 'trembled' at the sight of Samuel because they interpreted Samuel's arrival with a heifer as an indication that a murder occurred in their territory and that a legal action was being initiated . . . " Bergen, *1, 2 Samuel*, 178; cf. Deut 21:1–9.

11. 1 Sam 15:35.

12. Saul's affliction by an evil spirit has striking similarities to the psychotic disorder called manic-depressive. It is sometimes labeled as bipolar disorder. Saul fluctuates between hyperactivity and mental depression.

13. Modern medicine recognizes the therapeutic value of music in both mental and physical health. In the ancient classical world, music therapy was a standard part of treatment regimens.

14. Exod 2:1–10; cf. Acts 7:20–22.

invitation was extended to Jesse and his sons. Before sitting down for the communal meal following the sacrifice, Samuel proceeded with his divine commission to anoint the next king of Israel. Yahweh did not indicate to Samuel beforehand which of Jesse's sons was the chosen one. In a memorable scene, seven sons in succession stood before Samuel. Much to Samuel's surprise, Eliab the firstborn, who apparently possessed striking physical features like Saul, was not the divine choice. Instead, Yahweh reminded Samuel of the indispensable requirement for kingship: "The LORD does not look at the things human beings look at. People look at the outward appearance, but the LORD looks at the heart" (16:7). All seven failed to pass muster, truly "a perplexing situation."[15]

Schlepping with the Sheep

Samuel inquired, "Are these all the sons you have?" (16:11). Jesse answers: "There is still the youngest, he is tending the sheep." Jesse's response conveys far more meaning than he was aware. Following a divine pattern of election in the patriarchal narratives, not the elder but the younger was chosen. Isaac rather than Ishmael, Jacob rather than Esau, Ephraim rather than Manasseh, were chosen to be part of the Messianic line—nor was Solomon David's firstborn.

Furthermore, what David was doing at the moment was preparing him for the future. In the Hebrew tradition, political and religious leaders were likened to shepherds, a notion also found in the wider ANE culture. In fact, the relationship between shepherd and sheep provided a pattern for political leadership. A good shepherd puts the welfare of his flock above his own; indeed, he will risk his own life on behalf of his sheep. Here the well-known cadences of the twenty-third Psalm come to mind. The greatest leader of Israel prior to David was Moses, a man who spent forty years herding sheep in the desert *before* being commissioned to deliver Israel out of slavery and lead them to the Promised Land.[16] The prophet Jeremiah denounced the political leaders and self-proclaimed prophets of his day as unfaithful shepherds of Israel "who have led them astray and caused them to roam on the mountains."[17] In short, the mindset of a shepherd is essential to what it means to be a leader. It's no accident that in the NT the imagery of a good shepherd portrays the person and work of Jesus Christ.[18]

15. Bergen, *1, 2 Samuel*, 179.
16. See Acts 7:30.
17. Jer 50:6. See also Jer 23.
18. See esp. John 10:1–18; cf. 1 Pet 5:1–4.

Set Apart as King over Israel

The scene of David's anointing is briefly narrated. When summoned to the meal—notice that Samuel refused to eat until the youngest had appeared—David made his grand entrance. No doubt David's mother insisted he clean up and dress up before appearing before Samuel! The narrator purposely informs us that he was a fine-looking young man. There is no comment about his character; but Yahweh knows the heart and Samuel knows Yahweh well enough not to question his judgment. The inner voice of Yahweh tells Samuel, "this is the one" (16:12b).

Following long-established custom, Samuel anointed David's head with olive oil, a symbolic act conveying the idea of divine assistance through the Spirit of Yahweh. Kings, priests, and prophets were anointed with oil and thus set apart, or consecrated, for divine service. What the action symbolized is realized in what follows: "the Spirit of the LORD came on David in power" (16:13). No mention is made of any visible manifestation to onlookers, but no uncertainty exists as to the reality of the Spirit's presence in David's life. David's anointing was divinely directed with no input required by the elders of Bethlehem or of all Israel, for that matter. He was, after all, the man after God's own heart and that alone qualified him to succeed Saul. There is a nagging question: Will the Spirit remain with David or depart as happened to Saul (16:14)? The narrative supplies an unambiguous answer: "*from that day on*" (16:13).

The narrative raises a couple more questions. The actual anointing is said to have taken place "in the presence of his brothers" (16:13). Were the town elders present as well? If they were, what did they make of it? If they weren't, what did David's brothers think? Did they realize what Samuel had just done? In other words, are they in the know from the get go? We can't be certain. My supposition is they didn't understand it to be a royal anointing; they may have viewed it as a special blessing bestowed upon their youngest brother, though why it was him and not any of them remained a mystery and probably caused some resentment—the story of Joseph's coat comes to mind.[19] In hindsight, of course, it all became clear.

Summoned to the Royal Court

And so, the privately anointed king-to-be arrived at the royal court. He was not, however, a mere shepherd boy who just happened to be a skillful lyre player; he brought much more to the king's table than that. Besides

19. Gen 37:3–4; cf. 1 Sam 17:28–29.

being very articulate and handsome, his reputation as a courageous warrior preceded him—the very thing Saul urgently needed for his inexperienced army. Above all, however, was the general perception shared by the members of the court that Yahweh was with David. We hear echoes of young Joseph in Potiphar's house: "The LORD was with Joseph so that he prospered ... [and] his master saw that the LORD was with him and that the LORD gave him success in everything he did, Joseph found favor in his eyes and became his attendant" (Gen 39:2–3). Worth noting is the fact that Joseph, who also was "well-built and handsome" (Gen 39:6), was only seventeen when sold into slavery (Gen 37:2). When David faced Goliath (our next chapter), he was not yet twenty.[20] Not surprisingly, we read that "Saul liked him very much, and David became one of his armor-bearers" (16:21). Amazing! The future king was not only ushered into the court of King Saul; he became his indispensable, right-hand man. David was being groomed for bigger and better things!

20. Cf. 1 Sam 17:33 with Num 1:3.

5

A STAR IS BORN

Taking Down Goliath

In his youth did he not kill a giant,
and take away the people's disgrace,
when he whirled the stone in the sling
and struck down the boasting of Goliath?
For he called on the Lord, the Most High,
and he gave him strength to his right arm
to strike down a mighty warrior,
and to exalt the power of his people.

—SIRACH 47:4–5 NRSV

THE EXPRESSION "David and Goliath," referring to an apparent mismatch between two opponents, is a widely used and recognized idiom, part of our cultural heritage. The story behind the expression, however, is one of the most extraordinary events in the history of Israel. It rocketed David onto the center stage of national life, setting in motion eventual triumph over the Philistines and supremacy over the neighboring countries. Those raised in Sunday schools probably have memories of hearing it for the first time and seeing pictures of a shepherd boy with his sling and five smooth stones and an enormous giant encased in protective armor, armed with a huge spear and girded with a sword. Artists throughout the ages have sought to capture this epic duel on canvas or in sculpture. One thinks of Caravaggio's

44

masterpiece painting of David holding Goliath's head by his hair, and Michelangelo's world-renowned marble sculpture of young David just before taking on Goliath.[1] Let's revisit this moment in time and, with fresh eyes, reflect on what happened.

SETTING FOR THE STORY

The sacred historian locates this duel to the death in the Elah Valley, positioning the opposing armies and mentioning the sites involved in this dramatic "battle fit for the ages."[2] Visiting the area in person and reading the biblical account adds an unforgettable dimension to the story. One can see at a glance approximately where the opposing armies camped and the general area where the actual duel most likely took place.[3]

The Elah Valley was strategically important because it allowed access to the central ridge from the coastal plain. Traversing it eastward enabled one to proceed either up to Hebron or Bethlehem. If the Philistines could successfully push their forces up onto the central ridge, they would threaten Saul's capital at Gibeah and position themselves to gain control of the entire hill country. That would effectively cut off the northern tribes, rendering untenable any semblance of a united Hebrew kingdom. Saul realized the magnitude of the threat and mobilized his forces to repel the incursion. From the biblical description of the battle, it's clear that the Philistines occupied the southern slopes of the Elah and the Hebrews faced them on the northern slopes.[4] The scene was set for a decisive engagement.

1. Pictures can't capture its visual impact. I saw this colossal statue in person during a Tour of Italy, September 2017. Sculpted out of white marble, it stands seventeen feet high and towers above its pedestal in the Galleria dell 'Accademia in Florence, Italy. Michelangelo's David departs from earlier traditional poses by depicting a rather tense David just before his attack on Goliath. In his right hand, he holds a rock and, in his left, he grasps the end of his sling, which is slung over his left shoulder. One should also mention Bernini's famous life-size sculpture capturing the instant just before David hurls his sling. The dynamic sense of movement and emotional intensity are palpable.

2. Wright, *Understanding*, 41.

3. See Beitzel, *Moody Atlas*, map 57, 150; and Wright, *Understanding*, 40–42.

4. 1 Sam 17:3. On the northern slopes overlooking the Elah Valley, Yosef Garfinkel has excavated a site named Khirbet Qeiyafa. According to him, the Iron Age remains date back to David's time, perhaps even to Saul's reign. He further suggests that it is the biblical site Shaaraim, meaning "two gates," mentioned in 1 Sam 17:52 ("the Shaaraim road"). As it turns out, two gates were discovered, providing access to the fortified city of Qeiyafa. Although his interpretation of the finds is disputed, Garfinkel's hypothesis provides a plausible anchor point for Saul's forces deployed along the northern slopes of the Elah. Garfinkel et al., *In the Footsteps*, 17, 93–97.

What ensued, however, was a stalemate lasting forty days.[5] So why did the opposing forces face off so long before engaging? That requires a brief explanation. Armed conflict involving hand-to-hand combat was costly in terms of human lives—both sides generally suffered heavy casualties. Sometimes the winners came away with only a Pyrrhic victory.[6] The Philistines knew full well that even if they succeeded in defeating the Hebrews in battle, their losses would be heavy, hampering their attempt to subjugate the Hebrew heartland in the hill country. Following a well-established tradition in the Mediterranean basin, especially among the Greeks, contending armies chose champions who duked it out to the death. In principle, the outcome required the losers to submit to the victors. Better to lose a champion than an army! Homer's classic epic the *Iliad* illustrates this with several notable instances of one-on-one combat, the most memorable being the clash between Achilles and Hector. In the case of the Trojan war, however, neither side was prepared to accept the verdict of a single duel, and the carnage continued for some time. In due course, we will rehearse a similar incident in the struggle between David and Ishbosheth with a similar outcome, namely a continuation of hostilities.[7]

SEQUENCE OF EVENTS

The story itself unfolds in four interconnected scenes, displaying a marvelous literary artistry unrivalled in the ancient world. Carefully reading and rereading the narrative enhances our appreciation and enjoyment of the historian's storytelling skill.[8]

Scene 1: A Giant Challenges the Army of Israel

Attention is first drawn to the enormity of the Philistine champion. Looking like a character out of the pages of the *Iliad*, Goliath of Gath stepped forward from the ranks and threw down a challenge to single-handed combat—winner takes all.[9] Saul may have stood "a head taller than anyone else" in Israel

5. 1 Sam 17:17.

6. Named after Pyrrhus, a Greek king who won two battles against the Romans but incurred so many casualties he eventually lost the war.

7. 2 Sam 2:12–28.

8. "The writer deliberately employed certain narrative techniques that cause this story to achieve special prominence in the reader's/listener's mind." Bergen, *1, 2 Sam*, 187.

9. Although excavations have been carried out at Tel es-Safi, the generally

(9:2), but Goliath was a giant among men, standing "six cubits and a span" (17:4)—about nine feet, six inches![10] Added to his enormous height was his daunting armor and weapons. Wearing a bronze helmet, scale armor, leg greaves weighing some 125 pounds, and carrying a javelin and spear—the latter having a point weighing sixteen pounds—and advancing behind a shield bearer, Goliath was like a human tank! In addition to all that, he carried a sword unmatched in all Israel—a warrior and weapons without equal.

Goliath's challenge to the Hebrews was met with dismay and terror. What immediately jumps out at the reader is the frank recognition that Saul was also terror-stricken. Where was this Spirit-endowed leader who courageously led the Israelites against the Ammonites at Jabesh Gilead and drove the Philistines from Mikmash all the way down to Aijalon? Of course, the reader knows the answer. The Spirit of the Lord had departed from Saul, and he knew Goliath would make quick work of him. So, he declined the challenge, deciding to live another day. Understandably, the Hebrew troops were demoralized and humiliated. For forty days, Saul's army suffered in silence at Goliath's insolent challenge.[11]

Scene 2: David the Shepherd Arrives on the Scene

The narrator first reminds the reader about the family background of our hero. He then informs us of four additional facts:

- Jesse was now a very old man.

- His three oldest sons were serving in Saul's army and present at the standoff.

---

recognized location of Gath, no remains datable to the time of David had been found until just recently. Quite unexpectedly, Aren Maier, the director of the dig, now reports that a massive city with massive foundations and walls turned up about a meter beyond where they had been excavating for a number of years! He reckons that Gath was one of the largest cities during the Iron I in the entire Levant. See Borschel-Dan, "Colossal Ancient Structures."

10. Codex Vaticanus (LXX), 4QSam^a; and Josephus (*Ant.* 4.9.1[6.171]) provide an alternate figure: four cubits and a span (six feet, nine inches). Regardless of which reading is original, Goliath would have towered over the Israelites. Excavations at Iron Age I sites in the hill country of Israel have revealed homes with relatively low ceilings. Anthropologists have also studied skeletal remains at biblical sites. These findings suggest an average height of ca. five feet, five inches.

11. The forty days of taunting is probably not just an incidental detail; a period of forty days or forty years in Scripture often conveys the notion of testing and trial (See Gen 7:4, 12, 17; 8:6; 18:29; Exod 16:35; 24:18; 34:28; Num 13:25; Deut 2:7; Judg 13:1; 1 Kgs 19:8). Recall the forty days and forty nights preceding the temptation of Christ in the wilderness (Matt 4:2; Mark 1:13; Luke 4:2).

- David had been previously shuttling back and forth from his duties as court musician at Gibeah to his home in Bethlehem to tend his father's sheep.[12]

- David showed up on the scene of the confrontation at the request of his father, Jesse. His mission was to find out how his brothers were doing and report back. In addition, Jesse sent along some food for his sons and their unit commander.

David arrived at the Israelite camp just as the troops were forming the battle line. Once again, God's providence is at work behind the scenes. The echoes of Ruth showing up at Boaz's field not knowing whose field it was are unmistakable.

Leaving his supplies with the quartermaster, David caught up with his brothers on the front line. At that very moment, Goliath stepped forward and issued another defiant challenge to the men of Israel who collectively shrank back in fear—no one volunteered. But David heard it.

Scene 3: David Volunteers to Fight the Philistine Champion

A critical moment had come. God was about to do a great thing in Israel using a man after his own heart.[13] What follows makes the movie *Rocky* pale in comparison. The narrator mentions the reward for felling the Philistine champion three times, twice as a response to David's specific inquiry.[14] The reward was substantial: great wealth, marriage into the royal family, and exemption from taxes for the extended family of the victor. Such incentives would ordinarily have prompted a flood of volunteers; that no one stepped forward is a measure of how great the odds were stacked against any realistic hope of success. Only one man rose to the challenge, the one most would have probably considered the least likely to succeed, a young shepherd and lyre player from Bethlehem.

Word of David's willingness to take on the Philistine and remove the disgrace of Israel got back to Saul. When summoned, David self-assuredly informed the king, "Let no one lose heart on account of this Philistine; your servant will go and fight him" (1 Sam 17:32). Saul quickly tried to dissuade

12. "While Saul was fully occupied with military manoeuvres [Brit. Eng.] he would not need his minstrel, so David was back home for a while. The need to keep the army fed took David to the front and introduced him to the Philistine challenger." Baldwin, *1 and 2 Samuel*, 135.

13. In my mind, I'm hearing the lyrics of "Miracle of Miracles" from *Fiddler on the Roof*.

14. 1 Sam 17:25, 27, 30.

the youngster from such a foolhardy, suicidal mission. David countered by rehearsing his exploits while protecting his flock from ferocious predators, including a lion and bear. David possessed an unshakable confidence that the Philistine would prove no more difficult because he had committed a fatal mistake: he deified the living God. David confidently predicted the outcome: "the LORD . . . will rescue me from the hand of the Philistine" (17:37).

Saul couldn't help but admire the boy's courage. Though doubting David's triumph, he at least offered to improve the odds. He dressed his court musician and personal attendant in his own personal armor and gave him his sword.[15] They just didn't work. David was completely ill at ease with Saul's protective armor and sword. Instead, he opted for what he was used to, his shepherd's staff and trusty sling. To this he added ammunition: five smooth stones from the wadi Elah.

Scene 4: David Fells Goliath with One Smooth Stone

The reader should not imagine a child's slingshot. The sling David employed was a lengthy leather strap having a pouch in the center for the stone. The sling was not pulled back like a rubber band slingshot, but rather swung rapidly around the body until sufficient velocity was achieved and then one end of the strap was released, launching the projectile. A skilled slinger could exceed a velocity of one hundred miles per hour. The resulting impact could be lethal or at least knock an opponent unconscious if the stone struck the forehead. Therein lay the difficulty factor: the projectile must strike the target at a vulnerable spot.

We know from Scripture and extra-biblical sources that a slinger corps was a vital part of ancient armies, a sort of mini artillery corps. The Benjamites were legendary for their great accuracy with the sling: "seven hundred who were left-handed, each of whom could sling a stone at a hair and not miss" (Judg 20:16).[16] Assyrian wall reliefs depict slingers among their elite units who were apparently using an underhand delivery like a softball pitcher.[17] Today, in fast-pitch softball, men can reach a velocity of eighty-five miles per hour with an underhand delivery. In baseball, using an overhand delivery, some major league pitchers attain velocities of more than

15. Earlier we learned that only Saul and Jonathan had a sword or spear. To what degree this deficiency still existed for Saul's army is uncertain. I suspect that little had changed and none of Saul's soldiers possessed body armor made of bronze (1 Sam 14:22). They probably had homemade leather protective garments.

16. See also 1 Chr 12:2; 2 Chr 26:4.

17. See Pritchard, *ANEP*, pl. 101.

one-hundred miles per hour. For this reason, softball and baseball helmets
are required to protect one's head and, for the same reason, ancient soldiers
wore metal helmets. Goliath wore a bronze helmet with a small chink for
visibility. As 1 Samuel 17 attests, young David was a superb marksman, and
that is exactly where David's first smooth stone landed!

Goliath was at the very least knocked unconscious and fell face-down
on the ground. David rushed forward, stood over him, drew Goliath's sword
from its sheath and administered the *coup de grâce*. Dramatically signaling
his triumph, he cut off the Philistine's head and probably head it aloft for all
to see. The impact of David's smooth stone was felt by more than Goliath—it
was like a shot heard round the land. The Philistines panicked and fled to
their nearest cities for refuge with the Hebrews in hot pursuit and inflicting many casualties along the way.[18] The tide in a long war was beginning
to turn. The Philistine defeat could be likened to the Battle of Gettysburg
during the American Civil War.[19] Israel had a rising star who, along with
many other talents, was a born leader of men and a military genius. Israelite
morale soared as new hope was born. Nashon and Caleb would have been
extremely proud of their descendant.

SEQUEL TO DAVID'S VICTORY

The narrator briefly sketches three scenes following David's dramatic defeat
of Goliath.

Scene 1: David Displays Goliath's Head at Jerusalem and Takes Possession of His Weapons

The mention of David taking Goliath's head to Jerusalem has puzzled commentators because at the time Jerusalem was a Jebusite, not a Hebrew city.
Some suggest that the reference is proleptic, that is, it anticipates David's
action at a later time. To be sure, one of the first things David did as king
of all Israel was to capture Jerusalem, making it his capital city.[20] But in my
opinion, even before the capture, David sent a message loud and clear to
Jebusite Jerusalem: their autonomous city-state would not long be allowed

---

18. In ancient battles, most casualties occurred when soldiers were retreating or
fleeing because their backs were exposed to the pursuing forces.

19. Though two bloody years of war remained, the final outcome was inevitable.

20. 2 Sam 5:6–10.

to exist in the heart of the Hebrew homeland.[21] We will discuss this crucial event in more detail later.

A question also arises about Saul's query as to the identity of David's father.[22] Why, if David had already been shuttling back and forth to Saul's court in Gibeah as Saul's personal musician and armor-bearer, wouldn't Saul know who David's father was? In response, we should remember that Saul had been rapidly recruiting personnel for his expanding government and professional army. Though he knew David's name, it's understandable that he could have forgotten his father's name, especially given the fact that he also suffered from deep depression. Abner had even less personal contact with David and was completely preoccupied with military matters. At any rate, Saul needed to know the father's name of his prospective son-in-law. Family connections were extremely important in biblical times. Accordingly, the narrator caps off this section with another announcement of David's lineage: "I am the son of your servant Jesse of Bethlehem" (17:58), nicely framing David's introduction to the Goliath's story in 1 Samuel 17:12. In short, the most famous name in Israelite history emerged from obscurity. Before long, David's "name became well known" (18:30), a national hero.

Scene 2: Jonathan Makes a Covenant with David

Jonathan found a fellow traveler. David's unqualified trust in Yahweh created in Jonathan a kindred bond. "He loved him as himself" (1 Sam 18:1). Far from having homosexual overtones, we have the language of friendship and covenant: "Jonathan made a covenant with David" (18:2).[23] Ratifying his compact, Jonathan bestowed his own robe, armor, and weapons upon David as a gift. The irony of this should not escape us. David had previously rejected Saul's armor and weapons because he was not used to them. He accepted Jonathan's and by so doing acknowledged his new standing in the army of Israel. Indeed, one senses that Jonathan himself recognized the heir apparent to the throne. It was a remarkable gesture, later supported by Jonathan's oral recognition of David's right to the throne.[24]

21. See also Hoffmeier "Aftermath," 18–23.

22. 1 Sam 17:55–58.

23. See Arnold, *1 & 2 Samuel*, (1 Sam 18:1–4) in reply to those who interpret this passage as a veiled reference to a homosexual relationship.

24. 1 Sam 23:17.

Scene 3: Saul Promotes David to the Rank of a Commander in the Army

The last scene sets the stage for a dramatic reversal in David's fortunes. In the immediate aftermath of David's victory over Goliath, Saul capitalized on David's popularity by commissioning him to participate in several missions. He was so successful in these operations that Saul promoted him to the rank of commander, an appointment applauded even by Saul's officers. This meteoric rise in David's status had a serious downside. The popular adulation of the young hero increased Saul's insecurity and fear. This was especially stoked when a victory celebration in Gibeah exalted David's exploits over that of the king: "Saul has slain his thousands, and David his tens of thousands" (1 Sam 18:7).[25] Dark jealousy gripped the monarch's mind. He quickly came to an unsettling conclusion: "What more can he get but the kingdom" (18:8). The narrator laconically adds these ominous words: "And from that time on Saul kept a close eye on David" (18:9). The stage is now set for some of the darkest days of David's life.

---

25. One recalls Miriam and the women of Israel celebrating Yahweh's great victory at the Red Sea "with timbrels and dancing" (Exod 15:20) and the doomed daughter of Jephthah who greeted her victorious father "dancing to the sound of timbrels" (Judg 11:34).

6

FROM FAVORITE TO FUGITIVE

You can only be jealous of someone who has something you think you
ought to have yourself.

—MARGARET ATWOOD, *THE HANDMAID'S TALE*

THE THRILL OF VICTORY

THE AFTERMATH OF DAVID'S stunning defeat of the Philistine champion
Goliath witnessed an equally stunning rise to national fame. David became a
household name. Everyone knew about his amazing feat in the Vale of Elah.
The crowds adored him, the women sang his praises, the army of Israel and
Judah loved him and devotedly followed him in battle, and he met with one
success after another. His exploits eclipsed those of Abner, the commander
in chief of Saul's army and, for all practical purposes, David functioned as
such without the title. As the song from the Academy Award-winning 1955
movie *Oklahoma* has it: "Ev'rything's goin' my way." But things quickly took
a turn for the worse. Let's rehearse the sequence of events that ushered in a
drastically different situation.

A Green-eyed Monster Takes Control

The sacred historian sums up Saul's reaction to David's meteoric rise to fame: "Saul was very angry" (1 Sam 18:8); "Saul was afraid of David" (18:9); "from that time on, Saul kept a close eye on David" (18:12, 29); and "Saul . . . remained his enemy the rest of his days" (18:29). Fear and jealousy consumed Saul; he lived in constant dread of a changing of the guard. Samuel's denunciation constantly re-echoed in his tormented mind: "But now your kingdom will not endure; the LORD has sought out a man after his own heart and appointed him ruler of his people" (13:14). What was painfully clear to Saul was that the Lord had departed from him and was with David.

The pace of the story now accelerates. The narrator takes us through a harrowing series of close calls in which David barely eludes Saul's murderous attempts on his life. The scenes rapidly shift settings with one constant: God always provides a way of escape, and Saul becomes increasingly consumed with the necessity of eliminating his hated rival.

Saul's anger and paranoia quickly erupted. The day after the victory celebration in the capital, Saul "fell into a frenzy" (18:10 REB). As usual, David was summoned to play his lyre for the deeply disturbed king. A brief word of explanation is required. The NIV and TNIV translations say that Saul "was prophesying." I think the Hebrew verb is more accurately rendered "began to rave" or "fell into a frenzy." The problem is that the same verb form is used to convey differing nuances and only the context determines its precise meaning.[1] In this context, something like "raving" or "fell into a frenzy" fits better because "an evil spirit came forcefully on Saul" (18:10). In short, the dark side of Saul's personality emerged and he tried twice to kill David with his spear. Providentially, David escaped both attempts.

Foiled Plans to Eliminate a Rival

Regaining rational control, Saul tried a different tack to rid himself of David. Shrewdly exposing David to the constant perils of combat, Saul commissioned him to lead a thousand men. Surely, thought Saul, he will succumb. Quite the contrary, David was amazingly successful, which led to even more adulation for the rising star.

The time was overdue for the king to fulfill his promise to the victor over Goliath. Saul offered David his oldest daughter, Merab, in marriage. The invitation to become a son-in-law, however, came with a carefully

---

1. See Alter, *David Story*, 114, n. 10. See also ESV; HCSB; NRSV; NAB, "raged"; NJPS "began to rave"; REB, "fell into a frenzy."

calculated condition—a sort of catch-22.[2] David must commit to personal loyalty to the king and courageous service in battle. Once again, Saul cynically reasoned that sooner or later he would be killed: "Let the Philistines do that!" (18:17). The offer of marriage, surprisingly, was met with reticence on David's part. Like Saul, David was not from a prominent clan or family and he expressed unworthiness to accept such a high honor and privilege. But after two attempts on his life already, David must have had serious misgivings about being so intimately attached to the royal family! Besides this, David was acutely aware of his lack of resources—he had very little to offer as a bridal price other than personal service. One thinks of Jacob who likewise could only offer Laban his labor and toil as a bride price for the lovely Rachel.[3]

Saul probably hadn't anticipated David's reluctance, but after thinking about it, he decided on another plan, namely, a public insult and humiliation. Rather than giving Merab to David, at the last moment, he gave her to another man, hoping that publicly shaming David would result in his resignation from service and return home to Bethlehem. Saul could then get on with life without having to endure unfavorable comparisons to the young superstar. In fact, David did neither. Something unexpected happened in the royal family.

Romance in the Royal Court

"Now Saul's daughter Michal was in love with David" (1 Sam 18:20). In a striking passage of Scripture, the narrator tells us that another daughter of Saul's had fallen in love with this young, handsome hero. In no other historical narrative does the Bible explicitly tell us that a woman loved a man. To be sure, it doubtless happened often, but the Bible was written in a patriarchal culture and thus from a masculine perspective, so we rarely hear the feminine side of these stories. In the poetic book, Song of Songs, however, the bride does express her love, even erotic love, for her beloved.

When word got back to Saul about Michal's crush on David, he hatched another plan to eliminate his rival. He would use Michal as bait to lure David to his death. Simply stated, Saul again attached a precondition with a very high-risk component: he must kill one hundred Philistines.[4] The

---

2. Title of a satirical novel by Joseph Heller published in 1961. A catch-22 is a situation from which there seems to be no escape.

3. Gen 29:16–30

4. The modern reader is pulled up short by the mention of cutting off the foreskins of the Philistines as a trophy of war and system of tallying "kills." There is no

narrator informs us: "Saul's plan was to have David fall by the hands of the Philistines" (18:25). Saul initiated a behind-the-scenes influence scheme to encourage David the second time around to accept the offer of marriage. It worked: "He was pleased to become the king's son-in-law" (18:26). But Saul's scheme misfired. David not only met the quota, he doubled it! Saul had no choice—he gave Michal to David in marriage. Everything was turning up roses for David. He was now the king's son-in-law and not only won his battles, he outshined all the rest of Saul's officers in the process. There was no stopping this phenom. Saul was paranoid because "the LORD was with David" (18:28). Ironically, even though David described himself as "little known" (18:23), in reality, "his name became well known" (18:30).

Intrigue in the Royal Court

For Saul the situation called for drastic measures. The only remaining option was assassination and the best hit men would be members of the royal court. Saul ordered his son Jonathan and the king's personal attendants—probably his body guards—to carry out the hit. The plot seemed foolproof. David would have been completely caught off guard and a rag-to-riches story tragically cut short. But it didn't happen. God in his providence provided a way of escape for the future monarch.

David had two loyal allies in the royal court who came to his rescue. The first was, surprisingly, the heir apparent Jonathan, the one who had the most to lose if David became king. The second was David's young bride, Michal. Without them, David would never have survived the machinations of a deranged Saul.

In a similar way, the prophet Jeremiah would never have survived the bitter enmity of his enemies in Jerusalem had it not been for a few loyal, highly placed government officials and a faithful, foreign-born servant.[5] One also thinks of the Apostle Paul who was spirited out of Damascus by his followers and talked out of appearing at the theater in Ephesus by some city officials and his friends.[6]

---

way around it—mutilation was a regular part of ancient warfare demonstrating disdain for defeated enemies. Alas, modern wars are still not rid of this barbaric practice. Christianity historically helped minimize brutality and played a role in promoting an international code of behavior for humanitarian treatment in war. The theological basis lies in the truth that all human beings are made in God's image and thus are worthy of humane treatment, even in times of war. See Hill, *What Has Christianity Ever Done?*

5. Jer 7, 26, 37–38. See Helyer, *Life and Witness of Jeremiah*, 14.

6. Acts 9:25; 19:31.

Jonathan's Intervention

The king's direct order to kill David prompted an immediate response by Jonathan. He first tipped off David as to Saul's intentions and then planned a direct intervention. While David hid in the field, Jonathan appealed to Saul's "better angels" to relent on his assassination order.[7] Jonathan's appeal was twofold: David was completely innocent of disloyalty and his actions had only benefited the king. In short, there was "no [good] reason" (1 Sam 19:5) for killing David. Sometimes even unbalanced people can be persuaded by logic.[8] In this case, Saul agreed with his son and took an oath cancelling David's death warrant. Unfortunately, circumstances quickly changed and Saul's "dark angels" returned with a vengeance.

Michal's Intervention

War with the Philistines again broke out, and David forcefully and gallantly led the Israelites in a rout. David's success plunged Saul into another bout of mental disturbance ("an evil spirit from the LORD" [19:9]). As David played his lyre to soothe the manic monarch, Saul launched another spear at David. The agile David eluded the spear thrust and concluded that Saul was bent on murder—he must escape now.

David's escape is one of the most dramatic in Scripture featuring the second loyal supporter, David's wife Michal.[9] As David was planning his escape the next morning and saying his goodbyes to Michal, Saul was ordering his body guards to carry out a hit on David that very night. Obviously, Jonathan was left out of the loop. The assassins set up watch outside his room waiting for him to emerge. Meanwhile, Michal got wind of the assassination attempt and came up with a daring escape plan.[10]

The plan involved a drop and a dummy. Realizing there was not a moment to delay, she "let David down through a window, and he fled and

---

7. Phrase adapted from the title of a book by Pinker, *Better Angels*.

8. "Saul's paranoia and uncontrolled outbursts manifest themselves in an intermittent cycle. He is amenable to the voice of reason and conscience . . . [but at other times] will unleash another round of violent impulses." Alter, *David Story*, 118.

9. Arnold notes that "our story seems to have degenerated into a soap opera." Arnold, *1 & 2 Samuel*, loc. 5751.

10. So, how did Michal find out? Royal courts, ancient and modern, have their back channels of information. A Turkish film, *The Magnificent Century*, features the constant intrigue and flow of both reliable information and unfounded rumor that circulated throughout Suleiman the Magnificent's harem in the sixteenth century AD. Saul's royal court, though on a vastly reduced scale, was no different.

escaped" (19:12).[11] Probably well before dawn, Saul's henchmen banged at the door demanding that David come out. Michal answered: "He is ill" (19:14). They reported back to Saul who seized on this as the perfect opportunity to personally dispatch his hated rival: "bring him up to me in his bed so that I may kill him" (19:15).[12] They forced their way into David's room and discovered a life-size idol made to appear like a human![13] The delay allowed David just enough time to escape to Samuel at Ramah.[14]

Saul's frustration and wrath turned on his youngest daughter. She had to resort to a lie in order to escape severe consequences, perhaps even murder by her father.[15] She claimed David threatened her life if she did not cooperate. Whether he fully believed her or not, it was at least plausible and, at the moment, he was completely preoccupied, "hellbent on destroying David."[16] Before long, informants notified Saul of David's whereabouts and the pursuit continued.

This episode has some interesting parallels to one in the patriarchal stories involving Jacob and his favorite wife, Rachel.[17] Following long years of service and shrewd bargaining with Laban, his conniving father-in-law, Jacob decided to secretly escape to his homeland in Canaan. What is of interest is the role Rachel played in the clandestine flight. Before leaving, and

11. This calls to mind the escape story of the two Hebrew spies at Jericho. They used the house of a Canaanite prostitute named Rahab as a hideout. She had a room, like that of David and Michal, built into the side of the city wall allowing outside access without having to go through the city gate. When their presence was discovered, the king of Jericho demanded that Rahab bring them out. Instead, she hid them on the roof under stalks of flax. When the soldiers arrived, she told them the spies had already escaped, but perhaps they could yet be apprehended before crossing the Jordan River to the east. In fact, she had "let them down by a rope through the window" (Josh 2:15) and instructed them to climb up into the hills to the west of Jericho and hide out for three days before crossing the Jordan. The stratagem worked and Rahab not only became a follower of Yahweh, she became, like Ruth, an ancestress of David and Jesus. See Josh 2:1–24; 6:25; Matt 1:5. The Apostle Paul had a close call in Damascus in which "his followers took him by night and lowered him in a basket through an opening in the wall" (Acts 9:25; cf. 11:32–33). It should be noted that Paul, like David, had a number of close calls with death (2 Cor 11:23–33).

12. Saul's body guard could not violate the privacy of a royal princess without direct authorization from the king himself.

13. "She [Michal] adopts the familiar trick used by prisoners round the world of concocting a dummy to mask an escape." Alter, *David Story*, 120.

14. Ramah lay a mere two miles north of Gibeah. David hoped Samuel's presence would guarantee personal immunity and sanctuary.

15. Later in a fit of rage, Saul even hurled a spear with murderous intent at Jonathan, the designated heir! (1 Sam 20:33)

16. Arnold, *1 & 2 Samuel*, loc. 5737.

17. Gen 31.

unbeknownst to Jacob, Rachel stole the household gods, the equivalent to title deeds. Following in hot pursuit, Laban finally caught up with Jacob's family in the hill country of Gilead, east of the Jordan River. An angry Laban berated Jacob for secretly slipping off and then accused him of stealing the household gods. Jacob protested his innocence and vowed the death penalty for anyone in whose possession they might be found. All the tents were searched and only Rachel's quick thinking saved her life: she hid them under a saddle and sat upon it apologizing for not getting up: "I'm having my period" (Gen 31:35).[18] The ruse worked and Jacob was completely exonerated. Jacob and Laban settled their grievances and sealed it with a non-aggression pact between the two men and their respective families.

A troubling aspect in both stories of a loyal wife siding with her husband against her father relates to the remnants of idolatry still very much in evidence. Rachel's case is less egregious since it occurred well before the giving of the Mosaic Law with its explicit ban on idols. But Michal's possession of such paraphernalia is inexcusable and calls into question Saul's undivided loyalty to Yahweh.[19] Unfortunately, the history of Israel was replete with idolatry and religious syncretism, major violations of the Sinai covenant that eventually led to exile.

The Holy Spirit's Intervention

Saul dispatched soldiers to Ramah to arrest David despite Samuel's presence and protection. What follows is an extraordinary intervention by the Spirit of God. On four separate occasions, the last involving Saul himself, the arresting forces were overwhelmed by the Spirit and joined the prophets in ecstatic worship of Yahweh.[20] This experience so completely altered their attitudes that they simply ignored or forgot their mission! Especially astounding was its effect on Saul: "He stripped off his garments, and he too

18. The household gods Rachel stole were obviously much smaller than the life-size teraphim Michal had in her room.

19. Bergen suggests that Saul was quite aware of Michal's "idolatrous inclinations" and that is what Saul meant by her becoming "a snare to him" (1 Sam 18:21). Bergen, 1, 2 Samuel, 204. "What is especially shocking and revealing about the episode is the fact that, as late as the lifetime of David in the early tenth century B.C.E., the Israelites were still keeping and using idols despite the oft-stated loathing of Yahweh for polytheism and paganism." Kirsch, King David, 70.

20. The prophets associated with Samuel were probably part of "the school of the prophets," disciples who sought to maintain faith in Yahweh against the inroads of the Canaanite cults.

prophesied in Samuel's presence. He lay naked all day and all that night" (2 Sam 19:24).

This was the second time the Spirit came upon Saul and he prophesied. Recall that the first time was after Samuel anointed him king and "God changed Saul's heart" (1 Sam 10:9). The contrast between these two occasions is tragic and tells the tale. Saul's stripping off his royal robes depicts his divestiture as king over Israel. In short, his investiture was cancelled and his anointing annulled. The proverbial question, "Is Saul also among the prophets?" (1 Sam 10:11; 2 Sam 19:24) is easily answered. No, he is not.[21] Meanwhile, the delay at Ramah allows the newly anointed king, who is a true prophet (2 Sam 23:1 cf. Acts 2:30), enough time to escape back to Gibeah for one final appeal to Jonathan for help.

JONATHAN'S COVENANT WITH THE HOUSE OF DAVID

Chapter 20 is one of the most memorable in the entire story of David. Turning to Jonathan, the heir apparent and only male in the house of Saul he can trust, David pleads his innocence and spells out his extreme peril: "there is only one step between me and death" (1 Sam 20:3). For his part, Jonathan displays an unexpected naivete about Saul's true intentions, being under the impression that his father shares all his decisions with him (20:2). David's obvious distress causes Jonathan to reconsider: "Whatever you want me to do, I'll do for you" (20:4).

David devises a strategy for revealing Saul's secret strategy: he will absent himself from an expected dinner engagement with the king, and Jonathan must carefully observe how Saul reacts.[22] For his part, Jonathan will covertly convey the answer by ostensibly practicing his archery out in the open field. David will hide in a special hiding place toward which Jonathan shoots his arrows. If Jonathan informs the boy sent to retrieve the arrows that they fell on the near side of a certain rock, David should interpret that to mean: "you are safe, there is no danger" (20:21). If, however, the arrows fly beyond it, David should flee, "because the Lord has sent you away" (20:22). The name of the rock Ezel means, appropriately, "departure," a special touch not missed by Hebrew-speaking listeners and readers.

---

21. "The repetition of the saying invites comparison with the earlier occasion. Then what occurred was part of Saul's accession to the throne; here a humble and incapacitated Saul is debarred from using his royal authority to arrest David." Mackay, *1–2 Samuel*, 207.

22. The occasion was the monthly burnt offering marking each new moon (Num 28:11–15).

The answer was unmistakable: "Saul's anger flared up at Jonathan" (20:30) and he proceeded to make it crystal clear what should be done to David: "He must die" (20:31). When Jonathan protested, Saul hurled his spear at Jonathan. "Then Jonathan knew that his father intended to kill David" (20:33). He left the feast in anger and grief at Saul's shameful behavior. As planned, Jonathan relayed the message without anyone knowing.

Jonathan and David say their goodbyes in a poignant scene. Both men swear their covenant loyalty to each other and their families (20:42). By doing so, Jonathan virtually renounces his right of succession and acknowledges David as the legitimate king. What he asks of David is that when that happens, he would not wipe out Jonathan and his family, as typically happened in middle eastern dynastic changes. After parting in peace, Jonathan returns to a troubled household and David sets out on an uncharted course.

ASSISTANCE AND ASYLUM

David has nowhere to turn and few if any options. Just how long can he survive as a fugitive on the king's most wanted list? The rest of 1 Samuel provides the answer. The Lord will not abandon his chosen one. It won't be easy nor without its heart-stopping moments, but through it all the Lord remains faithful and proves himself to be David's hiding place and refuge. "Lord my God, I take refuge in you; save and deliver me from all who pursue me" (Ps 7:1; cf. Ps 11:1). Several psalms attributed to David reflect those dark days of desperation.

Assistance by the Priest Ahimelek

Fleeing southward along the ridge route, David turned aside at Nob, a priestly village just north of Jerusalem. Here he was met by an apprehensive priest named Ahimelek, alarmed that a commander in Saul's army would show up alone, unarmed, and unannounced. David claimed to be on a top-secret, last minute mission on behalf of the king himself—a patent falsehood.[23] Supposedly, what he urgently required, given the sudden and unusual nature of the mission, was food and weapons. Despite misgivings, Ahimelek volunteered both—consecrated bread from the altar and the great sword of Goliath having no equal in all Israel. "Thus armed with an

---

23. Alter, *David Story*, 131; Baldwin, *1 and 2 Samuel*, 146; Mackay, *1–2 Samuel*, 218–19; and Peterson, *First and Second Samuel*, loc. 2242; all acknowledge David lied, but Bergen asserts that "David was telling the truth" because the "king" in question was Yahweh—which stretches the truth, to say the least. Bergen, *1, 2 Samuel*, 221.

Excalibur of his own, and provisioned with holy bread, David left the priest of Nob in peace."[24]

Asylum with Achish King of Gath

Nourished andequipped, David fled to Achish the Philistine king of Gath for asylum. This is an unexpected move. Why on earth would David, the conqueror of Goliath of Gath the great Philistine champion, seek asylum there—seemingly tantamount to signing his death warrant? Needless to say, he hid Goliath's sword before showing up in Gath! But politics and war make strange bedfellows. Achish may have viewed David's request as a golden opportunity to reverse the fortunes of battle that had gone very badly for the Philistines since David joined Saul's army. By enlisting David's services as a loyal vassal, Achish could flip the script on the course and outcome of the conflict. In all likelihood, Achish already had intelligence about David's fall from favor. In short, David was *persona non grata* at Saul's court and to adapt an old adage, if you can't beat 'em, sign their best player! David's petition for asylum and Achish's hope for military success were quickly dashed. As one might expect, the attendants of Achish were hardly enthused by this new soldier of fortune, "the king of the land" celebrated in song as having slain many Philistines (1 Sam 21:11).[25] David picked up on their animosity and realized he had to escape.

How he pulled this off is the stuff of which legends are made. Attempting to fight his way out of Gath would have been pointless; he had to resort to a ruse that would result in expulsion from the city. Keeping his wits about him he pretended to be witless! He played the role of an insane person (21:13). In so doing, David gambled on a widespread view at that time about people who were deemed insane. Thinking them possessed by some alien spirit, people were extremely reluctant to execute such persons lest the demonic being wreak vengeance upon them. Fortunately for David, that was precisely the reaction he got. Achish now viewed David as damaged goods and of no military value whatsoever, concluding that the madman must go. David should be awarded an Oscar for his amazing performance! At the very least, one must be impressed by his quick thinking and ability to improvise on the spot, characteristics common to great leaders.[26] Beyond that, one must allow for divine intervention: "This poor man called, and the

24. Kirsch, *King David*, 81.

25. "Tens of thousands" is a poetic hyperbole.

26. The fictional character Captain Kirk of the starship *Enterprise* was renowned for his ability to think outside the box, even in the most life-threatening circumstances.

LORD heard him. He saved him out of all his troubles. The angel of the LORD encamps around those who fear him, and he delivers them" (Ps 34:6–7).[27]

Asylum in Adullam

After fleeing from Achish, David holed up in the cave of Adullam, located on the southwestern fringes of Saul's kingdom close to the frontier with the Philistines—a sort of no-man's land. According to the editorial notation for Psalm 57, this was the occasion prompting both a petition and a pledge: "Have mercy on me, my God, have mercy on me, for in you I take refuge. I will take refuge in the shadow of your wings until the disaster has passed" (Ps 57:1). The hideout served as a staging area for a small but growing ragtag resistance movement. In addition to his brothers and fellow clansmen, "all those who were in distress or in debt or discontented gathered around him, and he became their commander. About four hundred men were with him" (23:2).[28] David was acutely aware that his family was now at risk of royal retaliation. Notice where David transferred his family for safety: "he left them with the king of Moab" (22:3). Hardly an accident given the family history of David through his great-grandmother Ruth, a Moabitess.

Assistance by Gad and Abiathar

Two extremely valuable assets joined the rebel cause. It would be hard to overestimate the contributions of Gad the prophet and Abiathar the priest. They provided a direct link with Yahweh, enabling David to stay a step ahead of Saul's henchmen in hot pursuit. In Gad's first appearance, he functions as the virtual mouthpiece of Yahweh, directing David to leave Moab and return to a wooded area of Judah.[29] We will have occasion later, at the end of David's career, to hear Gad utter a word of judgment upon the king himself

27. The editorial notation at the beginning of Ps 34 notes that it was when he pretended to be insane before Abimelek, "who drove him away, and he left." Abimelek refers to Achish and may have been a dynastic name or title, like Pharaoh (cf. Gen 20:2; 26:1).

28. In a memorable description of this group, John Bright says: "His kinsmen rallied about him, together with malcontents, fugitives, and distressed persons of all sorts. Out of this flotsam, ruffians and desperadoes all, a tough fighting force of four hundred men soon emerged." Bright, *History of Israel*, 188–89.

29. I can't resist comparison to Robin Hood and his merry men in Sherwood Forest—though David's men were hardly merry most of the time! Kirsch characterizes Gad as "a master of guerrilla warfare. Like Mao Tse-tung and Che Guevara and Ho Chi Minh . . . " Kirsch, *King David*, 84. In my opinion, that's rhetorical overkill.

for a serious error in judgment (2 Sam 24:11–14). Gad's contributions went much further. In cooperation with David and Nathan the prophet, he later prescribed the Levitical liturgy and music for the temple.[30] He was also responsible for chronicling the events of David's momentous reign, a valuable primary source drawn upon by the historians of Kings and Chronicles.[31]

The story of Abiathar's defection requires special mention. He was the only son of Ahimelek to escape the massacre of the priests of Nob. Unfortunately, Doeg was present when Ahimelek assisted David. Responding to Saul's disparaging harangue against his officers for alleged disloyalty and sensing a generous reward, Doeg reported what he witnessed at Nob.[32] Saul trampled underfoot any notion of priestly sanctity and separation of power by indicting Ahimelek and his entire priestly family for high treason.[33] When Saul ordered their immediate execution, the officers refused. Not so Doeg the Edomite—he personally struck down eighty-five individuals.

Providentially, Abiathar escaped and relayed news of the grisly mass murder.[34] Feeling personally responsible, David offered him sanctuary. "As a result, king-elect and priest-elect join forces as fellow fugitives, and they forge a relationship that will last throughout David's reign."[35] As for Doeg, David rested in divine justice: "Surely God will bring you down to everlasting ruin: He will snatch you up and pluck you from your tent. He will uproot you from the land of the living" (Ps 52:5).

Abiathar brought much more than his priestly ministry to the rebel movement—he brought the ephod or priestly breastplate employed as a means of seeking specific divine guidance (1 Sam 23:6). This cultic item

30. 2 Chr 29:25.

31. 2 Chr 29:29.

32. "Doeg is an outsider who should have had more sense than to speak first in the midst of a family quarrel. But Doeg has news and he is exceedingly eager. He files his intelligence report. He breaks the silence. He thinks to advance himself by this ill-advised intervention." Brueggemann, *First and Second Samuel*, 158.

33. "Saul's behavior suggests something like a Captain Queeg scene from *The Caine Mutiny*. Saul's speech no longer shows any respect, regard, or trust for his best advisers and soldiers. He accuses them of not giving him information, of not reporting on how Jonathan has aided in setting up an ambush. Saul's charges against his Benjaminite supporters, as far as we know, have no basis in fact. But facts do not matter now to Saul. He is increasingly living in his own world of terrified fantasy." Brueggemann, *First and Second Samuel*, 158.

34. Alter notes the irony that "[Saul] is carrying out the ban he executed only imperfectly against Amalek . . . but the massacre is directed at his own innocent people." Alter, *David Story*, 139, n. 19.

35. Arnold, *1 & 2 Samuel*, loc. 6349. This close relationship ended when Abiathar backed the presumptuous Adonijah in his bid to succeed David. For this, Solomon banished him to the priestly town of Anathoth just a few miles northeast of Jerusalem.

was far superior to modern intelligence gathering devices and techniques because it linked to the Sovereign Lord, the one who knows all things both possible and actual.[36] If Goliath's sword had no equal in Israel, how much more could it be said of the ephod! Two episodes narrated in chapter 23 illustrate its crucial importance and the decided advantage it afforded David.

The first instance occurred when Philistine forces attacked Keilah, a neighboring Hebrew town. David's dilemma was understandable. His own situation was extremely tenuous. Should he add even more risk by engaging the Philistine forces? David consulted the ephod. The Lord answered: "Go, attack the Philistines and save Keilah" (23:1).[37] David's men, however, were alarmed by the prospect of being placed in double jeopardy and pushed back. David consulted the ephod again, just in case he had been mistaken. The answer was unambiguous and encouraging. It is a testament to their confidence in David as a leader that his men strapped on their weapons and followed him to Keilah where "he inflicted heavy losses on the Philistines and saved the people of Keilah" (23:5).

David and his men take up temporary residence in Keilah, probably enjoying a bountiful reward from a grateful populace. Being stationary as a fugitive, however, is not recommended for longevity.[38] Sooner or later you will be cornered with no escape. Saul's informants relay David's position in Keilah and Saul mobilizes his forces. David needs immediate divine guidance with regard to two hypothetical questions: (1) Will Saul actually attack? And (2) will the citizens of Keilah, under royal pressure, deliver David over to the king? The divine answer conveyed through the ephod was clear: yes, to both possibilities.[39] With not a moment to spare, David and his men evacuate and head for other hangouts. Note, however, that the little band of warriors has now increased to a battalion size force of six-hundred men. The movement is gaining momentum.

36. Many references support the doctrine of God's omniscience: e.g., Pss 139:7–8; 147:5; Prov 15:3; Jer 16:17; Acts 1:4; Heb 4:13.

37. Attempts to determine how inquiry by means of the ephod actually worked are mere conjectures owing to insufficient evidence. My suggestion is that the inquirer placed questions before the Lord requiring either a yes or no answer. Something in the ephod determined the answer. Some suggest that the ephod had a pouch with two objects inside, perhaps the Urim and Thummim. One indicated a "yes" and the other a "no." Was it like throwing two dice? We just don't know.

38. "[A] guerrilla army is always safest when it is on the move through the countryside." Kirsch, *King David*, 84.

39. Alter calls attention to the "political paradox of the situation": Saul enlisted the aid of those whom David had rescued to deliver up their deliverer. Alter, *David Story*, 142, n. 12.

David's flight from Adullam initiates a new phase during which Saul doggedly pursues his quarry in the desolate expanses of the Judaean Wilderness. That becomes the new chessboard upon which some of the most stirring stories in David's life story play themselves out. To these we now turn. But before continuing the saga, let's take stock of what has transpired.

OPPOSING TRAJECTORIES

The narratives in 1 Samuel 18:1 through 23:13 draw a stark contrast between the fortunes of the protagonists. The ancient historian explicitly states why this is so: The Spirit departed from the rejected king and dwelt upon the newly anointed king, David son of Jesse. The tragedy deepens as Saul clings desperately to power refusing to accept his rejection. A mentally unbalanced man doubles down on his efforts to eliminate his rival only to witness the uncanny survival of his nemesis. Assassination attempts all fail and David seems to lead a charmed life. Adding to Saul's irrational fear and hatred is the fact that those closest to him assist his adversary. Further isolating Saul, Samuel is no long available for guidance; no other prophet comes forth with a word from Yahweh, and after wiping out the priesthood at Nob, he has no link to Yahweh by means of an ephod. In short, Saul must go it alone and darkness settles upon his soul like a shroud. The reader anticipates the inevitable and tragic end.

INSTRUCTIVE TYPOLOGY

Christian readers of David's story should reflect on an important theological application. In many respects, followers of Christ are members of a resistance movement against the Dark Lord. Though assaulted by the "the powers of this dark world and . . . the spiritual forces of evil" (Eph 6:12), eventually, we'll celebrate a resounding victory by the Lamb of God, the Lion of the Tribe of Judah.[40] As with David, so with followers of Christ; the way forward may be fraught with hardship and peril, "but those who stand firm to the end will be saved" (Mark 13:13), and at the end, the faithful will receive "a crown of righteousness" (2 Tim 4:8) and "a share in his glory" (Rom 8:17). The Apostle Peter delivers our marching orders:

> Be alert and of sober mind. Your enemy the devil prowls around
> like a roaring lion looking for someone to devour. Resist him,
> standing firm in the faith, because you know that your fellow

40. Rev 5:5; 7:14–17; 19:11–16; 21:22–26.

believers throughout the world are undergoing the same kind of sufferings. And the God of all grace who called you to his eternal glory in Christ, after you have suffered a little while, will himself restore you and make you strong, firm and steadfast. To him be the power for ever and ever, Amen. (1 Pet 5:8–11)

7

CAT AND MOUSE GAME IN THE WILDERNESS OF JUDAH

Be merciful to me, my God, for my enemies are in hot pursuit; all day long they press their attack.

—PSALM 56:1

You, God, are my God, earnestly I seek you: I thirst for you, my whole being longs for you, in a dry and parched land where there is no water.

—PSALM 63:1

True courage is about knowing not when to take a life, but when to spare one.

—*THE HOBBIT*, J. R. R. TOLKIEN

Setting for Saul's Searches

AT 1 SAM 23:14, the scene shifts from the Shephelah to the Wilderness of Judah. The reader needs to know that the geography of these two regions differs dramatically. The western facing slopes of the Shephelah receive on average about twenty-four inches of precipitation a year and support abundant vegetation and crops. East of the water shed, the central ridge, the land lies in a rain shadow. As was mentioned in chapter 2 on Ruth, Bethlehem receives about twenty-three inches per annum. But a mere five-to-ten miles east of Bethlehem, in the Wilderness of Judah, the drop off is dramatic, amounting to only about eight inches and displaying a desert landscape. By the time one arrives at the Dead Sea, about fifteen miles east of Bethlehem, the total is only about one-to-two inches, an extremely arid region, much like Death Valley, California.[1] Obviously, the Wilderness of Judah looks nothing like a wilderness area in the Midwest or East Coast.

This becomes the new chessboard. David the hunted holds an advantage over his hunter—this is his backyard and he knows it like the back of his hand. As a young shepherd, he learned from firsthand experience where green pastures near springs and water holes in the deep wadis (canyons) could be found. He also knew the location of numerous caves, which served as convenient hiding places from Saul's spies trying to track his daily movements. And he could count on at least some of his fellow tribesmen to protect one of their own. The bottom line, however, as always, was God's hand upon his life: "Because you are my help, I sing in the shadow of your wings. I cling to you; your right hand upholds me" (Ps 63:7–8).

Scenarios in the Wilderness of Judah

First Samuel 23:14—26:25 moves us through another series of heart-pounding, narrow escapes. Because the narrator compresses the elapsed time, one receives the impression of constant movement from one hiding place to another. To be sure, there is some truth to that, but one must also realize that just as in protracted military campaigns, much of the time was rather uneventful. For example, the many letters and accounts of Civil War soldiers mention the tedium of military service. The long stretches of relative calm, however, could be suddenly shattered by moments of sheer terror. We turn now to several of these hair-raising episodes.

---

1. See Beitzel, *Moody Atlas*, 151–52, map 58; and Rasmussen, *NIV Atlas*, 114.

Hot Pursuit in the Desert of Ziph

At first, Saul had daily patrols searching for David and his men.[2] Two types of hideouts provided the fugitives temporary respite: wilderness strongholds and hill tops. The strongholds were probably small fortified towers that served both to keep track of and protect against raiding parties of desert tribes like the Geshurites, Girzites, and Amalekites.[3] Hill tops were good observation posts and allowed David's lookouts to spot Saul's patrols from a distance. Neither of these, however, provided permanent protection because once surrounded the chess game was over. The key to survival was literally staying one step ahead of Saul.

The narrator inserts Jonathan's last visit during this phase. At a place called Horesh, Jonathan and David said their final goodbyes and Jonathan encouraged David with a remarkable exhortation. "Don't be afraid . . . My father Saul will not lay a hand on you. You will be king over Israel, and I will be second to you. Even my father Saul knows this" (1 Sam 23:17). As it turned out, he was right about the first outcome, but sadly, not the second. In truth, given middle eastern politics, it was hardly a realistic expectation. Dynastic change rarely made room for members of the deposed regime, and if it did these retreads typically had short tenures, as was the case with Abner. Nonetheless, the covenant relationship between these two men of faith in Yahweh was renewed and they parted as friends, never to see each other again in this life. As we will see, after ascending the throne, David honored his covenant of friendship with Jonathan.

Close Call in the Desert of Maon

Not all the clansmen of Judah supported David and his band of buccaneers.[4] Whether arising from antipathy or anticipation of royal favors, some Ziphites notified Saul about David's whereabouts and promised to deliver up the fugitive. When Saul's forces arrived in the vicinity, David had already evacuated Horesh and fled to the Desert of Maon, probably not far from the Dead Sea. His new lair was relayed to Saul who promptly set off "in pursuit of David" (1 Sam 23:25).

2. 1 Sam 23:14.

3. For an example see the article by Schuster, "Israeli Soldiers."

4. "A close reading of the biblical passage reveals that men and women throughout the land of Israel—even his fellow tribesmen in the land of Judah—regarded David with suspicion and sometimes even hatred." Kirsch, *King David*, 89.

Saul's chase came within a whisker of succeeding. Just as his forces were "coming round the mountain" about to close in and capture David, a providential reprieve sprang the prey from the trap.[5] At that very moment, Saul received an urgent message: "The Philistines are raiding the land" (23:27). He had no choice; he broke off the attack and left to confront the new threat. Thereafter, the place of escape was fittingly named Sela Hammahlekoth, meaning "the rock of parting" (23:28). If the parting from Jonathan at Horesh had been "such sweet sorrow,"[6] the parting from Saul at the mountain of Maon was a blessed relief! And so, the mouse would live for another day.

Golden Opportunity at Ein Gedi

The scene now shifts to one of the most visited sites in Israel. Beginning near the top of high bluffs overlooking the Dead Sea, the Wadi Arugot and Wadi David slice their way down to the western shoreline. Along the course of these steep wadis are numerous caves and lovely waterfalls. Near the head of Wadi David is a life-giving spring, called En Gedi, the second of only two fresh water springs along the entire western edge of the Dead Sea. The name means "spring of the young goat" and refers to wild or mountain goats, extremely agile creatures well adapted to scrambling up rock cliffs.[7] As the spring water courses its way toward the Salt Sea [literal translation of the Hebrew], it transforms a narrow strip of desert into an oasis, providing a wide range of agricultural products, most notably dates.[8]

After repelling the Philistine incursion, Saul received an updated report about David's new hangout at En Gedi. Once again, he set out with an elite and formidable force of three thousand soldiers in tow. David was now outnumbered five to one and had very little wiggle room for an escape. Another adrenalin moment ensued.

5. 1 Sam 23:26. Kyle McCarter Jr. imagines Saul employing a pincher movement around the mountain in order to capture David and his men on the back side. David escaped before the pincher snapped shut. Cited by Alter, *David Story*, 145, n. 26.

6. Spoken by Juliet in Act I, Scene II, from Shakespeare's *Romeo and Juliet*.

7. Visitors to the national park of En Gedi delight in seeing the nimble ibexes along the cliffs. Because of the huge number of visitors every year, they have become quite used to humans and allow close approach. Unfortunately, too many tourists also feed the animals, something the park authorities expressly forbid.

8. This area was highly coveted and a major source of income during the reign of Herod the Great. In the Song of Songs, the woman likens her beloved to "a cluster of henna blossoms from the vineyards of En Gedi" (Song 1:14).

And then, something totally unexpected happened: a golden opportunity fell right into David's lap. With one sword thrust, he could have rid
himself of his royal dementor,[9] the source of both personal and communal
anguish. The circumstances are described in great detail because the sacred
historian considered this a defining moment for David's future career. He
accomplishes this by inserting a series of dialogues between David and his
men on one hand, and David and Saul on the other. These exchanges reveal the character of the dialogue partners far more effectively than a mere
chronicling.

Here is what happened. As Saul and his men were sweeping down the
wadi, nature called, and Saul turned aside to relieve himself in one of the
caves. Little did he know that David and his men had taken cover in the
deep recesses of that very cave. It must have required great restraint on the
part of David's men to keep their voices down. "This is the day the LORD
spoke of when he said to you, 'I will give your enemy into your hands for
you to deal with as you wish'" (1 Sam 24:4). With that green light flashing in
his mind, David crept close to where Saul was squatting. But as he stealthily
approached and saw Saul's royal robe temporarily cast aside, he changed his
mind. Quietly, David "cut off a corner of Saul's robe" (24:4) and slipped back
to where his men were waiting with weapons drawn.

The mention of the corner of Saul's robe recalls the moment when
Samuel turned to leave after rejecting Saul as king. "Saul caught hold of the
hem of his robe, and it tore" (1 Sam 15:27). Samuel discerned in this spon-
taneous act a symbolic action: "The Lord has torn the kingdom of Israel
from you today and has given it to one of your neighbors—to one better
than you" (15:28). David the chosen one delivered a dramatic confirmation
of that verdict.

The initial reaction of David's men was stunned disbelief. David carried only a corner of Saul's robe in his hand and no blood on his sword.
How could he have allowed a divinely orchestrated opportunity like that to
slip away and prolong their agony? Only the sheer force of David's charisma
and their personal loyalty prevented them from rushing forward and dispatching Saul on the spot. The historian tells us, however, that David was
conscience-stricken that he had even carried out a mocking gesture against
the Lord's anointed.[10]

The royal bloodhound of Benjamin "left the cave and went his way"
(24:7). But David seized the moment to plead his case. After Saul was well

9. With a tip of the hat to J. K. Rowling's terrifying figures in the *Harry Potter* series.

10. "Clearly, what David feels is that he has perpetrated a kind of symbolic mutilation of the king by cutting off the corner of his garment . . ." Alter, *David Story*, 148,
n. 6.

out of range, David called after him and, prostrating himself, delivered an impassioned defense of his loyalty to the king. Saul should not listen to those who accuse him of murderous intent, the facts speak otherwise. Given the perfect opportunity, as witnessed by the piece of royal robe, he did not lift his hand against the Lord's anointed nor would he ever do so. Furthermore, Saul was just wasting his time tracking down a nobody who posed no real threat.[11] Finally, the heavenly judge will rule in David's favor.

Saul had no defense, he could only admit wrongdoing: "You have treated me well, but I have treated you badly" (24:17).[12] He even acknowledged the inevitable: "You will surely be king" (24:20). All he could do was extract an oath from David that when it does happen, Saul's family would be spared the customary purge. David gave his word and with that another dramatic confrontation ended; Saul went home and David and his men went up to the stronghold.[13]

DISASTER AVERTED AND A NEW BRIDE ACQUIRED

Shortly after the En Gedi escapade, Samuel the prophet, the last of the judges and the king-maker king-breaker of Israel, passed away. It was the end of

11. Alter notes that a dead dog metaphor for someone worthless was proverbial. "David goes the idiom one better by saying he is scarcely more important that a single flea on the dead dog's carcass[!] . . . " Alter, *David Story*, 150, n. 15.

12. One recalls Judah's acknowledgment of wrongdoing against Tamar (Gen 38:26). Brueggemann links Saul's speech to a patriarchal story: "Saul's initial statement is a masterful narrative device. Why does he ask whose voice it is (v. 16)? Is it too dark to see? The language is powerfully reminiscent of Isaac, who was feeble and could not identify his son (Gen 27:18, 32). Is the question placed in Saul's mouth intended to recall Isaac?" Brueggemann, *First and Second Samuel*, 171.

13. That, of course, prompts a question: Where was the stronghold? The short answer is: we don't know. Klein assumes that David went back to the cave of Adullam. Klein, *1 Samuel*, 24:22. As does Gordon, *II Samuel*, 181. But that would put him in even more peril owing to its relative proximity to Saul's forces and the lack of an escape route once surrounded. Others suggest the imposing mountain stronghold of Masada, one of the most visited and impressive of all the sites in Israel. Beitzel, *Moody Atlas*, 151. To be sure, from the time of the Hasmoneans until Herod the Great, this natural rock fortress did indeed serve as a stronghold. Herod transformed it into a show piece palace and it was this site where the stirring story of the fall of Masada to the Roman legions of Silva occurred in AD 73. Flavius Josephus recorded this epic struggle in *J. W.* VII, 259–416. For my part, I doubt Masada is the stronghold referred to in our text. At that time, there was no access to water on its summit, an absolute necessity for survival. Furthermore, as already mentioned, staying on such a height would invite certain capture because there was literally no way off the mountain except for one difficult route. Once surrounded on top of Masada, the chess game would be at the point of "check." "Checkmate" would soon follow.

an era. For forty years, he had been a guiding, steadying influence during transitional and tumultuous times. Saul was now left to his own devices and his tragic demise would not long delay. Meanwhile, a state funeral with a period of national mourning postponed any immediate plans for renewed pursuit of David.[14]

Once again, David changed venue and moved farther south into the Negev of southern Judah.[15] At this time, another ally entered David's story. Her name was Abigail and she saved David from making a big mistake. In the process, she also became his third wife!

Here's how it came about. In the Negev of the Calebites lived a man named Nabal, a discredit to the honorable legacy of Caleb. Though very wealthy by the standards and culture of the day, he was "surly and mean in his dealings" (1 Sam 25:3). There is a wry sense of humor in the story involving the man's name. Elsewhere in the Hebrew Bible, the word *nabal* means "fool." But what parents would stoop to such meanness? Consequently, scholars suggest, on the basis of cognate languages, that the meaning intended by his parents was something like "chosen." However, because Nabal was such a jerk, the biblical meaning fit like a glove; behind his back, the neighbors quite agreed—even his wife, Abigail! "He is just like his name— his name means Fool, and folly goes with him" (1 Sam 25:25). The listener/ reader knows in advance that David's request will not be warmly received.

This episode helps us understand how David and his six-hundred outlaws could survive in such a desolate region. They essentially earned their keep by serving as a militia protecting the southern tribesmen and their flocks and herds from desert marauders. While probably not operating a protection racket,[16] they obviously did accept and expect food and drink donations. In this instance, when David heard about Nabal's sheepshearing festival, he seized on the opportunity to collect "tithes" for services rendered.

Nabal rebuffed David's request with a defiant and disparaging refusal. From Nabal's point of view, David was a nobody and he and his men were nothing more than rogues and traitors. Recall that Saul had set up a victory monument in Carmel "in his own honor" to commemorate his defeat

---

14. 1 Sam 25:1.

15. The Paran mentioned here can hardly refer to the Paran of Sinai (Num 10:12), much too far south to make sense of the narrative. Some LXX mss have "Maon" which makes good sense geographically. If Paran is original, it must refer to a site in southern Judah. See Beitzel, *Moody Atlas*, 152, map 58; Rasmussen, *NIV Atlas*, 114; and Schlegel, *Satellite Atlas*, map 5-3.

16. Suggested also by Alter, *David Story*, 153, n. 7. Kirsch likens David to "a shake-down artist." Kirsch, *King David*, 89-91. In my view, this reads too much modern urban culture into the narrative. At face value, David acts out of honorable motives.

of the Amalekites (15:12).[17] As it turns out, Nabal had property in Carmel and supported Saul because he struck down the Amalekites who periodically raided the region. When David's emissaries returned and reported the insult, he was incensed. Living in the desert is never easy; adding insult to injury is like a trip wire. He strapped on his sword and ordered four hundred of his men to do likewise and follow him. He was bent on revenge in which there would be no male survivors in the house of Nabal.[18]

"Abigail acted quickly" (15:18). She must head off David's attack and appeal to his conscience. This she does with masterful eloquence and execution. Without consulting Nabal, she quickly collected a generous quantity of provisions and dispatched them in advance of her personal appeal for mercy, reminding us of Jacob's strategy of appeasing his estranged brother Esau.[19] Abigail's entreaty demonstrates another instance of divine providence intervening in David's life: "As she came riding her donkey into a mountain ravine, there was David and his men descending toward her" (15:20). She intercepted him just in time to prevent mass murder in retaliation for a contemptuous insult. Although David exercised remarkable restraint at En Gedi, he lost his cool with a "surly and mean" man of much less standing than Saul.

Abigail's plea is a model of diplomacy. She first admitted that Nabal's boorish behavior was inexcusable, but she had not been present and so was unable to intercede. Then she emphasized that Yahweh himself had prevented David from personally avenging himself with bloodshed (25:26). The unstated assumption was that such behavior was beneath the dignity of Yahweh's anointed. A further unstated assumption was that killing a fellow tribesman and all his male heirs on the grounds of personal insult would not only be unjustified, it would invite tribal retaliation. Finally, she appealed to David to accept the provisions as a gift and apology.

Asking David's indulgence, she then proceeded to deliver a carefully crafted exhortation exhibiting remarkable theological conviction. Yahweh had anointed David to be king of Israel and promised a long-lasting dynasty. In the meantime, because of this divine appointment, Yahweh would preserve him through all his trials, "bound securely in the bundle of the

17. The Carmel in question was located in the Negev, not to be confused with Mount Carmel in the north.

18. The Hebrew expression rendered in English as "male" is literally "one who pisses against the wall," exactly the way the KJV translated it! All modern English versions substitute a less vulgar sounding term. It should be noted that in all instances where the Hebrew expression occurs the context conveys the notion of contempt, which is the nuance intended by David. In contemporary idiom, we might say David was pissed off!

19. Gen 32:13—33:15.

living" (25:29). The bottom line is this: trust the LORD God of Israel. Once again, the reader is reminded that this was precisely the thing Saul failed to do. She concluded with a pointed reminder: David should not acquire guilt for "needless bloodshed or of having avenged himself" (25:31). To this she added a final word: "remember your servant" (25:31).[20] He did.

Graciously and gratefully David acknowledged his indebtedness to Abigail, a woman of "good judgment" (25:33). She had spared him from committing an act of personal vengeance that doubtless would have greatly complicated his ascension to the throne. He accepted her gift, granted her request, and dismissed her in peace.

Ten days later, Nabal died of an apparent stroke. Abigail, "an intelligent and beautiful woman" (25:33), had been married to a fool, an extremely trying man.[21] It comes as no surprise then that shortly after Nabal's death, David proposed to her and she accepted. And so, it came about that Abigail, a woman who spoke "with wisdom and faithful instruction" (Prov 31:26), came alongside David at a critical point in his career. She brought to the marriage a theological commitment that complemented David's.[22]

HAKILAH HILL: ANOTHER OPPORTUNITY TO KILL SAUL

The scene shifts again to the Desert of Ziph facing the eastern desert of Jeshimon and overlooking the Dead Sea (1 Sam 26). Saul's Ziphite informers notified him that David had been spotted on a hill called Hakilah (location unknown). After mobilizing his elite forces, Saul arrived on the scene and set up camp on the road leading to Hakilah. David's scouts informed him of Saul's encampment. He then resorted to an incredibly risky undertaking. Taking Abishai his nephew (who later was appointed a commander in the army and celebrated as one of the three mighty warriors of Israel), he slipped into Saul's camp in the dead of night. Following standard procedure, Saul bedded down right in the middle of the camp surrounded by his commander in chief, Abner, as well as his personal bodyguard. Incredibly,

20. The notion that she is actually "proposing to David that she carry out a kind of contract killing of her husband, with the payoff that she will become the wife of the handsome young warrior and future king" owes more to modern novels and murder mysteries than reading the text the way it wants to be read. Alter, *David Story*, 159, n. 31.

21. "She clearly has been chafing over her marriage with a boorish, unpleasant, and probably older man, and she sees an opportunity here." Alter, *David Story*, 156, n. 25.

22. "Abigail is the perfect partner for this headstrong man, knowing how to be shrewdly discerning, politically efficient, and theologically astute." Brueggemann, *First and Second Samuel*, 181.

David and Abishai were able to penetrate the outer defenses and reach Saul's sleeping spot marked by his personal spear.

Some commentators hold that the narrator stretches the truth to the breaking point and engages in sheer invention for the sake of a good story. Before resorting to such skepticism, let's ask ourselves how the text itself wants to be read. The narrator quite straightforwardly attributes David's ability to penetrate Saul's perimeter to God: "They were all sleeping because the LORD had put them into a deep sleep" (26:12).[23] In short, this was another instance of divine intervention that both preserved David's life and provided one more opportunity for Saul to repent and step down.

As in the cave at En Gedi, so here in the camp, Saul was completely at David's mercy. Abishai speaks for all the rebels when he assures David: "Today God has delivered your enemy into your hands" (26:8). The temptation must have been enormous. But once again David's response was unchanged: "Don't destroy him! Who can lay a hand on the Lord's anointed and be guiltless?" (26:9). He was confident one of three things would happen: The Lord would strike him down, he would die of natural causes, or he would die in battle. Bible readers know what happened, and we will revisit that tragic episode in the next chapter. But first we conclude the camp story.

Two tokens, Saul's spear and water jug, were taken to serve as exhibits A and B of the mortal peril Saul had just survived owing only to David's mercy. After slipping back out of the camp and crossing over to the other side of the wadi, he woke up Saul's camp with a rude reveille. Abner was shamed for his shoddy security and reminded of the seriousness of his lapse. Saul was chastised for his baseless charges against David and his fruitless chases after "a partridge in the mountains" (26:20).

When David asked Saul where his spear and water jug were, the realization of what had just happened shook the king and his commander in chief to the core. Saul again openly admitted his sin and his folly. Abner remained silent.[24] David invited one of Saul's servants to retrieve the royal spear—no mention was made of the water jug, something you never leave home without in the desert! Saul could only utter a blessing upon David, a blessing no doubt with a bitter taste on his lips: "David, my son, you will do great things and surely triumph" (26:25).[25] "So David went on his way, and Saul returned home" (26:25). David would never see Saul again.

23. "It was a 'deep sleep' like Adam knew in the creation of Eve (Gen 2:21), of the kind Abraham knew in the promise of God (Gen 15:12)." Brueggemann, *First and Second Samuel*, 184.

24. "Abner answers not a word to God. He stands indicted, reduced to silence." Brueggemann, *First and Second Samuel*, 186.

25. "Saul's last word is a relinquishment of the future to David." Brueggemann, *First*

THEOLOGICAL REFLECTION

Before moving ahead with the story, we need to pause and reflect on David's two "missed" opportunities to kill Saul. Obviously, the narrator attaches great significance to them since they are described in great detail and we should ask why.

For the sacred historian, this was a defining moment, illustrating what it means to be a man after God's own heart. Two theological and judicial principles undergird the cave and camp episodes. (1) Yahweh alone raises up and removes kings. This sacral act means that the person of the king is to be honored, obeyed, and protected. To raise one's hand against the sovereign is an act of sacrilege and treason, punishable by death. (2) The king also owes complete allegiance to the sovereign God of Israel. Should the king commit high crimes and misdemeanors, he is answerable to the high king of heaven who will render impartial justice and punishment carried out by his chosen spokespersons. Under the provisions of divine kingship, the individual subject was not permitted to be the judge, jury, and executioner of royal transgressions.

This is precisely the stance David adopts in his encounters with King Saul—he doesn't take justice into his own hands; he entrusts himself to the one who will plead his case and vindicate his cause. The bottom line echoes the Abrahamic conviction: "Will not the Judge of all the earth do right?" (Gen 18:25).

Modern readers live in a quite different culture and era in which the old divine right of king's has been superseded by democratic, representative forms of government. Under a constitutional form of government, there are specific limitations on the powers of elected officials. Individual citizens are granted the right of free speech, including dissent from public policy. However, just as in biblical times, one may not lift a hand against duly elected officials, but rather, defer to due process of law through authorized channels and judiciaries. There are established, legal procedures for removing and punishing elected officials who violate the rule of law. No individual is above the law nor authorized to take the law into his or her own hands.[26]

If one were to ask what would Saul have done had the sandals been reversed, the answer is obvious—he wouldn't have hesitated for an instant. He didn't wait for Samuel to offer a sacrifice before battle and he didn't prevent his men from plundering the good stuff of the Amalekites. Therein lies the

---

and Second Samuel, 183.

26. On December 18, 2019, the United States House of Representatives passed articles of impeachment against President Donald J. Trump. The two charges were abuse of power and obstruction of Congress.

critical difference between Saul and David. Saul sought to be "the master of the house"; David sought to be a servant in the Master's house. As the book of Proverbs observes, "There is a way that appears to be right, but in the end it leads to death" (Prov 16:25). Saul chose the way that leads to death; David chose the way that, paradoxically, leads to life. As the Master said, "For whoever wants to save their life will lose it, but whoever loses their life for me will find it" (Matt 16:25).

Most of us will never be in situation quite like David's. But there may be occasions in which we are tempted to take justice into our own hands. Precisely in those moments we need to ask this question: What does it mean to be a person after God's own heart? David's inspired hymnody provides guidance. "I cry out to God most high, to God, who vindicates me. He sends from heaven and saves me, rebuking those who hotly pursue me—God sends forth his love and his faithfulness" (Ps 57:2–3). David's attitude mirrors that of his greater Son who, when betrayed and arrested, rebuked Peter, "Put your sword away!" (John 18:11). Jesus reminded his apostles that he had at his disposal "more than twelve legions of angels" (Matt 26:53), but he refused "the temptation to reach his God-appointed destiny by unauthorized and sinful means."[27] David's refusal to take Saul's life was one of his finest hours. It takes courage to know when to spare a life.

---

27 Mackay, 1–2 Samuel, 241.

8

SAUL'S SUICIDE ON MT. GILBOA

How the mighty have fallen!

—2 SAMUEL 1:27

First Samuel 27:1—Second Samuel 1:27 resolves the conflict and tension between two anointed kings coexisting at the same time: Saul the anointed but rejected king, and David the anointed but waiting-in-the-wings king. The section falls into four carefully crafted panels that toggle the reader between the respective destinies of the two protagonists, neither appearing in a panel together. They have gone their separate ways and Yahweh deals separately with them by bringing Saul's story to a tragic end and opening a door for David's further ascent to power. It breaks out as following:

- David's deployment as a Philistine vassal (1 Sam 27:1—28:2)
- Saul's desperation in the face of the Philistine threat (1 Sam 28:3–25)
- David's discharge from the Philistine army (1 Sam 29:1–31)
- Saul's death fighting the Philistines (1 Sam 31:1—2:27)

The tragic death of Saul in defense of Israel against their inveterate enemies, the Philistines, unifies the entire section. Saul began his career as king by successfully repelling Philistine forces from the central mountain ridge of Benjamin. It ended on Mount Gilboa with a futile attempt to repel the Philistines from the Jezreel Valley. The geopolitical implications of Saul's failure require further discussion. In the meantime, however, I pick up the threads of the narrative following the famous camp incident on Hakilah Hill.

David's Deployment as a Philistine Vassal

David the Doubter

Despite Abigail's confident assertion that Yahweh would protect David and bring him to the throne of Israel, and David's acting on this conviction by passing on yet another opportunity to be rid of Saul, he now began to waver and entertain second thoughts about his survivability. "One of these days I will be destroyed by the hand of Saul" (1 Sam 27:1). He decided to end the nerve-wracking cat-and-mouse game and once more seek asylum with Achish. The reader, of course, remembers what happened the first time. Why would David think it would be any different? As the saying goes, "fool me once, shame on you; fool me twice, shame on me." Earlier, however, we made the point that politics makes strange bedfellows. It's not as if Achish were the most gullible guy in Gath! Some things have dramatically changed. Earlier rumors of disaffection between the king and his famous commander have been substantiated by Saul's repeated searches aimed at capturing and killing David. Furthermore, a troubling reality persisted, Philistine inability to deliver a knockout blow to the kingdom of Saul. So along comes David the charismatic warlord with a corps of six-hundred fighting men offering his services as a vassal. The potential benefits far outweighed the risks. This man and his warriors really could change the course of the war. At the very least, he wouldn't be exerting his leadership skills on behalf of Israel.[1]

David the Devious Defector

David's defection ended a nightmarish existence: "[Saul] no longer searched for him" (1 Sam 27:4). But it brought with it a hellish kind of double life

---

1. Bergen recalls the adage, "My enemy's enemy is my friend." Bergen, 1, 2 Samuel, 260.

lasting a year and four months.[2] Owing to the size of his contingent,[3] David requested a transfer from Gath and received a billet in Ziklag, one of the satellite towns in the Philistine orbit.[4] According to the Chronicler, it was during this time that Benjamite defectors, even some relatives of Saul, augmented David's ranks—elite soldiers adept with bows and slings.[5] In addition, Gadites warriors "able to handle the shield and spear" and "the least was a match for a hundred, and the greatest for a thousand" (1 Chr 12:8, 14), along with some Judahites, allied themselves with David. The nucleus of a formidable fighting force was beginning to take shape in the Judean Negev. These defectors shared an unflinching loyalty: "We are yours, David! We are with you, son of Jesse! Success, success to you, and success to those who help you, for your God will help you" (1 Chr 12:18).

And so, from Ziklag, about twenty-four miles southwest of Gath, David launched attacks on the marauding desert tribes, the Geshurites, Girgizites, and Amalekites. In so doing, he and his men continued to protect the southern flanks of the tribe of Judah. This is not, however, what David told Achish. When required to report his activities to his overlord, David claimed his attacks were directed at various Judahite areas and clans, namely, the "Negev of Judah" or the "Negev of Jerahmeel" or "the Negev of the Kenites" (1 Sam 27:10). Of course, the only way David could pull off this deception was by making sure there were no survivors, neither "man or woman" (1 Sam 27:11). Consequently, all non-combatants—probably even children—were massacred, a grim and grisly undertaking.[6]

Some might defend his actions as a necessary evil in times of war, raising again the problematic issue of violence and war. Rather than devote considerable space to this perennial ethical and moral dilemma, I offer a few observations.[7] There is no indication in the biblical text that Yahweh directed David to defect; it was David's sense of despair and his flagging confidence in Yahweh's ability to protect him that prompted his decision. If

2. 1 Sam 27:7. "At one level David's policy has achieved success; he is no longer hounded by Saul—but at what cost? . . . David's period in Ziklag is a spiritual low-point characterized by deception and unnecessary slaughter." Mackay, *1–2 Samuel*, 260.

3. Alter estimates it could have been a group of two or three thousand. See Alter, *David Story*, 169, n. 5.

4. For a full discussion on the location of Ziklag, see Rainey and Notley, *Sacred Bridge*, 148–50.

5. 1 Chr 12:1–2.

6. "While the pragmatic wisdom of this policy is evident, his behavior is ethically indefensible." Mackay, *1–2 Samuel*, 261. Kirsch doesn't mince words: "The Bible leaves no doubt at all that he committed the kinds of atrocities that we call war crimes." Kirsch, *King David*, 104.

7. On this topic, I highly recommend Hays, *Moral Vision*.

David had held on just a bit longer, the problem would have resolved itself without his having to compromise his integrity or defend himself against accusations of treason. In fact, one of the main purposes of the narrator in his rather lengthy account of Saul's death and David's whereabouts is to answer allegations that David was directly or indirectly responsible for Saul's death.

To be sure, Yahweh preserved David during this time, but preservation doesn't amount to approval. Recall that David was not permitted to build the temple because he had "shed much blood on the earth in my sight" (1 Chr 22:7 cf. 28:3). Furthermore, David and his men very likely suffered repercussions on account of their despicable deeds—guilt is an inexorable bloodhound.

The number of US service men and women who return from active duty in war zones with PSTD speaks for itself.[8] Shakespeare captures the anguish of many a tortured soul when he has Macbeth utter the following words after killing Duncan in his sleep: "To know my deed, 'twere best not to know myself" (*Macbeth*, Act II, Scene II). In perhaps the most powerful line in English literature expressing guilt and remorse for murder, Lady Macbeth says, "Here's the smell of blood still. All the perfumes of Arabia will not sweeten this little hand" (Act V, Scene I). War and violence unavoidably foster moral ambiguities and raise ethical dilemmas.[9] When living under constant duress and fear, moral vision blurs and rationalization redefines right. Lady Macbeth only evades the problem when she tries to help her husband deal with his guilt and fear: "Things without all remedy should be without regard: what's done, is done" (Act III, Scene II). There's a better way.

So, how do we deal with moral failures? Those who stand outside the specific circumstances must take care. This is not the time to rush to judgment or hypocritically imagine we would have acted righteously. Great

---

8. An acronym for post-traumatic stress disorder. The estimated percentages are: Operation Iraqi Freedom, 20 percent; Gulf War, 12 percent; Vietnam War, 15 percent. Because many cases go unreported, these estimates are almost certainly lower than actual rates. Here is an excerpt of an interview with a US marine soon after he [unnecessarily] killed six men in a small room in Fallujah, Iraq (2004): "'My fiancée's worried that I'm not going to come back the same. I'll never tell her what things I did here. I'll never tell anybody. 'Cause I'm not proud of killing people. I'm just proud to serve my country. I hate being here but I love it at the same time.' The fiancée was right. He wouldn't come back the same. He thought his war was over, but a few months later, back in the safety of his childhood home surrounded by his adoring family, the dark secrets and all the guilt emerged from his mind." Sites, "Unforgiven."

9. For a sobering reflection on war in the context of Christian faith see Jones, "Living with War," 2–4.

empathy is required because we are all vulnerable and the Dark Lord knows our limits and weaknesses.

David the transgressor, moved by the Holy Spirit, points us to the only option that really works. "Have mercy on me, O God, according to your unfailing love; according to your great compassion blot out my transgressions. Wash away all my iniquity and cleanse me from my sin" (Ps 51:1). The Apostle John agrees: "If we confess our sins, he is faithful and just and will forgive us our sins and purify us from all unrighteousness" (1 John 1:9).

That brings us to an important principle in reading David's story in Scripture: not everything David the man after God's own heart *does* serves as an example for us to follow. His execution of non-combatants in the Negev is a clear case in point. This moral and spiritual low point in David's career serves as a warning "not to idolize any individual, no matter how successfully they have hitherto weathered the storms of persecution and temptation."[10]

But what David *says* when inspired by the Holy Spirit may be trusted fully. "Then I acknowledged my sin to you and did not cover up my iniquity. I said, 'I will confess my transgressions to the Lord.' And you forgave the guilt of my sin" (Ps 32:5). We have it on unimpeachable authority: "Blessed are those whose transgressions are forgiven, whose sins are covered" (Ps 32:1). An anonymous psalmist chimes in: "If you, LORD, kept a record of sins, LORD who could stand? But with you there is forgiveness, so that we can, with reverence, serve you" (Ps 132:3–4). The refrain of Psalm 136 (NAB) says it all: "His mercy endures forever."

David's Dilemma

David's double dealings come to an end with the ultimate dilemma, a worst-case scenario. The Philistines launch their most serious effort to subdue Saul's kingdom. Their strategy makes perfect sense. Rather than try another assault on the hill country and heartland of Saul's kingdom, they decide on a pincher movement designed to cut the Hebrew kingdom in half. The perfect place to execute this maneuver is the Jezreel Valley, the only valley that bisects Israel from west to east, from the Mediterranean coast to the Jordan Valley. By occupying the Jezreel, the Philistines divide and conquer. The southern tribes are cut off from the northern tribes and the Philistines can slowly strangle the hill country of Ephraim, Benjamin, and Judah. Saul, of course, knows immediately what is at stake—he must respond to the most serious threat of his reign.

10. Mackay, *1–2 Samuel*, 262.

And what of David? Achish requests David and his contingent to accompany him in the battle and serve as his personal bodyguard. Talk about a catch-22![11] The narrator leaves us hanging and the scene now shifts back to Saul.

SAUL'S DESPERATION IN THE FACE OF THE PHILISTINE THREAT

Saul's situation is desperate and one feels sympathy as his death, like a Greek tragedy, agonizingly plays itself out on center stage. The narrator reminds us Samuel was dead and buried. When Saul inquired of Yahweh, he "did not answer him by dreams or Urim or prophets" (1 Sam 28:6), and "terror filled his heart" (28:5). Only the dark side remained, but even that was problematic because earlier Saul had expelled "the mediums and spiritists from the land" (28:3).[12] But he was desperate and demanded that a medium be found somewhere so he could contact the departed Samuel, his last and only hope.

Saul's Deployment at Jezreel

Before we attend Saul's séance, let's take stock of what was happening on the ground. The Philistines camped at Shunem just below the Hill of Moreh. Saul bivouacked at the spring in Jezreel on the southern side of the Jezreel Valley, opposite the Philistines[13] From his vantage point, Saul could see what he was up against. The Philistines had a large, well-equipped army with a formidable chariot corp. The odds were heavily stacked against him. He would need divine intervention—but Yahweh was silent.

Saul's Séance

The prequel to the battle of Mount Gilboa is bizarre. It involves a dangerous, nocturnal visit behind enemy lines to consult a medium in the village of Endor. One recalls Gideon's daring night-time reconnaissance mission to the

11. Arnold wryly observes: "It is time for David to 'fish or cut bait.'" Arnold, *1 & 2 Samuel*, loc. 7516.

12. On the prohibitions against such illicit activity, see Lev 19:31; 20:6, 27; Deut 18:11.

13. Earlier Saul arrayed his forces on the northern slopes of the Elah Valley opposite the Philistines on the south. This time the Philistines were on the north and the Hebrews the south.

Midianite camp. He and his little band of three hundred were camped in the same general vicinity as Saul and his army (Judg 7:9–15). Unlike Gideon's encouraging intel, Saul's sortie reveals the worst possible outcome.

With two bodyguards and wearing a disguise, he circuitously slips into Endor and demands that the medium conjure up a departed spirit. Suspicious, she reminds the mysterious visitors of Saul's ban on all mediums. Incognito, Saul assures the woman that no punishment would befall her for arranging a séance.[14] "Bring up Samuel" (1 Sam 28:11). Ironically, Saul's name means "to ask or inquire." The first time we meet Saul he is asking Samuel's help to find his father's donkeys—which he did. Now at the end of his life, he asks Samuel for help against the Philistines—which he didn't.

What happens next is debated. At face value the text says she recognized Samuel and realized it was Saul who stood beside her. He reassured her of immunity and asked, "What do you see?" Her answer: "a ghostly figure" looking like "an old man wearing a robe" (28:13). "Saul knew it was Samuel" (28:14).

If Saul thought Samuel would somehow bail him out of this impending disaster, he was bitterly disappointed and utterly devastated. The prophet didn't soften in the least his disdain for Saul's disobedience—in fact he virtually reiterated his earlier denunciation.[15] Sounding annoyed that Saul had even disturbed him, Samuel pronounced Saul's fate and that of his doomed army. Saul and his sons would join Samuel in Sheol (place of the departed dead) along with many of his soldiers.[16] The narrator portrays a broken, pathetic man: "Saul fell full length on the ground" (28:20). As he lay immobilized before Samuel's spirit, Saul's career has essentially come full circle. At Mizpah, Samuel the kingmaker stood beside him and extolled his virtues: "There is no one like him among all the people" (1 Sam 10:24). Now he lay prostrate before the prophet, a condemned king paralyzed by dread.

The dark night at Endor ends with the medium preparing and serving a meal fit for a king.[17] As it turns out, it's Saul's last supper. Afterward, "that

14. "No reader can miss the irony that Saul was both lawmaker and lawbreaker. Saul swore by the life of Yahweh—again an ironic contrast with the spirits of the dead he wanted to invoke—that no guilt would accrue to the woman because of her actions." Klein, *1 Samuel*, 271. See also, Kirsch, *King David*, 441.

15. 1 Sam 28:17; cf. 15:18.

16. Sheol is often depicted in the OT as beneath the earth. In this regard, the Hebrew view of life after death was similar to that of the ANE. However, a much more hopeful view of life after death for the righteous gradually emerges in the canon of the OT. As the NT triumphantly proclaims, the resurrection of Jesus "destroyed death and has brought life and immortality to light through the gospel" (2 Tim 1:10). See further, Helyer, *Yesterday*, 334–47.

17. Alter calls it "an odd and eerie juncture of the story." Alter, *David Story*, 179, n.

same night they got up and left" (28:25). The perceptive reader may hear an echo of these words in the Apostle John's account of Jesus' Last Supper: "And it was night . . . Come now, let us leave" (John 13:30; 14:31). The next day, Saul died on Gilboa and on a next day—a millennium later—Jesus died on Golgotha. There the similarity ends. Saul suffered defeat at the hands of the Philistines and lost his kingdom; Jesus, however, defeated "the powers and authorities" (Col 2:15) and initiated his glorious reign at the right hand of the Father as "ruler of the kings of the earth" (Rev 1:5).

David's Discharge from the Philistine Army

We backtrack and pick up the story of David and his men. Talk about a last-minute reprieve! At the assembly point of Aphek, located northeast of the modern city of Tel Aviv, the Philistines began their march northward to the Jezreel.[18] Achish and his contingent fell in at the rear of the column. Other Philistine commanders took note. Long harbored grudges and deep suspicions surfaced, and they angrily demanded that David's corps be mustered out and sent home: "He must not go with us into battle, or he will turn against us during fighting. How better could he regain his master's favor than by taking the heads of our own men" (1 Sam 29:4), an acrimonious allusion to David's cutting off Goliath's head in the Elah Valley![19]

They just may have been right. Our narrator doesn't tip his hand. In hindsight, this seems to be another instance of providential intervention in which David was spared having to make a gut-wrenching choice. One thing is certain: if David had fought alongside Achish in the defeat of Saul, his path to the throne would have been seriously impeded. I suppose in the aftermath of the Philistine victory, David might have been appointed as a Philistine vassal king over Judah. It's extremely unlikely the Philistines would have granted David sovereignty over all Israel since that would constitute a potential threat to their hegemony.[20] On the other hand, if David and his men had turned against the Philistines, could they have made a difference? My impression is that even that would have been too little to turn the tide without Yahweh's direct intervention.

24.

18. Aphek had also been the Philistine assembling point prior to the battle of Ebenezer (1 Sam 4:1). It was a march of approximately fifty miles.

19. Klein suggests another pun: "The one whom Achish proposed to make the 'keeper of his head' (or bodyguard) in 28:2 might actually cost many Philistines their heads." Klein, 1 Samuel, 277.

20. When David was finally proclaimed king over all Israel, the Philistines immediately mobilized and launched an all-out assault on the new king (1 Sam 5:17).

Once again, we are faced with a "what if" of history, one of those mysteries of divine providence. As it turned out, David was prevented from participating in the disastrous Battle of Gilboa, thereby allowing him to succeed Saul as king over all Israel. But that wouldn't happen soon. Only after a protracted (and bloody) process—something that unfortunately would repeat itself in the later history of the monarchy—does our hero realize his destiny.

Amalekite Sneak Attack

"So David and his men got up early in the morning to go back to the land of the Philistines, and the Philistines went up to Jezreel" (1 Sam 29:11). On the third day, David and his men arrived back at Ziklag.[21] They were greeted by the charred remains of dwellings, a pall of acrid smoke, and eerie silence. Their wives and children were nowhere to be found. A horrifying reality gripped them: a raiding party had swooped down on defenseless Ziklag in their absence. Retaliation is a way of life among desert tribes. As they say, "what goes around, comes around." David and his men were overwhelmed by grief, the sense of loss so intense they exhausted themselves in weeping.

In times of catastrophe, human nature cries out for an explanation and seeks to lay blame. David was an easy target. If he hadn't come up with the idea of serving as a vassal of Achish, the disaster wouldn't have happened in the first place. Their bitterness was so deep they actually spoke of stoning David. Like his great ancestor Caleb, David confronted a potentially life-threatening attack by his own people.[22]

What follows is another defining moment in David's life. "But David found strength in the LORD his God" (1 Sam 30:6). Psalm 70, attributed to David, affords a glimpse into the soul of a man who can withstand the most devastating and life-threatening of experiences:

> Hasten, O God, to save me; come quickly, LORD, to help me.
> May those who seek my life be put to shame and confusion: may
> all who desire my ruin be turned back in disgrace . . . But as for
> me, I am poor and needy; come quickly to me, O God. You are
> my help and my deliverer; LORD, do not delay. (Ps 70:1–2, 5)

21. It's approximately fifty miles from Aphek to Ziklag, about the same distance as Aphek to Jezreel. David and his men were fully loaded with weapons, supplies, and pack animals so it took them two full days of travel. Probably on the morning of the third day they arrived back at Ziklag.

22. Num 14:10.

David's demeanor somehow deterred even one man from lifting up his hand against him, Yahweh's anointed. The Spirit of Yahweh undeniably rested upon this man like full body armor. One is reminded of David's greater son, Jesus of Nazareth, who several times in his ministry passed unharmed right through the midst of hostile crowds (Luke 4:30; John 8:59; 10:39). Jesus knew with certainty what his destiny was; David, with less certainty, nonetheless kept reminding himself what Yahweh had promised him.

David's Remarkable Rescue Operation

Mourning gives way to action. David calls for the ephod and inquires of Yahweh: "Shall I pursue this raiding party? Will I overtake them?" Again, affirmative answers to both questions. All is not lost. A surge of optimism rejuvenates the devastated and disgruntled troops. With hope rekindled, they set off in search of the raiding party.

Fatigue, both physical and emotional, catches up with two hundred of them—they are totally spent. David leaves them behind at the Nahal Besor and pushes on in hot pursuit.[23] Divine providence accompanies them. They get a big break when they happen upon an Egyptian slave who accompanied his master in the raid on Ziklag but became ill and was left for dead in the desert. They revive him and receive valuable information. Sure enough, the raiding party are Amalekites and yes, he will lead them to their camp if they promise to spare his life and free him from his master.

David's men discover the Amalekite camp, totally distracted in celebration and feasting. Like banshees, David's warriors swoop down upon the unsuspecting Amalekites and fight them nonstop for twenty-four hours.[24] Only four-hundred young Amalekite men manage to escape on camels. The unbelievably good news is that all the women and children are safe. Furthermore, all the goods plundered from Ziklag are recovered along with additional plunder taken from other towns raided. It is a remarkable turn of fortune. You can be sure the men who spoke of stoning David never brought up the subject again!

On the way home, when the troops come back to the Nahal Besor to pick up those left behind, a dispute breaks out. Some "evil men and

23. The Nahal Besor drains the Negev basin centered in Beersheba and empties into the Mediterranean about five mi. south of Gaza. David would have crossed the Besor about twelve mi. south of Ziklag.

24. It may be that David and his men were wreaking vengeance upon the Amalekites at about the same time Saul's army was being destroyed by the Philistines. For a suggested chronology of 1 Sam 30—2 Sam 1:2, see Bergen, *1, 2 Samuel*, 285.

troublemakers" adamantly insist that those left behind are not be entitled to divide the spoils. David will have none of it. He lays it down as a statue that from henceforth all members of the army, whether serving on the front lines or guarding the supplies in the rear, are entitled to share equally in the spoils of war.

Displaying political savvy, David shares some of the plunder with towns and villages in Judah on whose behalf David's men functioned as border guards during the ordeal with Saul. Currying favor with his Juda-hite base was an essential strategy in reaching the ultimate goal. His fellow tribesmen will repay him by first anointing him as their king and later func-tioning as the heartland of the united kingdom.[25]

Saul's Death Fighting the Philistines

We return to Saul's last battle. Samuel's dire prophecy was fulfilled the next day and Saul's army suffered a catastrophic defeat. One may surmise that the Philistine chariotry broke through the Israelite lines and created havoc from the rear. Panic set in and full-scale flight followed: "the Israelites fled before them" (1 Sam 31:1). Since the Gilboa ridge gradually rises in a southeasterly direction, Saul's only hope of avoiding complete disaster was to retreat to higher ground where the Philistine chariotry would be less effective. Saul and his sons rallied the remaining soldiers and prepared for their last stand on the heights of Gilboa. But like Custer at the Little Big Horn, they were overwhelmed and "many fell dead on Mount Gilboa. The Philistines were in hot pursuit of Saul and his sons, and they killed his sons Jonathan, Abi-nadab, and Malki-Shua. The fighting grew fierce around Saul, and when the archers overtook him, they wounded him critically" (1 Sam 31:2–3).[26]

Realizing all hope was gone and his strength ebbing away, Saul deter-mined to avoid humiliation and torture. He ordered his armor-bearer to ad-minister the *coup de grâce*. The loyal armor-bearer could not bring himself to do it, a touching moment in an otherwise tragic scene. Saul, in a final act of desperation, fell on his own sword and his armor-bearer followed suit.[27] The king was dead.[28]

25. As we will discover, this also had a downside and was a major factor in bringing about the divided kingdom.

26. The LXX adds that Saul had been shot in the belly with an arrow.

27. In his suicide, Samson inflicted many Philistine casualties (Judg 16:30). Saul's suicide came in the aftermath of many Israelite casualties. It's worth noting that just before Samson died, he called out to the Lord (Judg 16:28). We hear no such cry from the derelict Saul.

28. The narrator draws a summary that is majestic in its terseness. "'Thus Saul died,

Jubilation reigned in Philistia. News quickly spread in public places about the decisive victory over Israel and the death of the Hebrew King Saul.[29] Saul's head was displayed in their towns and his armor adorned one of their temples. His dismembered torso was fastened to the wall of Beth Shan as a graphic warning: Philistia was the new master of the region and all who resisted would face the same fate as Saul.

David's Reaction to Saul's Death

Bearer of Bad News

News of Saul's death reached David "on the third day" (2 Sam 1:2).[30] Ironically, the bearer of bad news turned out to be a young Amalekite.[31] Readers familiar with the story of David know that two accounts of Saul's death are recorded. The narrator gives his version in 1 Samuel 31 and then recounts the story as told by an Amalekite in 2 Samuel 1. Not surprisingly, the accounts differ in details and commentators disagree on how to handle the discrepancies.

Without entering into an involved discussion, I offer my take. I think it highly unlikely the Amalekite version is completely true. That he could have been on the battlefield *before* Saul was dead stretches credibility to

---

and his three sons, and his armor-bearer, and all his men, on the same day together' (v .6). The sentence must be spoken slowly. There must be a pause with each phrase to grasp the massiveness of the death, its finality, and its majesty." Brueggemann, *First and Second Samuel*, 208.

29. David's lament actually decries celebration of Saul's death in the "market places" rather than the "streets" of Ashkelon. I have elsewhere argued for this transl. of the Heb. *huzzot* based on both archaeological and linguistic evidence. See Helyer, "Proclaim It Not," 11–22.

30. See also 30:1. It's more than a coincidence that many significant events in redemptive history happened on the third day. Abraham saw Mount Moriah, the place where he was to offer up his son Isaac on the third day. The Lord told the Israelites to prepare to meet before him at the foot of Mount Sinai on the third day. The left-over sacrifice on the altar was to be burned on the third day. Rehoboam asked the elders to come back and meet with him on the third day. The Second Temple was completed on the third day of the month of Adar. Esther appeared before the king on the third day. Of course, the most momentous event in redemptive history, indeed, world history, occurred on the third day when the Lord rose from the dead.

31. "As the story unfolds, an odd symmetry emerges. David has just struck down Amalek; an Amalekite says he has struck down Saul; David has this Amalekite put to death." Alter, *David Story*, 195.

the breaking point. That he was there *after* Saul died and made off with his crown and arm band is not in dispute. Stripping the dead has always been a gruesome way to gain loot. One thinks of the despicable innkeeper in *Les Misérables*, Monsieur Thénardier, who looted bodies after the Battle of Waterloo.

What motivated the Amalekite to make the one-hundred mile trek to find David and personally tell him what happened is obvious. He had his heart set on a king's ransom for turning over Saul's royal insignia and personally dispatching David's arch enemy and rival. Did he ever miscalculate! This unwitting Amalekite practically signed his own death warrant. Having just rescued wives and children from the clutches of Amalekite raiders, David was hardly well disposed to reward an Amalekite fortune hunter![32]

But despite David's understandable animosity, the Amalekite's immediate death sentence was justified on the grounds of shameless sacrilege: "Your blood be on your own head. Your own mouth testified against you when you said, 'I killed the LORD's anointed'" (2 Sam 1:16)—ironically, something he probably didn't do! The ultimate irony, however, is that an Amalekite stripped Saul of his royal insignia. Remember that Saul had been charged to strip the Amalekites of both life and property, but he defaulted on the assignment.[33] Samuel gets the last word: "To obey is better than sacrifice, and to heed is better than the fat of rams" (1 Sam 15:22).

Ballad of Sad News

David's tribute to Saul and Jonathan is one of the masterpieces of Hebrew literature. Almost certainly it assumed a place in the national heritage of Israel and was regularly performed on state occasions, perhaps when leading figures died. Composed as an elegy, it commemorates the life of Israel's fallen heroes, Saul and his son Jonathan. The piece is nicely framed by the threefold lament, "How the mighty have fallen!" (1 Sam 1:19, 25, 27) and focuses on the virtues and accomplishments of Saul, not his failures and shortcomings. In highly poetic language, the dirge celebrates and lionizes Saul and Jonathan as mighty warriors who triumphed over their foes.[34] The

32. We never hear about Saul's crown or arm band again. Out of respect I doubt that David ever wore them. They may have eventually been housed in David's palace as part of a royal collection. On a much more magnificent scale one thinks of the Crown Jewels of England in the Tower of London, also known as Her Majesty's Royal Palace.

33. 1 Sam 15:1–3.

34. Eugene Peterson observes that "if David had allowed Saul's hate to determine his life he would have been destroyed. He maybe wouldn't have been killed, but he certainly would have been damned—reduced, cramped, and constricted by vengeance . . .

women of Israel are summoned to bewail the deaths of these two champions whose victories clothed them in luxurious garments.

Especially poignant are the lines that speak of Jonathan. His loyalty to his father in life and death is paired with David's love for him as a faithful friend. Probably the most memorable passage is the following: "I grieve for you, Jonathan my brother; you were very dear to me. Your love for me was wonderful, more wonderful than that of women" (2 Sam 1:26).[35]

Four additional observations merit mention. The first is the curse on Mount Gilboa. As the scene of the tragic death of these heroes, David utters a curse upon its heights: no dew, rain, or showers (2 Sam 1:21). This poetic curse should be understood in terms of what David thought the site deserved to be rather than a dire prophecy of what it actually would be. I can assure the reader that Gilboa does not suffer from a lack of precipitation. It's a fertile, forested, and flowering region, especially noteworthy for its irises that bloom in the spring.

Secondly, there's good reason to believe that this lament also served an important function militarily.[36] Note that David "ordered that the people of Judah be taught this lament of the bow (it is written in the Book of Jashar)" (2 Sam 1:18).[37] Behind this reference to the bow lies a technique of archery volleying. That is, the various sequences involved in selecting an arrow, notching it, drawing back the bowstring, and releasing the arrow were performed rhythmically to the cadences of the song. The result was a lethal and regular stream of arrows. David probably picked up this technique from the Philistine archers and adapted it for his troops. Before long, David's archers could volley with the best of them. In retrospect, David's sojourn among the Philistines served to upgrade his rapidly improving army.[38] Though the

---

Saul's hate, instead of narrowing David and reducing him, in fact provided conditions in which he became large, expansive, and generous." Peterson, *Leap Over a Wall*, 117.

35. The LGBTQ movement appeals to this passage as evidence of homosexual love in the Bible. Given the clear and uniform OT stance against homosexuality, it's highly unlikely David and Jonathan had such a relationship without any censure whatsoever on the part of the narrator. The modern debate is distorted by western bias and fails to account for middle eastern cultural expressions in which close, male, non-sexual friendships are not at all unusual.

36. In what follows, I am indebted to Anson Rainey, under whom I studied the historical geography of Israel back in 1968–69.

37. Alas, this source has never been found though forgers have given it a go! If it should somehow be discovered, that would rank among the most important discoveries of all time!

38. As we will see, David also employed Philistine mercenaries and bodyguards in his professional army.

Philistines had won a great victory and greatly reduced the size and scope of Saul's kingdom, the tide was about to turn big time.

Thirdly, "We're now at the midpoint of the David story. David's lament over Saul and Jonathan functions as a pivot."[39] Lamentation is the prelude to exultation. David will build on the foundation laid by Saul, imperfect though it was, and erect upon his ashes a kingdom such as never before occupied the "Land Between."[40] The kings of the east will pay homage to the House of David.

Burial Befitting a King

Finally, I call attention to the bravery and devotion of some Gileadite warriors. They undertook an all-night forced march of some twenty-four miles round trip, during which they crossed the Jordan River, snuck up to the city walls of Beth Shan, and surreptitiously took down the mutilated corpses of Saul and his sons. These they carried back across the Jordan to Jabesh where they burned them and buried the bones under a tamarisk tree. The book of First Samuel ends on a note of mourning, "they fasted seven days" (1 Sam 31:13).[41] Saul's daring rescue of Jabesh at the beginning of his reign was not forgotten.[42]

Although Saul's reign fell far short of expectations and his death entailed suicide, decapitation, and dismemberment, in the end, he was accorded a burial befitting a king. David's moving tribute ensured that Saul's memory would forever be enshrined in the history of Israel.

39. Peterson, *Leap Over a Wall*, 121.

40. The land of Canaan functioned as a land bridge and was usually dominated by the great river valley civilizations of the Nile and the Euphrates. For a relatively brief moment in ANE history, an indigenous dynasty controlled its own destiny in this region, the House of David. The expression "Land Between" is indebted to the devoted labor of Jim Monson and the many helpful tools he created to help students better understand the role of this land in the unfolding of biblical history. See his *Geobasics* and, with Lancaster, *Regions on the Run*.

41. The biblical books Genesis, Deuteronomy, Joshua, and First Samuel end with a burial notice. Joseph "was placed in a coffin in Egypt" (Gen 50:26). The Lord buried Moses somewhere in Moab overlooking the Promised Land (Deut 34:6). Joshua was buried at Timnath Serah in Ephraim (Josh 24:30), and Joseph's bones were reinterred at Shechem (Josh 24:32). Eleazar, son of Aaron, was buried at Gibeah, Saul's capital (Josh 24:33). Of course, the most important burial notice of all times is the following: "So Joseph took down the body, wrapped it in some linen cloth, and placed it in a tomb cut out of rock. Then he rolled a stone against the entrance of the tomb" (Mark 15:46). But something happened "on the third day" that forever altered the seeming finality of death and burial.

42. 1 Sam 11:1–11.

9

WHEN A PLAN COMES TOGETHER

I love it when a plan comes together.

—HANNIBAL SMITH, *A-TEAM*

WE NOW COME TO the last segment of a connected narrative frequently labelled "the Accession Narrative" or "History of the Rise of David." Beginning in 1 Sam 16:1 and running to 2 Sam 5:5, the sacred historian weaves together a skillfully crafted story centered on a Bethlehemite shepherd boy from the House of Jesse who rose from relative obscurity to become the shepherd king over the House of Israel.[1] Linked to the rise of David is the parallel story of the fall of the House of Saul. There really is nothing quite like it in the literature of the ANE. Generations of Jews and Christians have reflected on and vicariously relived the individual stories that comprise the larger narrative. The extraordinary power of David's story to inspire and instruct never diminishes. In the words of the writer of Hebrews, "And what more shall I say . . . about David . . . who through faith conquered kingdoms, administered justice, and gained what was promised . . . ?" (Heb 11:32–33).

Here is how this final segment breaks out:

- First Step: Tribal King of Judah (2 Sam 2:1–7)

---

1. The imagery of a king as a shepherd was widespread in the ANE. See, e.g., Ezekiel 34.

- Civil War between the House of David and House of Saul (2 Sam 2:8—3:5)

- Abner Offers to Broker a United Kingdom (2 Sam 3:6–21)

- Two Murders Threaten to Derail the Deal (2 Sam 3:22—4:12)

- Last Step: King at Last! (2 Sam 5:1–5)

FIRST STEP: TRIBAL KING OF JUDAH

The aftermath of Saul's death left all Israel in a quandary. Israelites living in the Jezreel and surrounding areas fled eastward to Gilead for sanctuary.[2] Abner, who somehow escaped death at Gilboa, took Ish-Bosheth, the only surviving son of Saul, and installed him as king in Mahanaim, east of the Jordan Valley.[3] He was king of all Israel, but in name only.

David also faced a dilemma. What should his next move be? He consulted the ephod and divine guidance was promptly forthcoming. Hebron, revered as the site of patriarchal traditions, was the next stop. There Abram had purchased a burial plot for his beloved Sarah.[4] He, along with Isaac and Rebekah and Jacob and Leah, were also interred in the Cave of Machpelah. In all likelihood, it was the largest of the towns of Judah and included satellite towns. Also, worth noting is the tradition that Caleb, one of Judah's most celebrated warriors, initially captured Hebron and received it as his ancestral portion. During the process of tribal allotments, it was designated both a city of refuge and a Levitical city.[5] Clearly, Hebron was a strategic choice. Accordingly, David and his two wives, Ahinoam and Abigail, along with his men and their families, evacuated Ziklag and "settled in Hebron and its towns" (2 Sam 2:3).[6]

---

2. 1 Sam 31:7.

3. How Abner managed to evade death on Mount Gilboa is never mentioned. He was, after all, Saul's commander in chief. And how did Ish-Bosheth also survive? I suspect that Abner knew full well how the battle would turn out and had some sort of escape plan. Whether Ish-Bosheth was even there at Gilboa is moot. One gets the impression from the narrator's brief description that he was inept as a warrior. Saul had a premonition about the outcome and probably wanted to make sure at least one son survived.

4. Gen 23.

5. Josh 15:13–14; Josh 20:7; Josh 21:11.

6. "That he did this with the Philistines' consent is certain, for he was their vassal and could hardly have taken such a step without their approval." Bright, *History of Israel*, loc. 5223.

David's careful currying of Judahite goodwill soon paid dividends. "The men of Judah came to Hebron, and there they anointed David king over the house of Judah" (2 Sam 2:4). This was a significant step forward, but not yet the endgame. Overcoming the resistance of the tribe of Benjamin and the continuing loyalty of northern tribesmen remained a major obstacle.[7] Lingering rumors and suspicions about the circumstances of Saul's death must be addressed.

David took great pains to exonerate himself and demonstrate his continuing respect for Saul. His first act as king of Judah involved a diplomatic embassy to the people of Jabesh Gilead. He dispatched messengers to convey his personal gratitude for their heroism and loyalty to Saul. To this he appended a prayer for divine blessing and a personal promise of royal goodwill. He concluded with a carefully worded update: "Saul your master is dead, and the house of Judah has anointed me king over them" (2 Sam 2:7)—a thinly veiled invitation for them to consider following suit.

CIVIL WAR BETWEEN ISRAEL AND JUDAH

It took seven years and six months to take the last step in David's rise to kingship over all Israel. Civil wars are characteristically bloody and brutal and this one was no exception. The House of Saul, propped up by the powerful Abner, still commanded loyalty among the Benjamite's and many northern tribesmen. The narrator condenses this prolonged power struggle into one brief encounter: the ordeal at the Pool of Gibeon.

The narrator treats us to an extended account of this confrontation between the rival combatants. The reason soon becomes apparent. What happened that day set in motion a blood feud that eventually eliminated the strongman Abner from the equation of royal succession. Let's first set the stage. Gibeon was one of the Hivite cities that deceived Joshua and was able to negotiate a treaty with the invading Hebrews.[8] After the deception was discovered, they were enslaved and eventually assimilated into the tribes of Benjamin and Ephraim. The location of Gibeon, just off the N-S watershed route, made it a strategic town to control the entire central ridge. Both the House of Saul and the House of David coveted this important choke point. No surprise then that the contending forces of Abner and Joab collided at this junction.

7. "So long as a king from the house of Saul still reigned, David would remain only a tribal chieftain, and his path to the throne of all Israel would still be barred." Kirsch, *King David*, 435.

8. Josh 9.

There was a pool in Gibeon where they faced off.[9] Just like earlier at the Vale of Elah, so here, Abner suggests an ordeal by combat to determine the outcome rather than engaging all the troops and incurring large casualties. Instead of just two warriors, however, each side selected twelve. This grim duel to the death apparently involved the combatants grabbing their opponent's head with one hand and wielding a sword with the free hand.[10] Unfortunately, this gladiatorial combat ended in a tragic draw—all twelve of the fighters were killed! As you can imagine, an indecisive outcome precipitated an all-out battle, which was "very fierce" (2 Sam 2:17) and resulted in resounding victory for David's men.

What happened next was critical. David's three nephews were in hot pursuit of the fleeing Israelites. Asahel, the fleet-footed one, set his sights on running down and killing Abner. This young man bit off far more than he could chew, but youthful overestimation of one's abilities is a common failing. Asahel was faster than Abner but hardly a match for the wily veteran. Abner tried twice to warn off Asahel, but to no avail. Abner waited until Asahel was right behind him before he "thrust the butt of his spear into Asahel's stomach, and the spear came out through his back. He fell there and died on the spot" (2:23).

That momentarily brought the pursuit to a screeching halt. Joab and Abishai, however, with revenge now intensifying their burning hatred for Abner, resumed the chase. As the sun was setting, Abner was able to rally his forces and regroup on a hilltop. Storming the hill would have entailed great loss of life. Abner appealed to Joab's better judgment and called for a ceasefire. Joab reluctantly accepted. Joab and Abishai counted up their losses and took Asahel's body back to the family tomb in Bethlehem and buried him. Then after an all-night march, they arrived in Hebron at daybreak. It had been a bittersweet victory. Still, David lost only twenty men compared to three hundred for Abner, an ominous bellwether signaling that Abner's days were numbered—Joab and Abishai would make sure of it.

---

9. Most tour groups don't visit Gibeon because it is in the Palestinian Authority. But for those who do, the story of this confrontation at the Pool of Gibeon comes to life. One can see the very large shaft, thirty-seven feet in diameter and eighty-two feet deep, carved out of the limestone with a spiraling set of seventy-nine steps descending to the water eighty feet below street level. For background see Thompson, "Gibeon, Gibeonites," 1:863–64.

10. See Anderson, 2 *Samuel*, loc. 1143, for an examples of this kind of combat in the ANE.

Abner Advocates for a United Kingdom under David

The narrator tersely summarizes the situation: "The war between the house of Saul and the house of David lasted a long time. David grew stronger and stronger, while the house of Saul grew weaker and weaker" (2 Sam 3:1). Not only did David grow stronger militarily, his royal household multiplied with his harem increasing to six and his sons now numbering six as well.[11] David would not lack for claimants to his throne—setting the stage for yet another bitter struggle for succession near the end of David's life. But all in due course.

Falling Out between Abner and Ish-Bosheth

As might be expected, the relationship between Abner and Ish-Bosheth deteriorated. Abner had nothing but contempt for Ish-Bosheth, who was no Saul. This led to a major transgression on Abner's part and sealed Ish-Bosheth's doom. Abner began "strengthening his own position" (2 Sam 3:6), and was, for all practical purposes, Saul's successor. He made this very clear by sleeping with one of Saul's concubines named Rizpah, a virtual declaration of kingship.[12] Ish-Bosheth called him out but Abner reacted angrily, loudly protesting his loyalty to the house of Saul—after all, he hadn't handed Ish-Bosheth over to David *yet*—and expressing his disdain at being accused of an illicit affair—though he didn't bother to deny it! Ish-Bosheth backed down, "because he was afraid of him" (3:11). The die was cast. Abner had enough political smarts to know that even if he proclaimed himself the new king over the house of Saul, he would not prevail against David. Rather than go down that path, he decided it would be better to be a successful commander in chief for David than a defeated and disgraced king. Politicians are masters of self-serving agendas.

Abner's Overture to the House of David

Abner quickly set his plan in motion. He sent messengers to David offering to broker a united kingdom. Abner's question, "Whose land is it?" (1 Sam

---

11. 2 Sam 3:2–5. David's marriage to Maacah the daughter of Talmai king of Geshur was an astute political move, providing David an ally contiguous to Israel in the northeast.

12. "It was not simply a sexual act. It was a defiant public, political challenge that could not be ignored." Brueggemann, *First and Second Samuel*, 226.

3:12) is ambiguous. Either Abner considered himself as the real power in the north or he was alluding to the divine oracle proclaiming David as the legitimate king. Whatever Abner's meaning, David agreed to the overture with one caveat: he demanded that his wife Michal be returned to him or the deal was off. In fact, David demanded that Ish-Bosheth himself authorize the transfer. Ish-Bosheth had no bargaining chips or chutzpah; he meekly granted the request.

In one of the more heart-rending scenes of the David story, Paltiel followed behind David's wife, Michal, weeping as in a funeral procession and turned back only after forced to do so by Abner.[13] Dynastic politics run rough shod over matters of the heart. As for Michal's feelings in the matter, they remain unexpressed, once again reflecting the predominantly masculine orientation of a narrator living in a strongly patriarchal society. I think she was excited by the prospect of being reunited with his first love and being back where the action was in the royal court of David. As it turned out, however, the tragedy of annulling Paltiel's marriage to Michal was compounded when David and Michal later had a serious falling out and ended their days estranged. We can only hope Paltiel later found comfort and joy with a new wife. At any rate, by reuniting with his former wife Michal, David son of Jesse solidified his position as legitimate successor to Saul.

Two power blocs in Israel first had to be persuaded. The first would be more easily amenable, the northern tribesmen. In fact, Abner already knew full well what their sentiments were: "For some time you have wanted to make David your king. Now do it!" (2 Sam 3:17–18). They were on board.

The other constituency, the tribe of Benjamin, was more problematic. The narrator doesn't elaborate on the particulars of Abner's pitch, other than to say he spoke to the Benjamites *in person*" (3:19). In all likelihood, the sheer force of his personality and status—he was after all the most illustrious Benjamite—carried the day. They acquiesced and threw their support behind David. I suspect, and later details tend to confirm, that pockets of Benjamite resentment against David persisted throughout his reign. For the most part, however, majority opinion supported David. Given the ongoing Philistine threat, there really was no viable alternative.

13. "There is scarcely a more striking instance of the evocative compactness of biblical narrative." Alter, *David Story*, 211.

Two Murders Threaten to Derail the Merger

Assassination of Abner

Blood feuds are nasty affairs. There have been some real donnybrooks in American history. One thinks of the famous Hatfield-McCoy feud of West Virginia-Kentucky. The Middle East, however, seems to have the longest, most persistent blood feuds in the world. People groups in the region nurse grudges for centuries. For example, some Palestinian Muslims speak of the Crusades as if still in living memory. They cling to the fact that it took the Muslims two-hundred years to drive the Crusaders out of the Holy Land and the State of Israel is not even one-hundred years old. They are biding their time until the opportune moment comes to exact revenge for the *nakba* (Arabic word for "catastrophe"), the unjust establishment of the State of Israel in 1948.

Joab and Abishai will not let Abner die peacefully. We know that sooner or later the score will be settled and Asahel's blood avenged. Our narrator expands on how the day of reckoning unfolded because of its threat to David's succession and its lingering consequences during David's reign.

After garnering support for David, Abner set off for Hebron with a delegation of twenty leading men. David's earlier shaming of Abner was forgotten,[14] a feast was enjoyed, and negotiations went swimmingly. Abner eagerly announced his intention to assemble the leaders of Israel to make a covenant of kingship with David.[15] Abner set off in peace and high spirits. The endgame seemed near at hand.

Ominously, Joab and his men were not present for the feast and negotiations; they arrived from a raid just after Abner departed. Was this fortuitous or deliberate on David's part? One wonders. At any rate, when they got wind of what just went down, they were incensed: "What have you done?" (2 Sam 3:24). They put the worst possible spin on Abner's visit, accusing him of reconnoitering David's military strength. Without waiting for David's reply, they stormed out and quickly hatched a plan unbeknownst to David. Sending messengers after Abner, they recalled him, presumably on the pretext of further instructions from David. Suspecting no danger or malice, Abner returned with the messengers to Hebron. Then, taking him aside privately, Joab stabbed and killed him. When word got back to David, he was beside himself. How could Joab sabotage the agreement with such

14. 1 Sam 26:14–16.
15. 1 Sam 10:25; 11:14.

a dastardly deed like that? The reader knows full well. First and foremost, revenge for killing his little brother (2 Sam 3:30). But there was something else not explicitly stated: Joab was not about to play second fiddle to Abner as commander in chief in a new united kingdom.

Abner's murder was a major crisis. If Benjamin backed out of the deal on account of this cold-blooded murder, sympathy might quickly shift away from David in the north. He must act immediately to clear his name of any involvement in the assassination. A national day of mourning was called and Joab and his men were ordered to lead the funeral procession in sack cloth and with loud weeping. This had to be a galling experience for Joab. One thinks of Haman's humiliation when he was forced to lead Mordechai's horse and proclaim Mordechai's honor in the streets of Susa.[16] David himself fasted and displayed profound and very public lamentation and sorrow. As in the case of Saul and Jonathan, David composed a lament, a lament, however, that focused on the cowardly and shameful nature of Abner's murder. It worked. "So on that day all of Joab's men and all Israel knew that the king had no part in the murder of Abner son of Ner" (2 Sam 3:37). But David's relationship to his fiercely loyal but cunning and self-serving nephew Joab had been irreparably damaged.[17] The assassination of Abner sowed the seeds of Joab's later demise—David's deathbed revenge.[18]

Assassination of Ish-Bosheth

The assassination of Abner stalled the progress of unification. A state of alarm and uncertainty spread throughout the north. For his part, Ish-Bosheth inspired no confidence. Few, if any, believed he was up to the task. His days were numbered and his assassination would be as gruesome as Abner's. Two military officers in charge of Saul's raiding parties decided to take matters into their own hands and end the stalemate. Baanah and Rekab, Beerothites of Benjamin, slipped down to Ish-Bosheth's palace in Mahanaim across the Jordan Valley in what is today Jordan. When they arrived, Ish-Bosheth was taking his afternoon nap in the "heat of the day" (2 Sam 4:5), which in this region often exceeds one-hundred degrees Fahrenheit. Under the pretext of getting some wheat, they entered his private quarters and stabbed him to death. Cutting off his head, they set out at night for Hebron, by way of the Arabah, a grueling trek of some sixty miles.

16. Esth 6:11.

17. "He is a man of the sword, who believes a little well-aimed killing will go further in state policy than a lot of words." Brueggemann, *First and Second Samuel*, 228.

18. 1 Kgs 2:5–6.

They requested an audience with the king and presented him with Ish-Bosheth's head. Like the Amalekite fortune hunter, the assassins badly miscalculated David's character. Instead of a king's reward, they were executed, dismembered, and their bodies hung up by the pool of Hebron, like Saul and his sons had been at Beth Shan. The speedy sentence once again sent a clear message to the north that David was not personally involved in the murder. Furthermore, Ish-Bosheth's head was interred in Abner's tomb in Hebron out of respect for his status as Saul's son and successor. Now the last son of Saul was dead and the final impediment to a united monarchy removed. It was time for the endgame.

King at Last!

The elders of Israel seized upon the only viable option. They came to Hebron and pledged their allegiance to David son of Jesse. Two facts solidified David's choice: he had served with distinction in leading the military campaigns under Saul, and he was divinely elected to kingship. The latter was revealed in a divine oracle, which was apparently common knowledge among the populace: Yahweh said "You will shepherd my people Israel, and you will become their ruler" (2 Sam 5:2). In short, he had impeccable credentials.

The coronation consisted of two distinct actions. The first involved writing a covenant of kingship, doubtless following the pattern of Samuel's scroll explaining "the rights and duties of kingship" when Saul was chosen king (1 Sam 10:25). The Deuteronomic regulations for kingship may have provided the essential substance of this document.[19] The second action involved a sacral anointing with oil. Abiathar, David's priest, probably performed the ritual.

It had to be a very special moment as Abiathar reflected on how divine providence had spared his life and brought him into David's inner circle. They had shared hard times together, but God was faithful and now he served King David as high priest for the entire nation of Israel. The lyrics of one of David's songs may have welled up in his heart: "Listen to my cry, for I am in desperate need; rescue me from those who pursue me. Set me free from my prison, that I may praise your name. Then the righteous will gather around me because of your goodness to me" (Ps 141:6–7).

The sacred historian wraps up the conclusion of the Accession Narrative with a chronological note. David was thirty years old when he became king over all Israel. Approximately thirteen years had elapsed since David's stunning victory over Goliath in the Elah Valley. Most of those thirteen years

19. Deut 17:14–20.

had been extremely difficult. Now a new day was dawning. In anticipation, the historian informs us that David had a long reign of forty years. His reign in Hebron lasted seven years and six months, and his reign over all Israel and Judah in Jerusalem would last thirty-three years. "Long live the king!"

Triumph of the Crucified Christ

Along the way, we have pointed out that the Bible is one grand narrative of redemptive history. Sometimes a particular story echoes in later developments of the overarching story. Here is another instance. Do we not hear a reverberation of this moment in the life of David's Greater Son? According to Luke's Gospel, Jesus was "about thirty years old when he began his ministry" (Luke 3:23). But more significantly, when the tribes of Israel tell David, "You will shepherd my people Israel, and you will become their ruler" (2 Sam 5:2), one is reminded of the Master's words as recorded in John's Gospel: "I am the good shepherd. The good shepherd lays down his life for the sheep . . . I am the good shepherd; I know my sheep and my sheep know me" (John 10:11, 14).[20] And it is John who crafts a profound paradox in his Apocalypse whereby in the person of Christ we have the two powerful images of "the Lion of the tribe of Judah, the root of David . . . [who] has triumphed" and "a Lamb looking as if it had been slain, standing in the center before the throne" (Rev 5:5–6).

By the power of the Spirit, David the shepherd of Israel accomplished great things for the people of Israel, and they experienced many triumphs over their enemies, as we shall briefly recount in the next chapter. But there would be some major disappointments and setbacks. He was, after all, a flawed human being who at times succumbed to his lower nature and made faulty choices at critical moments. The truly good news is that Jesus the Son of David never failed or faltered and his triumph over the world, the flesh, and the devil was total: "The kingdom of the world has become the kingdom of our Lord and of his Messiah, and he will reign for ever and ever" (Rev 11:15).[21] Hallelujah!

---

20. "The metaphor of shepherd and sheep introduces an entire theory of governance and power. That theory receives its most remarkable embodiment in the vocation of Jesus, who is the good shepherd whose death is interpreted as a complete sacrifice of the shepherd for the sheep: The good shepherd lays down his life for the sheep" (John 10:11). Thus the metaphor is pushed to its interpretive limit, a limit obviously not approached by David." Brueggemann, *First and Second Samuel*, 226.

21. Cf. Matt 25:41; John 12:31; 16:33; Eph 6:12; Heb 2:14; 1 John 3:8; 5:4–5.

10

THE HOUSE OF DAVID

On that day the Lord made a covenant with Abram and said, "To your descendants I give this land, from the Wadi of Egypt to the great river, the Euphrates."

—GENESIS 15:18

INTRODUCTION

THE HOUSE OF DAVID supplanted the house of Saul and a new day dawned. This new day completed the transformation of a loosely confederated tribal system into a centralized government, a monarchy, that flexed its muscles from the Nile to the Euphrates. The Abrahamic promise came to fruition when the Davidic Empire controlled the great land bridge between Europe, Asia, and Africa.[1]

Second Samuel 5–10 falls into the following episodes:

- David Captures Jerusalem (5:6–16)

- David Defeats the Philistines (5:17–25)

- David Transfers the Ark of the Covenant to Jerusalem (6:1–23)

1. "The reigns of David and Solomon in the tenth century BC represent the golden age in Israelite history. Then, briefly, Israel earned a place among the imperial powers of the near east." Gordon, *I & II Samuel*, 224.

- David Receives a Covenant Promise from Yahweh (7:1–29)
- David Dominates the Levant (8:1–14; 10:1–19)

David Captures Jerusalem

David's first recorded action as king over all Israel was a game-changer. The conquest and establishment of Jerusalem as the capital city of the united monarchy unified the tribes and set the course for the rest of Israel's history with after effects extending into succeeding ages and beyond. Nothing would be quite the same thereafter.

Historical Background of Ancient Jerusalem[2]

The site of ancient Jerusalem was, like virtually all cities ancient and modern, determined by geography. Perched on a limestone ridge, just off the Judean water shed, protected on three sides by steep valleys, and supplied by a perennial spring called Gihon, it afforded a viable place of habitation. Already in the prehistoric era, there is evidence of human occupation near this spring. During the Early and Middle Bronze Ages, Canaanites dwelt on the site and the ancient city first appears in historical records in the Ebla archives (ca. 2,500 BC). Then in the nineteenth century BC, the city crops up in Egyptian texts called *The Execration of Asiatic Princes*.[3] Its Egyptian name, *Urushalim*, is similar to its later Hebrew name, *Yerushalayim*. In addition, for the first time, we have evidence of a well-fortified city with defensive walls, towers, and water system. Portions of these may be seen today in the City of David excavations. This was the city that the patriarchs knew and where Melchizedek lived.[4] At most, it consisted of about eleven acres of densely populated living space.

During the Amarna Age (fourteenth century BC), Jerusalem was a relatively important city in the hill country of Canaan. From correspondence between Egypt and Canaan, called the El Amarna Texts, we learn that the

---

2. The following section is adapted from Helyer, *Mountaintop Theology*, 131–32.

3. These texts are magical curses uttered upon Egyptian enemies. Pottery bowls inscribed with the names of enemies were smashed in a symbolic gesture depicting their destruction. Apparently, a not very cordial relationship existed between Pharaoh and the king of Jerusalem at the time! See Pritchard, *ANET*, 329.

4. Gen 14:18. Salem is a shortened variant of Jerusalem (Ps 76:2). See also Hebrew 7.

name of one of Jerusalem's kings was Abdi Heba.[5] In the days of the Judges (thirteenth–eleventh century BC), a people group called the Jebusites occupied the site and called it Jebus.[6]

During the conquest of Canaan, Joshua defeated a coalition of kings headed up by Adoni Zedek, the king of Jerusalem.[7] The Israelite tribes, however, were not able to occupy the city itself.[8] Long after the settlement of the Israelite tribes, the Jebusites still controlled their city—a foreign enclave in the Hebrew heartland.[9] The Jebusites called a fortress just below the summit Zion, perhaps meaning "fortress."[10] The summit just to the north of Jebus was probably Mount Moriah where Abraham had prepared to sacrifice his son Isaac.[11]

King David ended this untenable geopolitical situation in about 1,000 BC, when he captured the fortress and astutely chose it as his new capital— renaming it the City of David, a royal city unencumbered by tribal claims and rivalries, though originally allotted to Benjamin.[12] In the OT, the name Zion is frequently used poetically to refer to the entire city, but its primary name is Jerusalem.

The Capture of Jebus

David's capture resulted from a combination of insider information and considerable courage. Strong defensive walls and a tower complex protected the vulnerable Gihon spring and its pool.[13] The Jebusites were so confident in their ability to keep David at bay that they taunted him: "You will not get in here; even the blind and the lame can ward you off" (2 Sam 5:6). But David knew that the fortifications, strong as they were, had a weak spot; namely, "the water shaft" (5:8). Water carriers from within the city descended down

5. In the Canaanite dialect of the Amarna Letters, the city is named *Ur-salimmu*. For two letters mentioning Jerusalem by name, see Pritchard, *ANET*, 488–89, (EA, no. 287 and 489, EA, no. 290).

6. Judg 19:10–11; 1 Chr 11:4.

7. Josh 10:1–5.

8. Josh 15:63; Judg 1:21.

9. Judg 19:10–14.

10. See Mare, "Zion," 6:1896–97.

11. Gen 22:2.

12. Josh 18:16.

13. See Reich, *Excavating the City*, esp. the inside cover for map and plan of water system.

a shaft or tunnel with steps to the reservoir to fill their buckets.[14] A majority view holds that somehow David's men gained access to the reservoir and then climbed up the water shaft into the city.[15] According to the Chronicler, David promised that whoever led the attack would become commander in chief.[16] Joab rose to the occasion and led the charge up the water shaft into the city. Once inside, they made quick work of the defenders.[17]

Joab's extraordinary exploit won back his job as commander in chief. Owing to David's extreme displeasure over Abner's assassination, he had probably relieved Joab of his command. But now the king could hardly renege on his promise. Few characters in the Bible are as resilient and resourceful as Joab. We will have occasion to witness this in coming episodes.

Before we leave this incident, a further word about the enigmatic statement: "That is why they say, 'The blind and lame' will not enter the palace" (2 Sam 5:8).[18] What does the Jebusite taunt have to do with David's palace? The difficulty lies in the fact that the original readers know the back story, something lacking for modern readers. It may mean that David banned all Jebusites, collectively called the blind and lame because of their taunt, from his new royal residence. If, on the other hand, the Hebrew word rendered "palace" should be translated "temple," some suggest the ban may be an editorial comment explaining the later practice of forbidding the blind and lame entry into the Solomonic temple.[19] But clearly the prohibition didn't

14. See further Ben-Dov, *Historical Atlas*, 40–45, 59–62.

15. There are other translations for the Heb. word *tsinnor* rendered "water shaft" in the HCSB, ESV, NAB, NIV, NRSV, and "water channel" in the NJPS. These include "grappling hook" (NEB) and "windpipe" (McCarter, *II Samuel*, 140). The latter refers to slitting the throat. On this understanding, David did not want any maimed survivors. See further Gordon, *I & II Samuel*, 227. I think the majority view is most likely correct. Whether, however, the water shaft refers specifically to Warren's shaft discovered in 1867 is uncertain owing to difficulties of dating the various shafts and tunnels.

16. 1 Chr 11:6.

17. Bergen, *1, 2 Samuel*, 321, provides a plausible scenario for what he calls "a military marvel." This explanation is also favored by Alter, *David Story*, 222

18. Brueggemann notes that "the conclusion drawn in verse 8 seems to have no necessary connection with the statement in verse 6. The three references to the blind and lame (5:6, 8) are strung together without a visible connection." Brueggemann, *First and Second Samuel*, 240. Peterson was intrigued by medieval Rabbi Gersonides' explanation that the blind and lame were grotesque figures mocking blind Isaac and lame Jacob. Supposedly they were hydraulically driven by the Gihon water system and appeared to prowl the walls of Jerusalem warding off all possible invaders. Apparently, this view was widely held by medieval Jewish exegetes. Peterson says "this is an admittedly imaginative reconstruction of a difficult text." Peterson, *Leap Over a Wall*, 131–34; esp. 133. In my opinion, it's much too fanciful to be plausible and serves more as an example of rabbinic ingenuity.

19. Being analogous to the Pentateuchal prohibitions disqualifying blind and lame

apply to disabled or handicapped people in general since David permitted Mephibosheth, Jonathan's crippled son, to dine at the royal court the rest of his life.[20]

Whatever the precise meaning of this difficult text, the Evangelist Matthew appears to allude to this episode when he narrates Jesus' triumphal entry and cleansing of the temple.[21] Only Matthew's Gospel mentions that "the blind and lame came to him at the temple, and he healed them" (Matt 21:14).[22] Perhaps adapting a Jewish hermeneutical technique called *gezerah šawah*, in which one passage is explained by another having similar words, Matthew may link King David's military conquest of the "blind and lame" with an oral tradition about the Son of David's healing the "blind and lame" in the temple precincts (Matt 21:14).[23] In so doing, Matthew intentionally contrasts and magnifies the work of David's greater Son who introduces a new era in redemptive history.[24]

David Defeats the Philistines 5:17–25

When all the tribes came together and anointed David as king over all Israel, this sent a shock wave through Philistia. Up to this point, David had been regarded as a loyal vassal protecting the southern and eastern flanks of Philistia. Now it became clear that David was no longer content to remain a tribal king and Philistine vassal. A reconstituted Hebrew kingdom must be confronted posthaste, lest Philistia forfeit her hard-won hegemony over the land bridge of Canaan.[25]

---

priests from serving in the tabernacle. See Lev 21:18.

20. 2 Sam 9:11.

21. Matt 21:1–17.

22. Worth noting is the fact that in John's Gospel Jesus performs only two miracles in Jerusalem: the healing of an invalid (John 5) and a blind man (John 9). The site of the healings, the Pool of Bethesda and the Pool of Siloam, were probably ritual immersion pools for the Jewish pilgrims before they entered the Temple.

23. On Jewish interpretive techniques, see further Helyer, *Exploring Jewish Literature*, 436.

24. "As the only recorded healing by Jesus in the temple this is surely significant of his bringing a new era in which the old ritual barriers give way to God's purpose of universal blessing." France, *Matthew*, 305–6.

25. "The new state had at once to fight for its life. The Philistines understood perfectly that David's acclamation constituted a declaration of independence on the part of the reunited Israel. And this they could not tolerate. They knew that they would have to destroy David, and destroy him at once." Bright, *History of Israel*, loc. 5271.

The Philistines twice attempted to defeat the Judean upstart who would be king over all Israel. Both attempts ended in decisive victories for David's forces. The Philistine strategy appears to have been to sever David's fledgling kingdom in two, much like they had done successfully against Saul in the Jezreel Valley. They reoccupied footholds on the north-south water shed route cutting off the northern tribes from Benjamin and Judah and sent patrols in search of the elusive David. For his part, David retreated to his new stronghold, the fortress of Zion.[26] Meanwhile, the Philistines deployed their forces in the Rephaim Valley, hoping to maximize the effectiveness of their vaunted chariot corps. Like Saul at Jezreel, David surveyed the situation and realized what he faced. But in contrast to Saul, David had a direct line of communication with Yahweh the supreme commander of Israel.[27] Once again, a twofold response to a two-fold question: "Go, for I will deliver them into your hands" (2 Sam 5:19).

The precise location of Baal Perazim is unknown, but possible sites include the hilltops of Mar Elias (817 m) or Tantur (832 m), not far from the modern suburb of Giloh.[28] These heights provided a defensible position from which David's forces unexpectedly swooped down on the Philistine army deployed in the Valley of Rephaim. David's tactics recall those of Deborah and Barak in which the tribesmen of Naphtali and Zebulun positioned on top of Mount Tabor rushed down the slopes and fell upon the Canaanite forces bivouacked below them. Barak's charge was preceded by a torrential thunderstorm that virtually immobilized Jabin's chariotry.[29] The fact that David says, "As waters break out, the LORD has broken out against my enemies before me" (5:20) may hint that a thunderstorm likewise preceded David's attack upon the Philistines and the resulting quagmire neutralized the Philistine chariots, allowing David's infantry to operate unimpeded.

Undeterred, the Philistines renewed their efforts to deliver a knockout blow. Once again, the Philistines deployed in the Rephaim and David consulted his chief intelligence officer, the LORD of Hosts. This time the strategy was different. Yahweh told him not to launch a frontal assault but slip

---

26. "The claim often made that this refers to the stronghold at Adullam (compare 1 Sam 22) is unlikely because the battle here is entirely in the immediate vicinity of Jerusalem. This would have to be the stronghold within the city, referred to in v. 9. David can 'go down' to it because his residence in Jerusalem could be topographically above the stronghold." Alter, *David Story*, 223.

27. See Josh 5:14.

28. This significant victory is later recalled by Isaiah: "The Lord will rise up as he did at Mount Perazim, he will rouse himself as in the Valley of Gibeon—to do his work, his strange work, and perform his task, his alien task" (Isa 28:21).

29. Judg 5:4.

around the main force and attack from the rear "in front of the poplar trees" (5:23). The timing of the attack was critical: "As soon as you hear the sound of marching in the tops of the poplar trees, move quickly, because that will mean the LORD has gone out in front of you to strike the Philistine army" (2 Sam 5:24). The "sound" probably refers to strong winds forcefully buffeting the trees and imparts a mysterious, divine dimension to the narrative. One recalls the strong east wind that blew before the crossing of the Red Sea and the later theophany experienced by Elijah on Mount Sinai.[30] But "the wind in the willows" may also point to the approximate time of day when David's attack occurred.[31] I say this because one of the regular features of the climate in the hill country of Judah during the summer months involves the late afternoon winds. As temperatures rise during the morning and mid-day, the heat can become quite oppressive up in the hill country. However, around four o'clock in the afternoon, the sea breezes from the west finally reach the summit and the temperature delightfully drops. I have experienced this phenomenon many times, and you can almost set your clock by it. In short, David's surprise attack from the rear did not take place in the heat of the day, allowing his forces the stamina to drive the Philistines all the way back down to the coastal plain. The bottom line is this: the Philistine gains accompanying the defeat of Saul at Gilboa were lost in two disastrous battles with David. He was now king of the mountain and that was just the beginning of his ascent to the summit of an even higher mountain.

David Strengthens His Position

Second Samuel 5:9–16 summarizes Davidic upgrades to his new capital. Besides having renamed the citadel after himself, he enlarged and enhanced the city. Chief among the enhancements was a palace fit for a king of a united monarchy. An ally came forward whose services proved to be invaluable. Hiram of Tyre, king of the neighboring country just to the north (modern Lebanon), provided both expertise (carpenters and stone masons) and materials (cedar logs). Built with beautiful rose-tinted Judean limestone and adorned with aromatic and attractive cedar wood, David's new palace dominated the skyline of Jerusalem and projected an aura of magnificence—a

---

30. Exod 10:13; 15:10; 1 Kgs 18:45; 19:11.

31. A reference to Kenneth Grahame's famous children's novel. I call the reader's attention to the fact that the precise meaning of the Hebrew word rendered "poplars" in the NIV is uncertain. ESB, HCSB, and NRSV have "balsam trees." REB has "aspens," the NAB has "mastic trees," and the NJPS has "*baca* trees." It's just possible Alter has it right in translating the Heb. as "the willows"! See Alter, *David Story*, 224.

far cry from King Saul's very modest royal residence at Gibeah that looked more like a military outpost than a palace. The narrator summarizes the scope of what was happening by saying, "And he became more and more powerful, because the LORD God Almighty was with him" (2 Sam 5:10).[32] What's important to note is that David didn't let these accomplishments go to his head; he never forgot the source of his success. "David knew that the Lord had established him as king over Israel and had exalted his kingdom for the sake of his people Israel" (5:12).[33]

The narrator caps off this section with a family update: David's harem and offspring also expanded. To the earlier list of sons born in Hebron, eleven more were born in the new capital of Jerusalem, bringing the total to more than the tribes of Israel. David surpassed the grand patriarch Jacob!

TRANSCENDENT JERUSALEM

David "took up residence in the fortress and called it 'the City of David'" (5:9). It would be hard to overstate the importance of this event in the larger scope of redemptive history. Old Testament history from David to Zedekiah unfolds with Jerusalem most often serving as the focal point. But parallel to its mundane history are texts in which Jerusalem transcends time and place and assumes a metaphysical and theological reality quite apart from its geographical coordinates. The book of Psalms and the great prophets Isaiah, Jeremiah, and Ezekiel give voice to this new, transcendent dimension.[34] Jesus and his apostles weave these prophetic strands into a wonderful tapestry depicting a New Jerusalem as the final destiny for the redeemed people of God. Of course, it was in the historical Jerusalem that the central events of salvation history would unfold; where Jesus, as the Apostles' Creed states, "suffered under Pontius Pilate, was crucified, dead, buried. He descended into hell. The third day he rose again from the dead. He ascended into heaven." These moments were anchored in terrestrial geography and history. And on the basis of these saving deeds in the historical Jerusalem,

---

32. "The message of 2 Samuel 5:10 is pivotal in the *David Story*. Up to this point we've been reading the story of the rise of David; from this point on we'll be reading the story of the reign of David." Peterson, *Leap Over a Wall*, 137.

33. "The change at this point in David's life was radical. Suddenly he was the central figure of his nation. All his life he had been marginal; now he was central . . . Would David change too? Would he change into a middle eastern despot? Or would he grow? The phrase 'greater and greater' signals David's maturity." Peterson, *Leap Over a Wall*, 135.

34. See Pss 46, 48, 76, 84, 87, 122, 137; Isa 2:1–5; 4:2–6; 25:1—26:4; 35:8–10; 52:1–10; 54:11–17; 60:1—62:12; 66:1–24; Jer 3:14–19; 31:6, 38–40; 33:1–26; Ezek 20:40; 40:1–4; 48:30–35.

Jesus prepared the way for a transcendent (but still tangible) New Jerusalem radiating with the glory of God (John 14:13; Rev 21:11).[35]

DAVID TRANSFERS THE ARK OF THE COVENANT TO JERUSALEM

If the establishment of a new capital of a united monarchy in Jerusalem ranks as one of David's most significant achievements, the transfer of the ark to the City of David is nearly on par. The combination of political and religious power centralized in one city functioned as a potent unifying force and created a mystical bond between people and city that has persisted to the present day. Today, hundreds of millions of people on the globe feel some sort of religious attachment to the city of Jerusalem, and for the three monotheistic faiths, Judaism, Christianity, and Islam, the Holy City elicits deep emotions.[36]

This intense emotion was palpable when David set about moving the Ark to Jerusalem. A Psalm written after David's time reflects back on this sacred moment.

> LORD, remember David and all his self-denial. He swore an oath to the LORD and made a vow to the Mighty One of Jacob: "I will not enter my house [palace] or go to my bed, I will allow no sleep to my eyes or slumber to my eyelids, till I find a place for the LORD, a dwelling for the Mighty One of Jacob." We heard it in Ephrathah, we came upon it in the fields of Jaar [Kiriath Jearim]: "Let us go to his dwelling place, let us worship at his footstool, saying 'Arise, LORD, and come to your resting place, you and the ark of your might. May your priests be clothed with your righteousness; may your faithful people sing for joy.'" (Ps 132:1–9)

Yahweh Strikes Down Uzzah

The transfer of the Ark, however, wasn't without mishap. David assembled a large delegation of young Israelite men, thirty-thousand strong—the precise

---

35. Cf. Gal 4:26; Heb 12:22; Rev 3:10; 21:2, 10–14. See further Helyer, *Mountaintop Theology*, 133–37.

36. I have both experienced and witnessed this phenomenon in tours to Israel. Many visitors have a strange sense of having come home when they visit Jerusalem, especially when they get their first glimpse of the Holy City.

number of Israelite soldiers killed when the Philistines had earlier defeated Israel and captured the ark.[37] He then arranged to transport the ark on a new cart from the house of Abinadab in Baalah (Keriath Jearim), where it had remained for twenty years following its return by the Philistines.[38] This grand procession with exuberant celebration and music came to a crashing halt, however, when the Levite Uzzah, Abinadab's son, was struck down by the Lord.

What caused this unexpected tragedy? When the ark nearly tumbled off the cart because the oxen pulling it stumbled, Uzzah took hold of the Ark to steady it. This seemingly innocuous action performed with the best of intentions resulted in his instantaneous death. David, shocked and angry, called the place Perez Uzzah (outbreak against Uzzah). "How can the ark of the Lord ever come to me?" (2 Sam 6:9). Fearing further divine reprisals, he left the ark in the house of Obed-Edom the Gittite for three months.

After three months, when word came that the Lord had blessed the house of Obed-Edom, David interpreted this as a sign that the transfer should go forward. In the interim, David learned the cause of the divine outbreak: there had been a major violation concerning the manner in which the ark ought to be transported.[39] The Mosaic Law clearly stipulated that it should be carried only on the shoulders of Kohathite Levites. Furthermore, none must touch it except for the Aaronide priests. In retrospect, David's first attempt to transfer the ark resembled that of the pagan Philistines when they returned the ark to Beth Shemesh.[40] Careless and casual should not characterize the way one approaches the holy things of a Holy God.[41]

The second amended attempt went without calamity. Amid great rejoicing, David led the way "leaping and dancing before the Lord" (2 Sam 6:16). The ark was placed in a specially prepared tent, presumably near the royal palace.[42]

---

37. 1 Sam 4:10–11. See Alter, *David Story*, 225.

38. 1 Sam 7:1–2.

39. Num 4:4–6, 15; 7:9.

40. 1 Sam 6:7–12. See Bergen, *1, 2 Samuel*, 329.

41. This reminds the reader of Aaron's two sons Nadab and Abihu who "offered unauthorized fire before the Lord, contrary to his command. So fire came out from the presence of the Lord and consumed them, and they died before the Lord" (Lev 10:1).

42. Cf. 2 Sam 12:20. It was not where the temple would later be built on the summit of Mount Moriah, just to the north of Jerusalem. David had to purchase that location (2 Sam 24:18–25).

Michal Despises David

There was, however another incident that marred David's celebration. When Michal observed his behavior leading the procession, "she despised him in her heart" (2 Sam 6:16). This surprising reaction reflects Michal's lukewarm commitment to Yahweh and betrays an understanding of kingship more in accord with that of the surrounding nations. She protested about David's immodest behavior before "the slave girls" (6:20), but I think she was primarily disgusted with David's divesting himself of his royal insignia as he led the procession in worship. To Michal this was humiliating and unbecoming to his kingly dignity and office. Humility before Yahweh was not one of Michal's virtues.

In response, David affirmed his willingness to humble himself even more before Yahweh. This profound difference in outlook resulted in estrangement, a sad ending to a relationship that began with passionate love. The narrator laconically notes that "Michal daughter of Saul had no children to the day of her death" (6:23), probably implying more than simply saying Michal was incapable of having children. In all likelihood conjugal relations between them ceased.[43] In retrospect, one wonders if the narrator's description of Michal as "daughter of Saul," rather than "David's wife" unmasks her ambivalent loyalty to Yahweh, something she shared in common with her father.[44]

DAVID RECEIVES A COVENANT PROMISE FROM YAHWEH

First Samuel 7 is one of the great mountain peaks of biblical revelation. Brueggemann goes so far as to affirm, "I judge this oracle with its unconditional promise to David to be the most crucial theological statement in the Old Testament."[45] The reason for its importance comes down to this: it shapes the rest of redemptive history. Here is how the chapter unfolds.

---

43. The fact that Michal was Saul's daughter and therefore any sons would be potential heirs to the throne may also be involved. David pointedly reminded Michal that Yahweh had chosen him rather than her father Saul as king (6:21). McCarter thinks one of the principal reasons for verse 23 is "to show that the blood of the house of Saul was never mixed with that of the house of David." McCarter, *II Samuel*, 476.

44. See again 18:21. Bergen notes that "Michal's rejection of David actually was symptomatic of an underlying problem in her relationship with God." Bergen, *1, 2 Samuel*, 333. Gordon notes that "the basic problem was that Michael did not share her husband's enthusiasm for the ark: 'like father, like daughter.'" Gordon, *I & II Samuel*, 234.

45. Brueggemann, *First and Second Samuel*, 258.

- Historical occasion (7:1–3)
- Divine promise to David and his dynasty (7:4–17)
- David's prayer and response (7:18–29)

Historical Occasion

Chapter 7 probably doesn't follow chapter 6 chronologically. The reason is fairly obvious. When one looks at chapters 8 and 10 and compares them to the opening of chapter 7, the "rest from all his enemies around him" (2 Sam 7:1) must have been later in David's reign, subsequent to the wars narrated in the following chapters.[46]

The occasion for the Davidic covenant grew out of David's heartfelt desire to build a temple worthy of the God of Israel. The disparity between the outward appearance of his cedar-paneled royal palace and the rustic tent housing the ark of God was disconcerting, and David sought to rectify the inequality. At this point in the narrative, a new figure suddenly appears, a prophet and royal adviser named Nathan, whose lineage is never given. He will play a leading role in two subsequent events of great importance. David shares his desire with Nathan who is immediately on board with the proposal. "But that night the word of the Lord came to Nathan" (7:4). This revelatory word involved an important change of plans.[47] The initial divine response came in the form of a query: "Are you the one to build me a house to dwell in?" (7:5). The implied answer was "no" without any explanation forthcoming. Instead, what follows is a historical retrospect that seems to express Yahweh's preference for a mobile tent rather than a fixed building.

The parallel passage in Chronicles simply repeats the earlier account in Samuel. Later, however, the Chronicler adds a further revelatory word in which David's fitness to build the temple is directly addressed. In short, David was denied the privilege on the following grounds: "You have shed much blood and have fought many wars. You are not to build a house for my Name, because you have shed much blood on the earth in my sight" (1

---

46. See Bergen, *1, 2 Samuel*, 335.

47. This episode lays to rest any notion that prophets simply by virtue of being mouthpieces of Yahweh were unerring in their opinions and even proclamations. Nathan went with what seemed right in his own eyes at the moment, but it turned out be contrary to God's will. This reminds us of Jeremiah's anguished conflicts with the false prophets who claimed to speak in the name of Yahweh but in fact led the country astray. See Helyer, *Life and Witness of Jeremiah*, ch. 4. The Apostle Paul cautions the Thessalonian believers: "Do not treat prophecies with contempt but test them all; hold on to what is good, reject whatever is harmful" (1 Thess 5:19–22).

Chr 22:8). We previously discussed this troubling issue in David's rise to power.[48]

Divine Promise to David and His Descendants

Yahweh's denial of David's desire must have stung, but what was promised in its place completely erased any momentary disappointment and flooded his heart with adoration and praise. The revelatory word falls into three distinct parts.

The first part recaps David's amazing rise to power, all thanks to Yahweh's divine guidance and intervention. The journey had not been without dangers and difficulties, but in every case, enemies had been overcome with the Lord's help.

The second aspect consisted of a fourfold promise of continuing divine blessing.

1. David's name (fame and reputation) would place him among the world's greatest achievers.

2. Israel's place as a nation would be firmly established.

3. Israel's protection against enemies would be guaranteed.

4. Israel's peace would be secured.

The patriarchal promises to Abraham, Isaac, and Jacob were partially realized through the accomplishments of a shepherd boy who simply took Yahweh at his word and purposed to honor him with his life. When placed in the larger context of redemptive history, one can see that the complete fulfillment of these four promises are only realized in David's greater Son, the Lord Jesus Christ.[49] Indeed, the fulfillment in Christ far exceeds the divine promises vouchsafed to David through the prophet Nathan. Paul's prayer for the Philippian believers gives voice to this glorious destiny: "I pray that the eyes of your heart may be enlightened in order that you may know the hope to which he has called you, the riches of his glorious inheritance in his people, and his incomparably great power for us who believe" (Phil 1:18–19).

The third part of the revelatory word plays on the nuances of the Hebrew word for house [bayt]. As mentioned previously, there are several

---

48. See ch. 8, pp. 3–6.

49. "These promises, however, were not fulfilled in David's lifetime: later prophets understood them to refer to a future period (cf. Isa 9:7; 1:5; Jer 23:5–6; 33:15–16)." Bergen, 1, 2 Samuel, 339.

distinct meanings this word can convey depending on context. Three of them figure in this section. The setting for the divine oracle is the "palace" (lit. "house") of David. Instead of David building a "house" (i.e., temple) for Yahweh, Yahweh promises that he will build a "house" (i.e., dynasty) for David. The consolation for David's being denied the right to build a temple for Yahweh consists in the fact that at least his son and successor will be granted the honor. As it turns out, David was given a free hand to plan and prepare for the construction of this magnificent edifice: "So David made extensive preparations before his death" (1 Chr 22:5). In many ways, he played a much larger role than his son Solomon. As always, Yahweh's gifts and grace are exceedingly generous![50]

The climactic feature of the third part of the Davidic Covenant centers on the everlasting nature of this divine arrangement between Yahweh and the House of David. Quite in contrast to the historical course of events in which the House of David eventually succumbed to its powerful eastern neighbors, the divine word insists, "Your house and your kingdom will endure forever before me; your throne will be established forever" (2 Sam 7:16). Only when this promise is read through the lens of the NT do we have its ultimate fulfillment. There can be no doubt that the NT proclaims Jesus of Nazareth as the legitimate heir of the House of David, the one who realizes the Kingdom of God on earth and who eventually triumphs over all his foes at the grand finale of redemptive history.[51] Jesus told Pilate "my kingdom is not of this world" (John 18:36). In so saying, he points to a new reality that breaks into history: a kingdom that transforms and transcends the historical manifestation of the kingdom of God under the House of David. This is not to imply that the spiritual realm replaces the material and the latter simply disappears—far from it, matter still matters! God created human beings as material-spiritual beings living in a material world open to and influenced by the spiritual realm. The end-game is not a Gnostic abolition of matter, but a perfect symmetry of matter and spirit in which evil is banished and goodness reigns (Rev 21:5). "Oh, the depth of the riches of the wisdom and knowledge of God! . . . to him be the glory forever! Amen" (Rom 11:33).

50. One thinks here of Yahweh's forbidding Jeremiah to marry (Jer 16). As it turns out, this was a severe mercy in that he was spared the anguish of his wife and children suffering and dying during the siege of Jerusalem. See further Helyer, *Life and Witness*, 45–47.

51. See Matt 1:1–17; 21:9; 22:42; Luke 1:32, 69; 2:4; John 7:42; Acts 13:34; 15:16; 2 Tim 2:8; Rev 5:5; 22:16; Rom 1:3.

David's Prayer and Response

David's response to Yahweh's divine promise falls into three parts and provides another glimpse into the heart of a man after God's own heart.

In worshipful wonder he first asks a question: How can it be that Yahweh should choose me, a nobody, to be a somebody in his great plan? What blows David's mind is that Yahweh's promise is not just about him individually, but about his descendants, a dynasty that lasts forever!

Then he essentially recites the famous Shema: "there is no God but you" (2 Sam 7:22 cf. Deut 6:4). Besides an incomparable God there exists an incomparable people, the people of Israel. Only they among all the peoples of the world have been redeemed by Yahweh and set apart as a living testimony to his incomparable greatness (22:23–26).[52] David's great affirmation must now be read in light of the further revelation of the NT whereby this incomparable Israel has been greatly augmented and reformulated by the grafting in of Gentiles in order to form a New Israel.[53]

David concludes with an expression of his perfect confidence in Yahweh's ability to carry out all the provisions of his covenant promise. There can be but one outcome: "the house of your servant will be blessed forever" (7:29). Once again, we turn to Psalm 132, the second half of which celebrates this divine covenantal promise to David.

> The LORD swore an oath to David, a sure oath that he will not revoke: "one of your own descendants I will place on your throne. If your sons keep my covenant and the statutes I teach them, then their sons will sit on your throne for ever and ever." For the LORD has chosen Zion, he has desired it for his dwelling saying, "This is my resting place for ever and ever; here I will sit enthroned, for I have desired it . . . Here I will make a horn grow for David and set up a lamp for my anointed one. I will clothe his enemies with shame, but his head will be adorned with a resplendent crown." (Ps 132:11–18)

The Christian who reads this knows the identity of the horn and anointed one whose head is adorned with a resplendent crown. "Crown him

---

52. See Isa 43–44. "David's focus on Yahweh's incomparability leads to an awareness of Israel's derivative incomparability. Israel is distinctive because Yahweh is distinctive. In Israel, but more specifically in David, Yahweh has enacted a *novum* in world history." Brueggemann, *First and Second Samuel*, 260.

53. See inter alia Rom 11; Gal 6:16; Eph 2:11—3:6; 1 Pet 2:4–10. "All David's people must pray this prayer of grateful astonishment." Brueggemann, *First and Second Samuel*, 260.

with many crowns, The Lamb upon His throne . . . And Hail Him as thy matchless King thru all eternity."[54]

DAVID DOMINATES THE LEVANT

Chapters 8 through 10 summarize a series of wars in which the House of David established itself as king of the mountain. The entire region was either subservient to or in alliance with Israel. Neither the kingdom along the Nile nor the kingdom along the Tigris-Euphrates could threaten Davidic domination of the land bridge. The major trade routes passing between Asia, Europe, and Africa were now controlled by Israel. This resulted in a dramatic increase of revenues and a corresponding rise in the standard of living for many Israelites. Militarily, none of Israel's immediate neighbors posed a serious threat. Yahweh fulfilled his pledge to David.

According to the superscription of Psalm 60, David composed a song that celebrates God's aid in overcoming his enemies:

> Moab is my washbasin, on Edom I toss my sandal; over Philistia
> I shout in triumph. Who will bring me to the fortified city? Who
> will lead me to Edom? Is it not you, God . . . Give us aid against
> the enemy, for human help is worthless. With God we will gain
> the victory, and he will trample down our enemies. (Ps 60:8–12)

Philistine Threat Eliminated

The sacred historian gives scant space to the subjugation of Philistia, which is somewhat surprising since, of all the surrounding nations and peoples, they had posed the most serious threat to the united kingdom.[55] In 2 Samuel 21:15–22, however, the narrator appends a short account of four additional military engagements with the Philistines. Presumably, these were also part of David's early campaigns against the arch enemy.

They are noteworthy for recording the exploits of four Hebrew warriors against vaunted Philistine champions. One in particular stands out because an exhausted David is nearly killed by "Ishbi-Benob, one of the descendants of Rapha" (2 Sam 21:16).[56] Only the timely intervention of

---

54. Matthew Bridges and Godfrey Thring, "Crown Him with Many Crowns." See Luke 1:69; 4:18; Acts 4:27; 10:38; Heb 1:9; 2:7, 9; Rev 14:14; 19:12.

55. 2 Sam 8:1. "The Philistines were Israel's most foreboding foreign threat during David's lifetime." Bergen, 1, 2 Samuel, 447.

56. Youngblood links this with 1 Chr 20:6–8 and holds that the descendants of

Abishai, David's cousin and celebrated member of the "Thirty," rescued the imperiled monarch. Owing to this close call, David's men vowed, "Never again will you go out with us to battle, so that the lamp of Israel will not be extinguished" (2 Sam 21:17)—another indication of the affection and esteem in which David's men held him. David thereafter heeded their request.

In 2 Sam 8:1, the Hebrew term Metheg Ammah ("a cubit bridle") may refer literally to a place name (unknown) or a bit one places in the mouth of a horse to control it. If, however, the term functions metaphorically, it may refer to Gath as the "bridle" (leading) city of the Philistines or to David's effective control over the Philistines. Whatever the precise meaning, the point seems clear enough: David the former vassal was now the overlord.[57]

Moabites Subjugated

There is another very brief description recounting the conquest of Moab. That an armed conflict occurred is unexpected since David had earlier transferred his parents to his great-grandmother Ruth's homeland to protect them from Saul. The cause of the war is unstated but it must have been serious given the severe reprisal meted out to the Moabite army after their surrender—two-thirds of their troops were put to death. The upshot was that Moab became a vassal state paying tribute to David.

Arameans Subjugated

The Arameans presented a more formidable foe and at least two large engagements had to be fought to determine the outcome. To the north of Israel lay a federation of Aramean states centered in Zobah, Damascus, and Hamath. Hadadezer of Zobah lost a battle to David on the Euphrates River, which in itself is noteworthy in that David's reach now extended to this important waterway. Alarmed, the Aramean kingdom of Damascus came to Hadadezer's assistance and another large battle ensued. The result was a sweeping victory for David and the reduction of the Aramean states to the status of vassals paying substantial tribute to Israel. Another Aramean king, Tou of Hamath, who had been at war with Hadadezer, sent congratulations and sought an alliance with David, clearly acknowledging David's superior

---

Rapha were giants. Youngblood, *1 & 2 Samuel*, loc. 1059. The Chronicler says he was "a huge man with six fingers on each hand and six toes on each foot—twenty-four in all" (1 Chr 20:6), a veritable multi-digital man of war!

57. Cf. 1 Chr 18:1 and LXX translation of 2 Sam 8:1. See further Kobayashi, "Methegh-Ammah," 8:800.

status with costly gifts.[58] Tribute flowed into David's coffers in the form of silver, gold, and bronze articles that David dedicated to Yahweh—some of which may have later adorned the temple.[59]

Edomites Subjugated

The long-standing enmity between Edom and Israel flared into war and David devastated the Edomites. Somewhere in the region of the Dead Sea he inflicted eighteen-thousand casualties. The entire region was garrisoned by Israelite troops and Edom became a vassal state. Twice in this section the historian sounds the recurring motif in the story of David's rise to power: "The LORD gave David victory wherever he went" (2 Sam 8:6, 14).

Ammonites Subjugated

The fullest treatment of a war with Israel's neighbors is the Ammonite war. Paradoxically, this was both a high-water mark and a breach in the dam for David's career.

The occasion that sparked the war grew out of a diplomatic blunder of major proportions. Here is an instructive example of how not to conduct foreign policy! We learn, rather surprisingly, that Nahash the Ammonite king had shown kindness to David. Recall that Saul's first exploit was delivering the citizens of Jabesh-Gilead from the cruel demands of Nahash.[60] Perhaps Nahash supported David during his years as a fugitive. This makes good political sense in that Nahash probably viewed David as a thorn in Saul's side and an impediment to any expansionist ideas by the Saulide government.

At any rate, when Nahash died, his son Hanun succeeded him on the throne. David apparently hoped to continue the good relations and dispatched an embassy conveying condolences to the new monarch. Unfortunately, this good faith gesture was interpreted by Hanun's military advisers in sinister terms. "Hasn't David sent them to you only to explore the city and spy it out and overthrow it?" (10:3). Hanun apparently agreed with their assessment and proceeded to humiliate the Israelite delegation by cutting

---

58. Alter suggests this was an advance payment of tribute and was intended to "ward off any possible military thrust of the expansionist Israelites against his own kingdom." Alter, *David Story*, 238.

59. Cf. 1 Chr 22:2–5, 14.

60. 1 Sam 11.

off half of each man's beard and cutting short their tunics, exposing their private parts.

When news of this egregious violation of diplomatic protocol reached David, the die was cast. A state of war now existed between the neighboring states. Hanun was forced to face up to the serious consequences of his ill-advised insult of the House of David. He scrambled to solicit the aid of the Aramean states Beth Rehob and Zobah—at considerable expense, no doubt—and prepared for the inevitable invasion. It was not long in coming. David mustered the entire army and commissioned Joab to reduce this arrogant monarch and his state to servitude. Note carefully that David did not personally accompany the troops at this point.

The battle outside Rabbath Ammon showcased the extraordinary military leadership and savvy of Joab and his brother Abishai. Caught in a pincer between the allies, the Arameans behind and Ammonites in front, Joab quickly divided his forces between himself and Abishai. He personally led the assault on the more dangerous Arameans to his rear while Abishai attacked the Ammonite forces in front of the city. The strategy succeeded and the Arameans were swept from the field while the Ammonites, dispirited and in disarray, fled behind the walls of their fortress city.[61]

The stage was set for a prolonged siege, but that had to be postponed for the time being. The Arameans, licking their wounds, tried one more time for a knockout blow. Recruiting Arameans living beyond the Euphrates River (modern day Iraq), Hadadezer deployed his troops at Helam under the command of Shobak. David called up the army and advanced to engage them.[62] The result, once again, was a resounding victory for the army of Israel. The Arameans finally came to grips with reality and submitted to the House of David.

David was now the undisputed king of the mountain. Alas, his success at the summit was short-lived. The seeds of his decline had already been sown and would soon produce a bitter harvest.[63]

61. Rabbath Ammon (modern Amman, Jordan), was, like Jerusalem, surrounded by deep valleys and presented a formidable challenge to would be besiegers.

62. Helam lays about forty-five miles east of the Sea of Galilee up on the Golan.

63. The reader will have noticed that I skipped the section dealing with David's honoring his covenant with Jonathan in the matter of his son Mephibosheth. I will deal with this more fully in the next section.

11

THE BATHSHEBA AFFAIR

Have mercy on me, O God, according to your unfailing love; according
to your great compassion blot out my transgressions. Wash away all
my iniquity and cleanse me from my sin. Against you, you only, have
I sinned and done what is evil in your sight; so you are right in your
verdict and justified when you judge.

—PSALM 51:1–4[1]

THE AMMONITE WAR GROUND on to its inevitable conclusion: military resistance was crushed and the capital city besieged. Joab was in charge of
the invasion "but David remained in Jerusalem" (2 Sam 11:1). As the saying goes, "idleness is the devil's workshop." One evening on the roof of his
palace in Jerusalem a "fatal attraction" took place with fatal consequences.

The narrative of the Bathsheba affair is a masterpiece of Hebrew literature. Though I have already praised the writer's skill, I must add an additional accolade: this story is without peer in the literature of the ancient
world.[2] With economy of words, our narrator draws us into a story with

---

1. The superscription to Ps 51 ascribes the Psalm to David and places it "when the
prophet Nathan came to him after David had committed adultery with Bathsheba."

2. "The writer has pulled out all the stops of his remarkable narrative art in order to
achieve a brilliant realization of this crucially pivotal episode." Alter, *David Story*, 249.

timeless relevance, a story as old as Eden and as current as the evening news.[3] The account unfolds in five scenes.

SCENE 1: SUCCUMBING TO LUST (11:1–5)

How this adulterous liaison came about requires some geographical background. The ancient city of Jerusalem lies on a limestone spur, the eastern hill, now located outside the sixteenth century AD Ottoman Turkish walls of the Old City. Today, at the northern extension and summit of the ridge lies the splendid Dome of the Rock, where Solomon built the First Temple. At the time of our story, the summit belonged to a Jebusite named Araunah who used it as a threshing floor. About four-hundred yards to the south lay the northern city wall of ancient Jebus (Jerusalem), where the fortress of Zion was located. Nearby, David built his palace and placed the ark of the covenant in a specially made tent. Today, this area is part of the City of David excavations in which tantalizing clues about this ancient site are slowly being uncovered.[4] The elevation drops off considerably, about 1,640 feet, as one moves southward down the ridge from the temple mount to the valley bottom where the Ben Hinnom Valley joins the Kidron.[5]

The point of this geographical digression is to help the reader understand the relative location of David's palace with respect to the home of Uriah the Hittite. While we don't know where Uriah's home was, Eilat Mazar has identified what she believes is David's palace near the northernmost (upper) part of the ancient city, overlooking the lower city like an observation post.

From his rooftop vantage, "he saw a woman bathing. The woman was very beautiful" (2 Sam 11:2). He was immediately infatuated and inquired about her family and status. She came from a prominent family; in fact, her father, Eliam, was one of David's chief warriors, and her grandfather was none other than David's chief advisor, the highly regarded Ahithophel, about whom we will hear more shortly. Even after learning she was already married to Uriah the Hittite, also one of his elite soldiers belonging to the

---

3. Peterson reminds us that "it's a story that's been repeated, with variations, over and over through the centuries." Peterson, *Leap Over a Wall*, 184.

4. Mazar, *Preliminary Report*, 1–87.

5. The slope of the original ridge was artificially altered when Herod the Great built a great retaining wall in order to create a large platform and increase the area surrounding the Second Temple. Today, one may sit on the southern steps of the temple mount and view the ancient City of David below.

celebrated circle of Thirty, David summoned her to his palace and then slept with her.[6]

The key verbs of the primal sin in the Garden of Eden ("saw . . . took . . . ate") re-echo in this story ("saw . . . took . . . slept"). And just as Achan in the days of the conquest under Joshua "*saw* in the plunder [what belonged to Yahweh] . . . "*coveted* them and *took* them" (Josh 7:21), so David saw and took what belonged to Uriah. James, the half-brother of Jesus and leader of the early Jerusalem church, offers a penetrating analysis of what happened in terms of a sequence so common to humanity we can only respond, "been there, done that." "Each of you is tempted when you are dragged away by your own evil desire, and enticed. Then, after desire has conceived, it gives birth to sin, and sin, when it is full-grown gives birth to death" (Jas 1:14–15). That is precisely what happened: David was dragged away and enticed by his sexual lust; it conceived and gave birth to sin and sin spawned a lethal brood.

Scene 2: Scrambling to Cover Up (11:6–25)

The deed was done, the milk spilled, the toothpaste out of the tube. Compounding the sin were circumstances that only worsened the situation. The narrator informs us that Bathsheba was performing a ritual bath undertaken by Israelite women following their menstrual cycle. Typically, this is when a woman ovulates. In this case, it took only one sexual encounter and she conceived. When she experienced the tell-tale signs of pregnancy, she sent word to David.[7] He now faced a crisis—a moral crossroad. What was to be done? In the novel *Les Misérables*, Jean Valjean also faced a moral dilemma, a crossroads experience. He could stay silent and let an innocent man go to prison, or he could come forward, acknowledge his real identity, and go back to prison himself. The musical version highlights this moment of decision with the haunting song, "Who Am I?" Valjean did the right thing; David didn't.

Like Adam, David tried to hide his sin.[8] Acting like a king "such as all the other nations have" (1 Sam 7:5), he resorted to a cover-up scheme. This, however, proved far more difficult than he imagined. As the Scripture

---

6. 2 Sam 23:8, 24, 39.

7. "After this affair Bathsheba returned to her house, and as far as David was concerned, the relationship was, apparently, at an end." Klein, *1 Samuel*, 11:1154. In the entire episode, Bathsheba says but two words in the Hebrew text: *harah anoki*. By using a contraction we can render it in English as "I'm pregnant."

8. Gen 3:7.

warns, be sure "your sin will find you out" (Num 32:23). This man who had passed numerous tests of character along the way stumbled badly this time. He sent word to Joab requesting a personal meeting with Uriah in Jerusalem—an unusual request that must have set off an alarm bell in Joab's mind. Nevertheless, he complied. In spite of his faults, Joab was a loyal soldier and several times served as the go-to guy when David required bailing out.

When Uriah appeared before the king, David first asked routine questions about how Joab and the soldiers were doing and how the war was going. Then, abruptly, David dismissed Uriah and granted him permission to visit his wife. The reader wonders if Uriah suspected something was amiss. My impression is he didn't. Afterall, David's track record of devotion to Yahweh had been so exemplary, it was unthinkable he would betray Uriah and flagrantly violate the seventh commandment of the Sinai Covenant: "You shall not commit adultery" (Exod 20: 14).

David calculated that Uriah would have sexual relations with his wife and the child would be reckoned as Uriah's. End of crisis. But David miscalculated and, ironically, Uriah thwarted the scheme with his steadfast commitment to upholding a rigorous code of conduct for Israelite soldiers engaged in war, namely, abstinence from sex.[9] Instead of sleeping with David's wife, "Uriah slept at the entrance to the palace" (2 Sam 11:9). When David summoned him again and asked why he hadn't gone home, Uriah emphatically restated his resolve: "I will not do such a thing!" (11:11). The contrast between David's breach of faith and Uriah's steadfast faithfulness leaps off the page. How the mighty have fallen! Shamelessly, David tried a third time, making Uriah drunk.[10] Again, he refused, leaving David in a quandary.

The depths to which one may sink in trying to avoid public exposure and shame are shocking. With a letter Uriah himself carried to Joab, his field commander, David signed Uriah's death warrant. In short, at David's express command, Joab positioned Uriah in such a way as to ensure his death. A Qumran scroll (4QSama) adds an even more damning dimension to the account by adding that Uriah was Joab's personal armor-bearer. The shameful scheme worked and Uriah fell in battle. David's hypocritical comment to Joab absolving him of any guilt in the matter reflects a cynicism we can scarcely imagine from the man after God's own heart—a total travesty.

9. Deut 23:10; 1 Sam 21:5.

10. "Uriah drunk is more pious than David sober!" Klein, 1 Samuel, 152, citing Ackroyd, 2 Samuel, 102. Bergen notes that "David could have learned this technique, ironically enough, from a study of the Torah's account of the origins of the Ammonites (cf. Gen 19:30–38), the very people Uriah was now fighting." Bergen, 1, 2 Samuel, 366.

After Bathsheba finished mourning her husband, "David had her brought to his house, and she became his wife and bore him a son" (2 Sam 11:27). Except for David, Bathsheba, some members of the court, and Joab, no one else knew the truth about the child's paternity—except, of course, Yahweh.[11]

From a public relations standpoint, the crisis appeared to have been "handled." Far from it, as it turns out. This murder won't go unpunished because Yahweh won't allow it. "But the thing David had done displeased the LORD" (11:27). The king blatantly abused his power and broke three of the Ten Commandments explicitly (murder, adultery, and covetousness) and, in the process, transgressed several more.[12] For this inexcusable abuse of power, he will be forced to descend into personal purgatory.

SCENE 2: STANDING BEFORE THE JUDGE

For the second time in the David story, the prophet Nathan appears on the scene. This time his mission is fraught with personal danger. He is tasked with confronting the most powerful man in the Levant and charging him with high crimes and misdemeanors. A divine impeachment case is about to explode right over David's head with repercussions that last to the end of his life.[13]

Nathan's Case Against a Rich Man

Nathan approached the king requesting his ruling in a civil case. In the Israelite system of government, the king served as the final court of appeal.[14]

11. The man sent to find out about Bathsheba probably knew and the messengers who were dispatched to escort her to the king's palace certainly knew. Alter is probably right that "the adultery can scarcely be a secret within the court." Alter, *David Story*, 251. Joab simply put two and two together.

12. On reflection one realizes that rarely do we transgress a solitary commandment in isolation from the others. Righteousness is a seamless garment that resists such compartmentalization. The rich young ruler was very naive in his assessment of his "righteousness" (Mark 10:17–21).

13. "However, very soon there arose far-reaching consequences which influenced many lives and, perhaps, altered the course of Israelite history." Klein, *1 Samuel*, 154. On December 18, 2019, the United States House of Representatives impeached President Donald J. Trump for abuse of power and obstruction of congress. The repercussions remain to be seen.

14. See 1 Kgs 3:16–28 and Ps 72 for illustrations of this function. This judicial role is still exercised by monarchs in the Middle East. Prior to the Six Day War, King Hussein of the Hashemite Kingdom of Jordan was put on the spot to render a verdict. The

In this capacity, David unwittingly played his part to perfection and in the process virtually convicted and sentenced himself.

The supposed case, in the form of a parable, is too engaging for a brief summary to suffice.[15] Let's see how it actually played out. Ostensibly, Nathan petitioned the king to adjudicate a case in which a wealthy man wronged his poor neighbor. There are warnings in the Torah that judges must be impartial in their judgments, favoring neither the rich nor the poor.[16] Here Nathan petitions the king to punish a rich man for trampling on a poor man's rights by stealing his property. In the alleged case, the rich man showed hospitality to a traveler by taking a little ewe lamb belonging to his poor neighbor—the only thing the poor man owned—and serving it to his guest for dinner. Adding to the despicableness of the deed, the narrator informs us that the lamb was a family pet. "He raised it, and it grew up with him and his children. It shared his food, drank from his cup and even slept in his arms. It was like a daughter to him" (2 Sam 12:2). For western readers it may seem odd that a lamb would be a family pet, but in ancient middle eastern culture, lambs were preferred pets. Contrariwise, dogs would never be considered pets. In fact, there isn't one positive reference to dogs in the OT![17]

David's Verdict against the Rich Man

David's reaction was kneejerk. He exploded with rage: "the man who did this must die!" (12:5).[18] The memory of cheapskate Nabal probably flashed

---

circumstances were that a Jordanian citizen living in the West Bank was accused of collaborating with the Israelis and imprisoned. His wife, in desperate straits, learned that the king was making an official visit to East Jerusalem (at that time the city was divided between Israel and Jordan). She was able to break through the cordon and throw herself at his feet and beg for clemency. This event was being carried live on Jordanian TV back in Amman. The king decided it was in his best interests to demonstrate mercy, so he granted a pardon.

15. The reader is justified in asking whether David viewed this case as hypothetical from the beginning or if he actually thought it was real. The fact that Nathan presented it in parabolic form doesn't immediately preclude its reality. Middle eastern rhetoric could adopt a parabolic form as a means of depicting an actual historical situation. One thinks here of Jotham's allegory or parable condemning Abimelek's unauthorized power grab (Judg 9:7–21).

16. Exod 23:3, 6; Lev 19:15; Deut 1:17.

17. This gradually changed as Jews assimilated to the larger Greco-Roman culture. Already in the Book of Tobit (2nd cent. BC) we have a reference to a pet dog (Tobit 6:2; 11:4). See Strong, "From Pets," 46–50.

18. David was probably not literally passing down a death sentence but rather expressing his outrage at the despicable nature of the deed. Klein calls attention to the English idiom, "he ought to be shot!" Klein, 1 Samuel, loc. 11162.

through his mind, triggering an instant animosity for another cold-hearted, wealthy skinflint (1 Sam 25:2–3). Of course, he realized his outburst was excessive, so he actually passed sentence in terms of the Pentateuchal stipulations for theft of livestock (Exod 22:1). In the case of stealing a sheep, fourfold reparation was demanded. So, the anonymous offender was required to recompense the anonymous victim with four sheep. File that sentence in your hard drive for now. We'll come back to it shortly.

Yahweh's Verdict against David

No sooner had David rendered his verdict than a bombshell exploded in the royal court. With remarkable courage Nathan announced Yahweh's verdict on David. The words, "You are the man!" reverberated in the court. The prophet proceeded to deliver Yahweh's lawsuit against the monarch's flagrant abuse of power. Analogous to the made-up case David had just decided, he, a powerful rich man, had stolen his neighbor's wife and compounded his crime by arranging the death of her husband. As awful as those crimes were, the ultimate indictment, twice repeated for emphasis, came down to this: David despised Yahweh and his word (12:9–10). He had repaid Yahweh's amazing grace with appalling ingratitude: "and if all this had been too little, I would have given you even more" (12:8).

David acted like a king "such as all the other nations have." As Samuel had warned, the king "will claim as his rights" the taking of their sons, their daughters, and a tenth of their crops and flocks.[19] But David went a step further—he took one of their wives. Saul "rejected the word of the LORD" (1 Sam 15:23) and now David "despise[d] the word of the LORD" (2 Sam 12:9). David was a man after Yahweh's own heart, but *he could still act just like Saul.* And the truth is, even under the new covenant, *believers are capable of acting just like Saul* by allowing the sin nature to take control (Gal 5:16–26).[20]

---

19. 1 Sam 8:7–18.

20. "The inspired text invites us to consider that we are all capable of such dark behavior." Arnold, *1 & 2 Samuel*, loc. 10659. "There are in every person, even after he is justified, two contrary principles, nature and grace, termed by St. Paul the flesh and the Spirit . . . Accordingly, believers are continually exhorted to watch against the flesh, as well as the world and the devil. And to this agrees the constant experience of the children of God." Wesley, "On Sin in Believers," 64.

David's Confession

To his credit, and in contrast to Saul, David dropped all attempts at cover up and denial. He abandoned his defenses and forthrightly acknowledged his guilt: "I have sinned against the LORD" (2 Sam 12:13). Therein lay the most important difference between Saul and David. Saul regretted his transgressions; David repented of his.

The time spent stonewalling exacted a huge emotional and physical toll. Psalm 32, attributed to David, describes someone who knows firsthand the consequences of denial: "When I kept silent, my bones wasted away through my groaning all day long. For day and night your hand was heavy on me; my strength was sapped as in the heat of summer" (Ps 32:3-4).[21] But then came the moment of truth. "Then I acknowledged my sin to you and did not cover up my iniquity. I said, 'I will confess my transgressions to the Lord.' And you forgave the guilt of my sin" (Ps 32:5). And with that he stepped out of his self-imposed dark dungeon into the glorious light of divine forgiveness. "Create in me a pure heart and renew a steadfast spirit within me. Do not cast me from your presence or take your Holy Spirit from me. Restore to me the joy of your salvation and grant me a willing spirit, to sustain me" (Ps 51:10-12).

David's Sentence Commuted but Not Dismissed

David's sin was forgiven and his sentence commuted—he was spared death, something that would hardly have been the case with an ordinary citizen (Lev 20:10). But he certainly didn't get off scot-free. In fact, in some respects, his sentence turned out to be worse than the death penalty. In short, his family became the source of indescribable personal anguish and tragedy. There is a certain symmetry in David's sentence: "You killed him with a sword . . . therefore, the sword will never depart from your house" (2 Sam 12:9-10). Or, from another angle, just as David destroyed Uriah's family; so now his own family would experience death and destruction. Furthermore, a deed done in secret would be followed by public humiliation.[22] The old Pentateuchal penal guideline applied: the punishment must fit the crime (Lev 24:20).

---

21. "It is possible that David has been miserable with guilt and actually welcomes Nathan's reproach." Arnold, *1 & 2 Samuel*, loc. 10814.

22. "David seized Bathsheba secretly; Absalom will seize David's wives publicly, for all to see." Bruggemann, *Second Samuel*, 281.

So, more specifically, what was his sentence? Like the sentence David passed on the rich man, a fourfold compensation was required. Though not explicitly spelled out, it's hardly a coincidence that four of David's sons died, three of them by the sword—a truly frightful price to pay.[23] No one can really claim David got away with it, and you can be sure David didn't see it that way. His anguish over Absalom's death opens a window into the intense emotional pain he endured. We'll revisit that tragedy shortly.

SCENE 4: ACCEPTING YAHWEH'S VERDICT

The first little lamb exacted was the illicitly conceived and unnamed son of Bathsheba. Shortly after Nathan pronounced Yahweh's judgment on David, the infant became ill.[24] David fervently interceded with Yahweh to spare the child's life and rigorously fasted to that end. He hoped against hope that Yahweh would relent. He did not. On the seventh day, the child died. Rather than railing against Yahweh, David acknowledged Yahweh's justice and bowed in worship before him (2 Sam 12:20).

Once again, we see the measure of the man. How often we wallow in our miseries, mostly of our own making, and bitterly react to the hand dealt us by divine providence. David shows us a more excellent way. Genuine worship is a spiritual restorative. Without it, we lose sight of the eternal and become completely absorbed in our temporal tragedies and troubles. A Davidic Psalm offers hope in hard times: "The LORD is close to the broken-hearted and saves those who are crushed in spirit. The righteous may have many troubles, but the LORD delivers them from them all" (Ps 34:18–19). A hymn by the German pietist Katarina von Schlegel captures well the libretto of David's hymnody: "Be still my soul—the Lord is on thy side! Bear patiently the cross of grief or pain; Leave to thy God to order and provide—In ev'ry change He faithful will remain. Be still, my soul—thy best, thy heav'nly Friend thru thorny ways leads to a joyful end."

Nothing will ever be the same for King David. He couldn't, like Superman in the movie, rewind the cosmic clock and undo what had been done. In terms of the larger David story, the high-water mark of his reign has been reached and from this point onward it slowly recedes. A new focus now dominates the narrative revolving around the question of David's successor. In fact, scholarly convention often designates the section 2 Samuel

---

23. The rabbis already drew attention to this correspondence. See *b. Yoma* 22B.

24. This chronological note requires the lapse of some months. It wasn't until after Bathsheba gave birth that Nathan appeared before David and announced Yahweh's indictment and sentence. Shortly thereafter the child became sick and died.

9:1 through 1 Kings 2:46 "The Succession Narrative." But before we tread David's Via Dolorosa, there will be a special birth and a national triumph to be savored. After all, the sun did come up tomorrow.

David consoled his wife Bathsheba and she conceived and gave birth to another son. He was given two names, both of which carry great significance in the larger story. Solomon means literally, "his peace" or "man of peace." The name is unexpected given that both David and Uriah were warriors. In hindsight, it appears prophetic in that Solomon's reign was marked by an extended period of peace in the land. His second name, bestowed by Yahweh himself and conveyed through Nathan the prophet was Jedidiah, meaning "beloved of Yahweh." How amazing that Yahweh's sentence upon David should be followed by this extraordinary demonstration of his grace and mercy. The repentant sinner was fully forgiven and continued to receive divine blessings. The account makes abundantly clear that Yahweh doesn't withhold grace from those who confess their sin and cast themselves on his mercy. "Great is thy Faithfulness" is something everyone can count on and David's life and psalms help us celebrate this profound reality: "For great is your love, reaching to the heavens; your faithfulness reaches to the skies" (Ps 57:10).

The David and Bathsheba affair reminds us that failure is not final. David was spared and led the nation for some years, though not without travail and trouble. Remarkably, David's successor will be none other than Solomon, son of Bathsheba.[25] She was not marginalized or quietly shunted aside and required to wear a scarlet letter "A" the rest of her life.[26] In fact, she played a major role in Solomon's accession to the throne. As already mentioned in the first chapter, she was an ancestress of David's greater son, Jesus of Nazareth.

Christian religious communities often struggle with transgressions of biblical sexual standards—vacillating between the extremes of being harshly judgmental on the one hand and completely non-judgmental on the other. The story of David and Bathsheba invites us to re-evaluate the way we handle sexual offenses within the church. The NT epistles chart a course that involves compassion without compromise. A delicate balance between discipline and restoration, between judgment and mercy, is difficult to

25. Brueggemann notes that "the placement of Solomon's birth in the narrative is stunning. Solomon is born so close to the sordidness, still within the echo of the prophetic lawsuit. Nonetheless, life begins again for this family." Brueggemann, *First and Second Samuel*, 283.

26. An allusion to Nathaniel Hawthorne's classic American novel, *The Scarlet Letter*, in which Hester Prynne, guilty of adultery, was required to wear a letter "A" (adultery) her entire life.

achieve and maintain but absolutely essential for the spiritual health of the believing community.[27]

SCENE 5: SETTLING THE WAR WITH AMMON

Meanwhile, Joab brought Ammon to her knees. After a year-long siege, he seized the citadel of Rabbah and its water supply. Further resistance was futile and the city was now ripe for the taking. Joab diplomatically sent word back to David—he knew which side of his bread was buttered! It was high time for David to come and personally claim the victory; otherwise, Joab would take credit. Rabbah fell and "David took the crown from their king's head, and it was placed on his own head." In addition, "David took a great quantity of plunder from the city" (2 Sam 12:30).

Hanun's serious miscalculation and insult brought national humiliation and servitude to a once-proud nation. Not until the sixth century BC did the Ammonites gain a measure of revenge when, as vassals of Babylon, they invaded parts of Judah.[28]

For a while, everything seemed hunky-dory. No foreign invasions, no catastrophic natural disasters, and no political upheavals. The standard of living soared and "Israel and Judah lived in safety, everyone under their own vine and fig tree" (1 Kgs 4:25). The united kingdom seemed invincible under the leadership of this seemingly invincible monarch. But the seeds of destruction had been sown. Before long, they sprouted and produced a bitter harvest. That will be the subject of our next chapter.

27. See 1 Cor 5:1–13; 6:12–19; 2 Cor 2:5–11; Gal 5:19; Eph 5:3; Col 3:5–6; 1 Thess 4:3–8; Heb 13:4; 2 Pet 2:14; Rev 2:14; 21:8; 22:15.

28. 2 Kgs 24:2.

12

FAMILY TROUBLES

The LORD, the LORD, the compassionate and gracious God, slow to anger, abounding in love and faithfulness, maintaining love to thousands, and forgiving wickedness, rebellion, and sin. *Yet he does not leave the guilty unpunished.*

—EXODUS 34:6–7

THE WHEELS ON THE King David Express begin to fall off. Like the catch phrase from ABC's *Wide World of Sports*, we have experienced "the thrill of victory." Now comes "the agony of defeat."[1] Before the Bathsheba Affair it's like we are right at the top of a gigantic roller coaster track. Suddenly, we plummet down the rails with our stomach in our throats! So, what happened? Nathan, speaking in Yahweh's name, called it precisely: "Out of your own household I am going to bring calamity on you" (2 Sam 12:11). A terrible toll—four "lambs"—was exacted for his transgression because his offense as the shepherd of Israel who must "not consider himself better than his fellow Israelites and turn from the law to the right or to the left" (Deut 17:20), was exceedingly grievous and disparaged Yahweh's extraordinary grace. While the descent into David's purgatory is painful, it provides penetrating insights into the fallen world we all inhabit. The tragic stories of three sons, Amnon, Absalom, and Adonijah unfold sequentially in 2 Samuel

---

1. This was a television sports anthology program that aired from 1961 until 1998. It was listed by *Time Magazine* as one of the top 100 television programs of all time.

13:1 through 1 Kings 2:46, by the end of which, the issue of succession is finally resolved. The Absalom story, however, is really the fulcrum around which everything else turns. Amnon was the prequel and Adonijah the sequel of a crisis that nearly toppled the House of David—Absalom's rebellion. This chapter will focus on Amnon and Absalom. The following chapter will conclude with the rest of the story: the succession of Solomon and execution of Adonijah.

AMNON: PREQUEL TO THE CRISIS

"In the course of time, Amnon son of David fell in love with Tamar, the beautiful sister of Absalom son of David" (2 Sam 13:1).[2] So begins the descent. David's firstborn son was Amnon, son of Ahinoam of Jezreel.[3] He was the heir apparent given his status as firstborn son. As it turns out, Amnon shared with his father a weakness in controlling his sexual desires.[4] The story that follows continues the high level of literary artistry we have come to expect.[5]

Like his father, Amnon saw a beautiful woman and lusted after her—the echoes of the Bathsheba affair are unmistakable.[6] He too faced an obstacle in that Tamar was a half-sister and under the stipulations of the Sinai law code such a union was forbidden:

> If a man marries his sister, the daughter of either his father or his
> mother, and they have sexual relations, it is a disgrace. They are

2. "The love in question will be revealed by the ensuing events as an erotic obsession—what the early rabbis characterized as 'love dependent upon a [material] thing.'" Alter, *David Story*, 265.

3. 2 Sam 2:2.

4. Baldwin titles 13:1—19:40 "Like father like sons." Baldwin, *1 and 2 Samuel*, 262. Kirsch reads between the lines and concludes that "the Bible allows us to understand that he was pampered by a doting father and feared by his many siblings. Perhaps that is why Amnon felt free to satisfy his every urge and impulse, no matter how grotesque or even criminal, and perhaps that's why nothing cautioned him against the longing he felt for his half-sister." Kirsch, *King David*, 206.

5. "The story is a masterpiece of drama, suspense, and irony." Howard, "Amnon," 1:196–97.

6. "The catastrophic turn in David's fortune began when he saw a beautiful woman and lusted after her. Now, the curse pronounced by Nathan on the house of David begins to unfold through the very same mechanism: a sexual transgression within the royal quarters resulting in an act of murder elsewhere. Several important terms and gestures here reinforce this link with the story of David and Bathsheba." Alter, *David Story*, 265.

to be publicly removed from their people. He has dishonored his sister and will be held responsible. (Lev 20:17)[7]

That should have deterred him, but like his father he seized forbidden fruit and, in the process, set off a chain of events that shook the very foundations of the House of David.[8]

The narrator tells the story of Amnon's incestuous rape with candor and precision, detailing Tamar's preparation of "some special bread" (2 Sam 13:6) for her supposedly sick half-brother. Amnon's lust for Tamar made him literally ill. This drew the attention of a certain adviser, Jonadab, Amnon's cousin. When he learned the cause of Amnon's distress, he laid out a devious strategy for Amnon to be alone with Tamar and satisfy his lust for her. Amnon carried out the ruse—even securing his father's unsuspecting permission for Tamar's visit to the crown prince's private quarters—and forcibly raped her.[9]

Suddenly, Amnon had a complete reversal in his feelings for Tamar and "hated her with intense hatred" (13:15).[10] Adding insult to injury, he had her thrown out of his dwelling: "Get this woman out of my sight" (13:17).[11] Though Tamar pleaded with Amnon and tried to bargain with him—"the king . . . will not keep me from being married to you"—Amnon refused to listen. Her desperate plea, "What about me? Where could I get rid of my disgrace?" (13:12), fell on deaf ears.

It didn't take long for news to get out; in fact, Tamar's actions spoke louder than words: "Tamar put ashes on her head and tore the ornamented robe she was wearing. She put her hands on her head and went away, weeping aloud as she went" (13:19).[12] Absalom, Tamar's brother, quickly sur-

---

7. Cf. Lev 18:9, 11; Deut 27:22.

8. Once again, we hear echoes of the primal sin (Gen 3:6–7).

9. Kirsch sides with scholars who put a sinister spin on David's permission and actually consider him a co-conspirator in the rape. See Kirsch, *King David*, 218. In my opinion, such a "reading against the grain" has little to commend it.

10. The sudden reversal from strong sexual attraction to even stronger sexual revulsion is by no means unique. Many such cases, clinical and literary, could be cited. In the latter category perhaps the best example in English is Shakespeare's Sonnet 129. "Enjoy'd no sooner but despised straight" (line 5).

11. One is reminded of the infamous line of President Clinton broadcast on TV in 1998: "I did not have sexual relations with that woman . . . " Kirsch comments that "at this ugly moment, among the most repugnant in all the Bible, the biblical author allows us to see that Amnon and Tamar are truly the children of David, if only because Tamar shares some of his best traits and Amnon some of his worst." Kirsch, *King David*, 218.

12. These demonstrations of grief and tragedy are typical in the Bible and the ANE. The reference to her torn ornamented robe dramatized her loss of status—forcibly stripped of her virginity. As Arnold notes, "Once she tears it, the robe symbolizes the

mised what had happened. His response was ominous: "And Absalom never spoke to Amnon again; he hated Amnon because he had disgraced his sister Tamar" (2 Sam 13:22).

Reports about "honor killings" especially in the Islamic cultures of South Asia, North Africa, and the Middle East surface now and then in public and social media.[13] The Amnon-Tamar affair reflects a similar cultural concept of honor and shame. In this instance, Absalom didn't kill his shamed sister; rather, he took her into his own home and bided his time. He waited to see what the king would do. David was furious, but that was as far as it went.

At the very least, the Torah called for banishment from the community and, one would think, disbarment from the line of succession.[14] David's inaction was rooted in his own moral failure with Bathsheba, hamstringing his ability to enforce parental and societal discipline.[15] Bookmark this in your mental browser: David's passivity in the face of moral outrage triggered a whole series of disastrous consequences.[16] When it became clear that David wouldn't punish Amnon, Absalom felt duty bound to take vengeance on his reckless half-brother for bringing dishonor on Tamar and the rest of the family. The Teacher of Ecclesiastes describes what happens in situations like this: "When the sentence for a crime is not quickly carried out, people's hearts are filled with schemes to do wrong" (Eccl 8:11). That is precisely what happened.

As it turned out, Tamar's mother Maacah was the daughter of Talmai, king of Geshur (2 Sam 3:3), an allied or vassal kingdom northeast of the Sea of Galilee, a fact that will come into play in the unfolding tragedy. Incidentally, there are only three women in the Bible named Tamar, two of

---

ruin of her life." Arnold, *1 & 2 Samuel*, loc. 11424.

13. "Honor killings are acts of vengeance, usually death, committed by family members against female family members, who are held to have brought dishonor upon the family. A woman can be targeted by (individuals within) her family for a variety of reasons, including: refusing to enter into an arranged marriage, being the victim of a sexual assault, seeking a divorce—even from an abusive husband—or (allegedly) committing adultery. The mere perception that a woman has behaved in a way that 'dishonors' her family is sufficient to trigger an attack on her life." Human Rights Watch, "Violence Against Women." "Men can also be the victims of honor killings by members of the family of a woman with whom they are perceived to have an inappropriate relationship, or by partaking in homosexual activity." Razzall and Khan, "Male 'Honour' Cases 'Underreported.'"

14. Lev 20:17.

15. In this regard, one thinks of Eli and Samuel's failure to discipline their deviant sons (1 Sam 2:12–17; 8:1–5).

16. "That imponderable silence is the key to the mounting avalanche of disaster in the house of David." Alter, *David Story*, 271.

whom suffered either sexual abuse or mishap. We've already reviewed the story of the first Tamar in the days of Judah, the tribal patriarch. He sought to prevent the widowed Tamar from marrying his third son, Shelah, under the provisions of the levirate marriage law. Tamar took matters into her own hands and wound up deceiving Judah and getting pregnant by him and giving birth to two sons, one of whom, Perez, was an ancestor of King David.[17] At least she fared better than her namesake, Tamar, the sister of Absalom. The latter lived out her days "a desolate woman" (2 Sam 13:20). Though beautiful, she was viewed as "damaged goods" and never married, a miserable consequence of Amnon's unbridled lust. Later, in a somewhat poignant aside, we learn that Absalom had a beautiful daughter whom he named Tamar.[18]

The Amnon-Tamar affair is a lived reality for multitudes in modern times—far more than we realize.[19] We are awash in a sea of unbridled sexuality and are reaping the whirlwind as a result.[20] Our greatest challenge—and there are many!—is to experience the liberating power of the Holy Spirit. "So I say, walk by the Spirit, and you will not gratify the desires of the sinful nature . . . The acts of the sinful nature are obvious: sexual immorality, impurity and debauchery" (Gal 5:13). Living in the world but not of the world is difficult; but if we default, we place ourselves at spiritual risk: "I warn you . . . those who live like this will not inherit the kingdom of God" (Gal 5:21).[21]

17. Gen 38:1–30; Ruth 4:18–22.

18. The chronology of Absalom's naming of his daughter, however, does not easily fit into the period after his sister's rape.

19. Revelations of sexual abuse by priests in the Roman Catholic Church have rocked that institution to the core. But all is not well in Protestantism either. The largest Protestant denomination, the Southern Baptist Convention, has recently revealed that sexual abuse by pastors and church leaders in that denomination has been widespread and covered up. Sexual abuse in cultic religious groups is notoriously prevalent. Rapes on college campuses are significantly underreported, as are those in the military.

20. Lewis Smedes wrote a revised edition of his book *Sex for Christians* (1994) in which he stated: "If I were writing today, I think I would mute my celebration of sex a little. I would not want to call off the party, but I should be more wary of the inevitable hangover. Sex is God's good gift; it is also one of the most powerful urges in the human arsenal. It is not at all clear that we are strong enough, smart enough, and good enough to know how to use it well. We all need help." Smedes, *Sex for Christians*, 231. The sexual crisis has only worsened since he penned these words—may his memory be blessed!

21. Cf. 2 Cor 13:3; 1 John 2:15.

ABSALOM: CRISIS THAT SHOOK THE HOUSE OF DAVID

Absalom Murders Amnon

Meanwhile Absalom nursed his hatred for Amnon. Then, after two years, he devised a plan to exact retribution, and, we should also note, eliminate the heir apparent and place himself next in line of succession by birth order. The murder was meticulously planned and executed.[22]

The king's sons apparently received land and livestock as part of their royal status, a perk for royalty both ancient and modern.[23] Absalom had a large herd of sheep on one of his estates at Baal Hazor, some fourteen miles to the north, and seized upon the annual sheep shearing as an opportune occasion to assassinate Amnon.[24] He personally invited the king and all his sons to attend the festivities, but David refused. Absalom persisted, however, and urged his father to at least allow his brother Amnon to participate. The king finally agreed, but only on the condition that all his sons join in the occasion. David couldn't have been oblivious to Absalom's bitter enmity against Amnon and so insisted that all the sons (and their attendants) be present, forestalling aggression. He failed to reckon with Absalom's determination to do away with Amnon at any cost and erase the stain against his family.

The stage was set. Absalom ordered his men to carry out the hit after the guests were "in high spirits" (2 Sam 13:28) and they ruthlessly complied. The rest of the royal sons, with their retinue, fled in panic on their mules to Jerusalem.

Modern readers may wonder how word of a massacre could possibly have reached the palace well before the sons arrived—and that without benefit of cell phones! The explanation is that a system of communication existed since the days of the settlement and judges.[25] Runners were regularly used for messages and hilltop signal fires relayed alerts and warnings along the central ridge of the country.[26] In this case, however, the message got gar-

22. 2 Sam 13:23–38.

23. For example, the royal family of the United Kingdom bestows estates and titles on their offspring. William and Kate are the duke and duchess of Cambridge and the newest royal couple, Prince Harry and Princess Meghan, are the duke and duchess of Sussex.

24. Cf. the story of Nabal in 1 Sam 25:2, 4–8.

25. Judg 3:27; 7:22–24; 12:1.

26. I will shortly discuss the story of two runners who relayed news of Absalom's death (2 Sam 18:19–32). In the days of Jeremiah, the prophet refers to signal fires: "Flee

bled along the way and by the time it reached Jerusalem, all the king's sons had supposedly been murdered. You can imagine the emotional impact on the king and his court. David tore his clothes, as did his attendants, and he lay on the ground completely overcome by grief.[27]

Our crafty adviser, Jonadab, alleviated the situation somewhat by assuring the king that only Amnon had perished and that Absalom had been intending to do this for some time. This despicable man ought to have been punished for his role in the sordid affair.[28] His "wisdom" was worldly and not the godly wisdom held in such esteem in the Bible.[29] At any rate, his assurance that all the other sons were safe was confirmed when they came wailing into the king's presence. David's grief was not dispelled—Amnon, the firstborn and heir apparent, was indeed dead. Loud wailing echoed throughout the palace and no doubt quickly spread throughout the city. For King David it was not temporary; he "mourned many days for his son" (2 Sam 13:37).

Absalom Recalled to Jerusalem

Meanwhile, Absalom made his escape to Geshur, seeking sanctuary under the protection of his maternal grandfather, King Talmai. Ironically, Absalom's exile from his homeland anticipates an exile he will force his father to endure.

David made no demands for extradition and initiated no overtures for reconciliation—even though he "longed to go to Absalom, for he was consoled concerning Amnon's death" (13:39). An uneasy stalemate stretched out to three years.

Finally, the go-to guy stepped in.[30] Joab knew that David longed for his son but just couldn't bring himself to grant a pardon and recall him to Jerusalem, so Joab resorted to a ploy of his own.[31] Knowing that a direct

---

for safety, people of Benjamin! Flee from Jerusalem! Sound the trumpet in Tekoa! Raise the signal [fire] over Beth-Hakkerem!" (Jer 6:1). Bergen suggests that the king's sons in their fear and panic took a circuitous route home thus enabling news to reach the palace before their arrival. See Bergen, 1, 2 Samuel, 385.

27. Recall the emotional impact of the Amalekite raid on Ziklag (1 Sam 30:4).

28. Peterson comments: "He is the kind of person who shows up so often in areas of religion and politics—a parasite on persons in power. People like this do nothing creative or responsible, but always seems to be on hand with insider gossip or information that may be of use." Peterson, First and Second Samuel, loc. 4146.

29. See Prov 1–4; 1 Cor 1:20; Jas 3:13–18.

30. Kirsch calls Joab a "political fixer." Kirsch, King David, 225.

31. Arnold offers another factor in Joab's motivation. "Absalom remains the crown

appeal on his part would probably be refused—owing to their strained relationship—he took a page from Nathan's playbook. He decided to bring another supposed case before the king for a ruling that would in effect shame him into doing the right thing. To expedite his plan, he enlisted the aid of a wise woman from Tekoa, a town only about five miles southeast of Bethlehem.

After coaching and costuming, Joab brought her as a supplicant appealing to the king for justice. By design, her petition bears a number of similarities to the exile of Absalom. In the alleged case, two sons of a widow quarreled and one killed the other. The clan then demanded the death of the killer, an outcome leaving the poor widow bereft of sons and patrimony. After hearing the case, David ruled in favor of the widow's request sparing the surviving son and pledging royal protection from clan vengeance. Displaying considerable eloquence, the wise woman then dropped a Nathan bomb: "Why then have you devised a thing like this against the people of God? When the king says this, does he not convict himself, for the king has not brought back his banished son?" (2 Sam 14:13).

David is no fool. He immediately senses the hand of Joab in this and forces the woman to fess up. Joab must have been standing nearby during the proceedings because the conversation now turns to him and David consents to Joab's request and issues an order to recall Absalom.

So far so good. But David couldn't take the next step. He refused to see Absalom. "Absalom lived two years in Jerusalem without seeing the king's face" (14:28). It was a fatal mistake.[32] The seeds of disrespect sprouted into utter contempt. The die was cast for an even greater tragedy to befall the House of David.

Absalom was in limbo and determined to break the impasse. Twice requesting Joab to again intervene on his behalf, Joab refused. In frustration, Absalom got Joab's attention big time—he set fire to Joab's barley field! Joab relented and went to the king, no doubt warning him that if something weren't done right away there would be hell to pay. Alas, that turned out to be the case anyway.

"Then the king summoned Absalom, and he came in and bowed down with his face to the ground before the king. And the king kissed Absalom" (14:33). I wish this were a story like Jesus' parable of the prodigal son who returned home to a father who "threw his arms around him and kissed him"

---

prince, and his absence from Jerusalem could complicate a smooth transition of royal power to a new leader when the time is right." Arnold, *1 & 2 Samuel*, loc. 11458.

32. "Absalom got rid of Amnon by killing him. Then David got rid of Absalom by shunning him. David lost his son Amnon because of the sin of Absalom. David lost his son Absalom by his own sin." Peterson, *Leap Over a Wall*, 196.

(Luke 15:20). The overjoyed father then hosted a rollicking celebration and feast because his son "was dead and is alive again; he was lost and is found" (Luke 15:24). Our narrator, however, says nothing further about reconciliation and reinstatement; instead, we fast forward "in the course of time" (1 Sam 15:1).[33]

This prompts several questions. What was Absalom's new status in the royal court? Was Absalom's obeisance feigned? Was David's kiss a genuine expression of his love for his son? The rest of the story answers the second and third questions; the first remains shrouded in ambiguity. The obeisance was feigned and David's kiss was sincere. The kiss, however, was too late.

Absalom's Rebellion

Despite the fact that Absalom was next in line, he must have sensed the throne was by no means a sure thing. So, he initiated an aggressive campaign of self-promotion and public airing of grievances against the king. Like a skilled politician, he embarked on a media campaign designed to make him a household name. This was not a hard sell because he had it all: good looks, great physique, glorious hair, and a gorgeous daughter.[34] His movements about the capital were choreographed, ostentatious, and well publicized. Had he lived in an era of TV and social media, he would have dominated the daily news! Coordinated with his public relations campaign, in which he "pressed the flesh" and "kissed the cheek" (2 Sam 15:5), he emphasized the king's repeated failure to administer justice and strongly hinted that if he were king things would certainly be much better. One can almost hear the campaign slogan, "Make Israel great again!"

Note that his appeal was aimed primarily at northern tribesmen. In other words, Absalom played on the long-standing tribal jealousies and rivalries going back to the days of the judges. He strongly implied that David showed favoritism to Judah at the expense of northerners. Absalom portrayed himself as a champion of the people against the privileged elite at David's court. It worked. "He stole the hearts of the people of Israel" (15:6).[35]

After four years of "campaigning," Absalom sensed the time was right for a coup. Once again Absalom made meticulous plans for this long-anticipated moment. The location chosen for his revolt carried considerable significance since Hebron was where David was first anointed king over

33. See Peterson, *First and Second Samuel*, loc. 4256–70.

34. The reference to Absalom's prodigious amount of hair anticipates Absalom's hair-raising murder!

35. Any resemblance to modern politicians, one in particular, is not a coincidence!

Judah.[36] The difficulty of leaving Jerusalem without stirring up suspicions was dealt with under the pious pretext of wishing to fulfill a vow he had made while in exile in Geshur. "If the LORD takes me back to Jerusalem, I will worship the LORD in Hebron" (2 Sam 15:8).[37] Ironically, he secured David's blessing for the pilgrimage—the third time David unwittingly granted permission for a wicked purpose.[38] Meanwhile, secret messengers positioned themselves throughout Israel awaiting word from Hebron. Another ploy to allay any suspicion of treasonous activity was an invitation to two-hundred Jerusalemites to accompany Absalom for the ceremonies. As the narrator is careful to note, they "went quite innocently, knowing nothing about the matter" (15:11).

One last piece in the coup now fell into place. Absalom secured the services of none other than David's most trusted senior adviser, Ahithophel of Giloh. Perhaps a Davidic Psalm alludes to his betrayal: "Even my close friend, someone I trusted, one who shared my bread, has lifted up his heel against me" (Ps 41:9). This surprising defection to Absalom will require later discussion.

The trumpets sounded and the secret messengers made their dramatic proclamation: "Absalom is king in Hebron" (2 Sam 15:10). This stunning development surprisingly fell on many receptive ears. In spite of the many achievements of King David, large numbers now threw their support behind the charismatic, handsome, and macho son of David. The rebellion would not be easily quelled. A showdown with dad was inevitable, and Absalom relished the prospect.

David's Flight from Jerusalem

Messengers reported the dire situation now facing the king: "The hearts of the people of Israel are with Absalom" (15:13). David did not dally; he sprang into action and took immediate steps, thereby averting a major disaster.[39] Relying on his many years of military experience, he quickly sized up his options and ordered an immediate evacuation and escape across the Jordan River. His personal bodyguard and loyal followers instantly obeyed. David's household abandoned the palace and trailed after the king. "But

36. 2 Sam 2:4.

37. One thinks of David's great desire: "One thing I ask from the Lord, this only do I seek: that I may dwell in the house of the Lord all the days of my life . . ." (Ps 27:4).

38. 2 Sam 13:6–8, 26–27.

39. "David shakes himself from his slumber of passivity, realizing he must move at once if he is to have any chance of surviving." Alter, *David Story*, 285.

David continued up the Mount of Olives, weeping as he went; his head was covered and he was barefoot. All the people with him covered their heads too and were weeping as they went up" (2 Sam 15:10). An extraordinary moment, unlike anything ever before witnessed in the capital city.

Those somewhat familiar with the site of ancient Jerusalem in David's day may be able to visualize the escape route. Almost due east of the ancient City of David, across the Kidron Valley and up on the crest of the Mount of Olives ridge lies a saddle, a dip in the elevation. This was the location of the main eastern route giving access to the Wilderness of Judah and the descent to the Jordan. Our narrator slows down the pace of the story and provides considerable detail that reads like an eyewitness account of this famous exodus from the City of David.[40]

The first group mentioned are the king's personal bodyguard, the stalwart Philistine contingents, renowned for their unflinching loyalty to David. As David paused at the edge of the city, near the bottom of the Kidron Valley, the Kerethites, Pelethites, and Gittites marched out before the king. One of the elite guards, a certain Gittite named Ittai, was a newcomer to the corps. David gave him the opportunity to return to Philistia rather than remain in an uncertain political situation. He emphatically declined: "Whether it be life or death, there will your servant be" (15:21).[41] This illustrates once again the intense loyalty that David elicited from those who served him, the kind of total commitment that will ultimately triumph over the whims of people swept up in Absalom's charm offensive. Staying power is the name of the game in politics.

David's Strategy to Undermine the Rebellion

David committed himself to Yahweh's will: "let him [Yahweh] do to me whatever seems good to him" (15:26). But he also took active steps to survive the crisis. The first priority was to escape with his household and elite bodyguard to the relative safety across the Jordan River in Gilead where he could regroup and reinforce his army. To achieve this, he needed reliable information about Absalom's intentions and movements. For this he had at his disposal three valuable allies: the high priests Abiathar and Zadok, and Hushai the king's "confidant" (TNIV) or "friend" (NRSV).[42] David prudent-

40. "The entire episode is unusual in the leisurely panoramic view it provides of the eastward march from the city." Alter, *David Story*, 286.

41. Peterson plausibly argues that Ittai was also a convert to the faith of Israel. See Peterson, *First and Second Samuel*, loc. 4441.

42. Hushai is identified as an Arkite, a clan living in Benjamin just south of the

ly decided not the remove the Ark of the Covenant from its dwelling place in Jerusalem. The high priests stayed behind and continued to perform their duties, protected by priestly immunity, all the while secretly serving as the king's eyes. Zadok's son, Ahimaaz, and Abiathar's son, Jonathan, also assisted as undercover agents relaying information to David. Hushai, however, was tasked with the critically important mission of "frustrating Ahithophel's advice" (2 Sam 15:34). As it turned out, Hushai answered David's prayer: "LORD, turn Ahithophel's counsel into foolishness" (15:31).

Interlude: Two Responses to David's Flight

Our narrator again slows the action in order to recount two diametrically opposed Benjamite responses to David's forced flight. The first involved Mephibosheth's steward Ziba. He was Johnny-on-the-spot with much-needed provisions and transportation for the rugged conditions and terrain of the Wilderness of Judah. David had two questions: Why had he done this and where was Mephibosheth? Ziba answered with an affirmation of personal loyalty and an accusation of disloyalty on the part of Mephibosheth. Given David's gratitude for the assistance rendered and lack of time for further enquiry, he immediately transferred Mephibosheth's estate to Ziba. There is good reason to believe this was undeserved, as we shall see later.

The second response was revealing because it openly expressed what some, especially in Benjamin, privately thought about King David. Shimei spewed out his spleen and raged against David "for all the blood [he] shed in the household of Saul, in whose place [he had] reigned" (16:8).[43] Adding to the insult, he lobbed stones and dirt at the disconsolate king traveling along the road below him. This was way more than Abishai's short fuse could tolerate, so he asked permission to cut off Shimei's head. David would have none of it, seeing in this humiliation a further outworking of his own transgressions: "for the LORD has told him to" (16:11).

---

border with Ephraim (Josh 16:2). His son Baana served as a district governor under Solomon (1 Kgs 4:16).

43. This may refer to Shimei's conviction that David had a hand in the death of Saul and his sons, Abner, and Ishbosheth. Perhaps it also includes the execution of the seven Saulides recorded in 2 Samuel 21 as retribution for Saul's massacre of Gibeonites since this episode is not precisely dated. I think, however, that this episode was toward the end of David's reign.

Hushai Thwarts Ahithophel's Advice

Absalom entered Jerusalem without resistance as the new king of Israel. What sweet revenge! The years of bitter exile and alienation had ended. But there was no time for celebration because pressing matters faced the newly acclaimed monarch. Ahithophel shrewdly outlined what Absalom must do to secure his grip on the throne. In short, he must preclude any possibility of future negotiation and reconciliation—there must be no turning back. To that end, Ahithophel strongly urged two actions to be undertaken at once.

David had left behind his concubines "to take care of the palace" (2 Sam 15:16). The first order of business called for Absalom to sleep with the royal concubines, thereby signaling a regime change. To this end, a tent was erected on the palace roof. The words of Yahweh's sentence upon David resound loud and clear: "Before your very eyes I will take your wives and give them to one who is close to you, and he will sleep with your wives in broad daylight. You did it in secret, but I will do this thing in broad daylight before all Israel" (12:12). David could scarcely have imagined, however, that the "one who is close to [him]" would turn out to be his own son.

Even more urgent was the unresolved fate of the deposed king. Ahithophel knew that as long as David lived, the possibility of his restoration to power was "a clear and present danger."[44] The only solution was to eliminate him once and for all. To this end, Ahithophel counseled immediate pursuit of David's fleeing family and followers with the objective of isolating the king and killing him. Once the king was dead, all resistance would collapse. Ahithophel put himself forward as the one to lead the operation, thereby eliminating any risk of Absalom being accidentally killed and thus bringing the coup to a crashing halt. Had the plan been carried out, it would likely have succeeded. But Yahweh was not finished with David yet—he would live to reign again.

David's planted agent Hushai assumed center stage. He faced two daunting tasks: (1) gain Absalom's confidence as a trusted adviser and (2) overturn advice that "seemed good to Absalom and to all the elders of Israel" (16:4). How Hushai pulled it off is a fascinating study in human psychology. The first he accomplished by sheer chutzpah. In short, he flattered Absalom as "the one chosen by the LORD" (16:18) and stated what seemed perfectly fitting, namely, that he should loyally serve the son just as he had loyally served the father. He struck just the right notes and just like that he was on the king's cabinet![45]

44. Title of a 1994 movie starring Harrison Ford.

45. Young Herod (later called the Great) got reinstated in the good graces of Octavian with a similar show of chutzpah. Herod had sided with Anthony in the power

Accomplishing the second task was even more challenging. Hushai began by flatly rejecting Ahithophel's counsel. One could have heard a pin drop! No one had ever before contradicted the sagacious Ahithophel. Hushai quickly followed up with a rationale for rejection and a counterproposal. First, Ahithophel's plan threw caution to the wind and risked too much in one hasty action. Hushai proceeded to spell out the inherent danger of an immediate pursuit. David and his loyal troops were seasoned military men. They will have anticipated the pursuit and were lying in wait for Absalom's relatively untested troops. An ambush with heavy casualties would create sudden panic leading to a disorderly retreat. At that point, all was lost because confidence Absalom would prevail against his father—whose reputation "all Israel knows" (2 Sam 17:10)—would be shaken.

Hushai's alternative proposal subtly appealed to Absalom's pride, something he had in abundance. What was called for was a convincing display of his leadership ability; after all, he had no previous military experience on his record, and this was the prime prerequisite for being king of Israel. By waiting until he could muster a massive army ("as numerous as the sand on the sea" is rhetorical hyperbole), he could be assured of a convincing victory while personally leading his troops in the battle. It would, in effect, confirm his kingship as nothing else could. In reality, Hushai's recommendation cleverly cloaked what Ahithophel so clearly understood: delaying the showdown was precisely what David needed to survive.

Absalom and the men of Israel swallowed the bait, hook, line, and sinker. "The advice of Hushai the Arkite is better than that of Ahithophel" (17:14a). Significantly, our narrator inserts an editorial comment revealing a theological conviction running like a scarlet thread throughout the story of David: "For the LORD had determined to frustrate the good advice of Ahithophel in order to bring disaster on Absalom" (17:14b).

Reading this story reminds us that there are indeed many mysteries in God's providence, sometimes, quite unexpected twists and turns.[46] What sustained David in the midst of the greatest crisis of his career was this abiding truth: "My times are in your hands" (Ps 31:15). The title to Psalm 3 says David composed it "when he fled from his son Absalom." "LORD, how many

---

struggle with Octavian. After Anthony's defeat at Actium, Herod sailed to Rhodes and sought an audience with Caesar (Octavian). In the words of the Jewish historian Josephus, he appeared "without his crown, in the dress and with the appearance of a commoner, but with the haughtiness of a king. He kept back nothing and spoke as man to man" (*J. W.* I, 391). In effect he boldly declared that he would now loyally support Octavian. Octavian believed him and Herod returned to Judea with his throne secure.

46. "There are hidden, powerful purposes from God that operate through Hushai, but they are not dependent on him or on any other human agent, because in the end the outcome was 'commanded.'" Brueggemann, *First and Second Samuel*, 314.

are my foes! How many rise up against me!" (Ps 3:1). Instead of being paralyzed with fear, David faced the crisis with remarkable calm: "I will not fear though tens of thousands assail me on every side" (3:6). In fact, he could even "lie down and sleep" (3:5). The source of this uncommon confidence and courage was not dredged up out of his own inner resources: "But you, LORD, are a shield around me" (3:3) and "from the LORD comes deliverance" (3:8). Timeless truth for temporal trials.

Having overturned the counsel of Ahiqthophel and successfully offered an alternative, Hushai was now privy to Absalom's intentions. He informed Zadok and Abiathar what was coming down. It was imperative for David's people to cross the Jordan immediately and make preparations for Absalom's impending and massive attack. The message was relayed to David, though not without its moments of high drama; in fact, the narrator entertains the reader with a short suspense thriller featuring a female servant and the two sons Jonathan and Ahimaaz.

The latter were staying just outside the southern city walls at En Rogel in order to evade surveillance. Absalom's security forces were probably suspicious of the high priests' loyalty and kept a close eye on their movements. An unnamed female servant somehow got word to the spies, but a young man spotted them and informed Absalom. For several harrowing hours, the whole mission was in jeopardy. They set out at once by way of the wilderness road, knowing full well Absalom's men would be in hot pursuit. After cresting the Mount of Olives and starting down the descent to Bahurim, they realized their pursuers were gaining on them. Providentially (note that word again), they knew a man in Bahurim who was loyal to David and who had a well in his courtyard. The lads climbed down into the well and the man's wife placed a cover over the top.[47] When the security forces arrived, she sent them off on a wild goose chase. The young men reached David later that night and relayed Hushai's urgent message. By daybreak, all were safely across the Jordan. That operation basically saved the day for David. Now it would just be a matter of time before Absalom's day of reckoning arrived.

Meanwhile back in Jerusalem, a dark night of the soul descended upon Ahithophel. His counsel had been rejected and he was dejected—so much so he lost all hope. Why? He knew with near certainty that Absalom's coup would fail. And he also knew what would happen to him when David returned. Rather than face the public humiliation, he followed in the footsteps of Saul and decided to commit suicide. The narrator laconically concludes

---

47. One recalls Rahab hiding the Hebrew spies on the roof of her house under stalks of flax (Josh 2).

with these melancholy words: "He put his house in order and then hanged himself" (2 Sam 17:23).[48]

So, why did Ahithophel join the rebellion in the first place? A little probing suggests there may be more than first meets the eye. According to the genealogy in 2 Samuel 23:34, Ahithophel was the father of Eliam, one of David's celebrated Thirty. In 1 Chronicles 3:5, a certain Ammiel is listed as Bathsheba's father. Could Ammiel be the same person as Eliam? One can't be certain but on linguistic grounds, it's at least possible. If so, that makes Ahithophel Bathsheba's grandfather and supplies a missing motive for his defection. Perhaps an aggrieved grandfather explains his participation in the coup. An intriguing but uncertain possibility.

Typology and David's Flight

Before concluding the story of Absalom's rebellion, let's pause and review the entire episode in light of the larger context of Scripture. It seems to me we hear an echo of this story in the Gospel of Luke. David's exodus from Jerusalem corresponds, in a contrastive way, to Jesus' entrance into Jerusalem at the beginning of passion week.

Dr. Luke narrates the event as follows:

> When he came near the place where the road goes down the Mount of Olives, the whole crowd of disciples began joyfully to praise god in loud voices for all the miracles they had seen: "Blessed is the king who comes in the name of the Lord!" (Luke 19:37)

Then in what follows we have this remarkable observation—unique to Luke:

> When he approached Jerusalem and saw the city, he wept over it and said, "If you, even you, had only known on this day what would bring you peace—but now it is hidden from your eyes." (19:40–41)

Can it be mere coincidence that King David should climb the slopes of the Mount of Olives weeping and then centuries later King Jesus the Son of David should descend the same slopes weeping? It's like a signpost in redemptive history—David the fleeing king weeping because his own sins had

---

48. There are only three recorded suicides in Scripture, though Job, Jeremiah, and possibly Jonah seriously considered it, and the Philippian jailer was about to attempt it when Paul intervened (Acts 16:27–28). Besides Saul and Ahithophel, Judas joins the list of suicides (Matt 27:3–5; Acts 1:18–19). He, too, took his life because of remorse and, in my opinion, loss of all hope in national liberation led by Jesus of Nazareth.

found him out, and Jesus the entering king weeping because the sins of his people had blinded their eyes to his saving mission. "You did not recognize the time of God's coming to you" (Luke 19:44).

To this we must add an historical-eschatological epilogue. David did triumphantly return from exile to Jerusalem (2 Sam 20:3) and Jesus will also triumphantly return from his place at the right hand of the Father to establish the New Jerusalem (Acts 1:11). David's flight is another typological moment in the grand meta-narrative of redemptive history.

Absalom's Rebellion Is Crushed

"Pride goes before destruction, a haughty spirit before a fall" (Prov 16:18). So the sages of Israel warned. Absalom, quite oblivious to his limitations, allowed his overweening pride to lead him like a lamb to the slaughter. Wanting to demonstrate military prowess and personally deliver the *coup de grâce* to his father, he walked right into a trap.

Geographical Setting

A little geography goes a long way in helping the modern reader make sense of what happened. David's forces safely arrived in Mahanaim, the old Trans-jordanian capital of Ishbosheth during the civil war with David (2 Sam 2:8–9). Located on the east side of the Jordan River Valley in the region called Gilead, the hills reach comparable heights to their counterparts on the west bank and, in biblical times, were heavily forested. Joshua allotted the area to half the tribe of Manasseh, but in the course of time, many Ephraimites migrated eastward and resettled there. In fact, they called the area where the battle was fought the Forest of Ephraim reflecting this demographic shift. The fortified city of Mahanaim rests on a steep ridge overlooking the Jabbok River and affords a secure site for redeploying and readying a battle plan that would increase the odds of success.

Echoes from the Past

While holed up at Mahanaim, I think a story from Israel's storied patriarchal past replayed in David's head. For it was at Mahanaim on the Jabbok River that Jacob paused and prepared for his potentially life-threatening reunion with Esau.[49] Recall that Esau threatened to kill Jacob for deceiving

49. Gen 27:1–42; 28:12–22; 32:1, 22–32.

and supplanting him as the principal heir and head of the family. Jacob's exodus from Canaan was accompanied by an appearance of angels and a theophany[50] and his return was welcomed by another angelic appearance and theophany.[51] These bookend experiences conveyed Yahweh's inviolable promise: "I am with you and will watch over you wherever you go, and I will bring you back to this land. I will not leave you until I have done what I have promised you" (Gen 28:15).

On that memorable occasion, Jacob wrestled with a mysterious nocturnal visitor who with a mere touch wrenched Jacob's hip out of its socket and then proceeded to change Jacob's name to Israel because he had "struggled with God and with human beings and [had] overcome" (Gen 32:28). At dawn, just before the visitor vanished, he blessed Jacob. At that moment, Jacob realized it was God himself who had appeared in human form. "I saw God face to face" (Gen 32:30). For the rest of his life, he walked with a limp but he now knew beyond a shadow of a doubt that Yahweh's blessing rested upon him and his angels were watching over him. It was a defining moment for Jacob. As it turned out, he was reconciled with his brother Esau and returned to the promised land.

Although the narrator doesn't mention a theophany experience for David, there are some striking similarities between Jacob's experience at Mahanaim and David's preparations at the same place for a showdown with his vengeful son. The confrontation with Absalom would turn out to be a defining moment, but sadly, a tragic one. David regained his kingdom but lost another beloved son. And even though he knew Yahweh was still watching over him, for the rest of his life he was emotionally crippled and never fully recovered.

Loyalists Support Their King

David's cause was greatly assisted by loyalists on the east bank. Three individuals were singled out as stalwart supporters who resupplied David's fighting force, demonstrating that the displaced monarch was not without adherents who would go to extraordinary lengths to reinstate their king.

Shobi arrived from the capital city Rabbah (Amman) with supplies. He was an Ammonite prince whose father Nahash had been on friendly terms with David. Recall that Hanun, another son of Nahash, insulted David and thereby brought about the eventual incorporation of Ammon into Greater

50. Gen 28:12–22.
51. Gen 32:1, 22–23.

Israel.[52] It may seem odd that Shobi came to David's aid given the latter's severe treatment of the Ammonites after the Ammonite War. But David probably had appointed Shobi as regent after deposing Hanun, and Shobi returned the favor by remaining loyal to his benefactor and overlord.[53]

Makir and Barzillai were probably Israelites from the tribe of Manasseh who lived in Upper Gilead. Makir of Lo Debar had previously provided sanctuary for Jonathan's son Mephibosheth. David recalled Mephibosheth to the royal court in Jerusalem and restored to him the estates of his grandfather Saul. Makir repaid David's kindness to Mephibosheth with critically needed supplies. The eighty-year-old Barzillai from Rogelim was singled out for special commendation and even offered an opportunity to retire in Jerusalem near the palace, an offer he graciously declined, wishing instead to die and be buried in his homeland (2 Sam 19:14–38). In sum, the timely assistance of these three Transjordanian backers was a major factor in David's survival.

Battle in the Forest of Ephraim

In what follows, I reconstruct this famous battle by piecing together what can plausibly be inferred about the battlefield and tactics. David's elite forces were greatly outnumbered but superior in experience and skill. To minimize the disparity in numbers, it was essential to select an advantageous position from which to fight.[54] The wooded heights of the Forest of Ephraim provided just such a redoubt. This forced Absalom's untested recruits to climb up the forested slopes to engage David's troops. As typical, David divided his army into three corps with Joab, Abishai, and Ittai as commanders. In my view, the primary strategy involved positioning expert archers on the front line of each corps. As the forward ranks of Absalom's army labored up through

52. 2 Sam 10:1–14; 12:26–31.

53. See also Dempster, "Shobi" 5:1224–25.

54. One thinks of the catastrophic defeat of the Union army at Fredericksburg, Virginia, in which Union troops attempted to cross the Rappahannock River and then assault the Confederate troops entrenched on the heights. It was a massive slaughter, the worst Union defeat of the war. At the decisive battle of Gettysburg, the Union commander George Meade carefully selected the ground he wanted to defend against Robert Lee's desperate attempt to win the war with one decisive victory. Lee's attacks on the Union flanks positioned on the high ground failed on days one and two. On the third day, Lee rolled the dice and ordered an attack on the Union center deployed on Cemetery Ridge. Known as Pickett's Charge, 12,500 Confederate soldiers crossed an open field and then charged up an incline to the fortified ridge line. The attack was repulsed with heavy losses and the tide of the war dramatically shifted in favor of the North. As in real estate, so too in battle, location is everything.

the thick stands of trees, they suddenly walked right into a withering volley of arrows and suffered numerous casualties. The shock of such sudden carnage completely unnerved those still standing and they broke ranks and ran back into the ranks moving up behind them. This created a domino effect. Soon all the ranks broke formation and fled for safety. But no safety can be found in turning your back on the enemy in ancient warfare; in fact, the odds of being killed increase. Joab's battle-hardened veterans pursued the fleeing soldiers, inflicting heavy casualties—the text says twenty thousand were slain that day. The enigmatic statement that "the forest swallowed up more men that day than the sword" (2 Sam 18:8), may mean that most of Absalom's army "got lost in the forest" in their panicked flight.[55]

Whereas the narrator quickly summarizes the outcome of the battle, his real interest focuses on the demise of Absalom. To this end, he zooms in and graphically describes the events leading up to Absalom's execution. Before doing so, I backtrack momentarily and remind the reader of David's final instructions to his troops as they marched out of the city to the battlefield: "'Be gentle with the young man Absalom for my sake.' And all the troops heard the king giving orders concerning Absalom to *each of the commanders*" (18:5).

During the chaotic flight of the Israelite forces, Absalom "happened to meet David's men" (18:9).[56] As they were giving chase, Absalom's fabulous flowing hair got snagged in the branches of an oak tree. The mule kept running but Absalom was left hanging—literally by his hair. The vainglorious usurper was no longer in control of his future; ironically, he dangled at the mercy of his father's warriors. In a remarkable display of restraint, they held off killing Absalom. Instead, one of them reported what had happened to Joab. Joab reacted with disgust that the soldier hadn't dispatched Absalom on the spot. Had he done so, Joab claimed, he would have handsomely rewarded him. To this the soldier replied that he wouldn't have laid a hand on the king's son for "a thousand shekels" (18:12), given the king's strict orders

---

55. Vannoy, "2 Samuel," n. on 18:8. If the narrator intended to say the forest was the reason for most of the deaths, it's hard to imagine what that might have entailed. Gordon offers this possibility: "The treacherous terrain—which apparently included large pits (v. 17)—over which the battle spread is held responsible for more casualties than the fighting itself . . . we may see here a suggestion that nature was enlisted on the side of David." Vannoy, *I & II Samuel*, 284. This strains credibility—even if there were large pits in the region, could they account for that many casualties? Some conjecture that the fleeing Israelites were so panicked they mistook their fellow Israelites for David's forces and killed one another (cf. Judg 7:22; 1 Sam 14:20; 2 Chr 20:23). This seems even more improbable.

56. Once again, an expression that implies a divine director of the drama.

to spare Absalom's life.⁵⁷ Joab had no patience for scruples or sentiment.⁵⁸ He arrived on the scene and promptly plunged three javelins into Absalom's heart. Joab's armor bearers followed suit and Absalom mercifully died quickly—a fate not often afforded traitors! For all practical purposes, the coup was crushed.

Joab called off the chase. The surviving Israelites slipped back across the Jordan to their homes. Absalom's body was unceremoniously tossed into a pit and covered with a pile of stones—an ignominious end to an inflated ego.⁵⁹ The narrator adds a footnote. Absalom, a classic narcissist, had already erected a monument to himself in the King's Valley.⁶⁰ Reflecting the voice of a near contemporary, the narrator adds, "and it is called Absalom's Monument to this day" (2 Sam 18:18).⁶¹ And so, for many years Absalom had two tombs: a magnificent monument in the capital bearing his name and an unmarked, distant, and deserted rock pile.⁶² Both famous and infamous, Absalom was enamored with vanity and his life amounted to vanity.⁶³

Good News/Bad News

Our narrator remains in close up mode as he describes the aftermath of the victory in the Forest of Ephraim with two juxtaposed scenes: two couriers compete to be the first to convey the news of Absalom's defeat and a grief-stricken father reacts to the news of Absalom's death.

57. Brueggemann notes that the unnamed soldier was in a catch-22, caught between king and commander. Brueggemann, *First and Second Samuel*, 320.

58. "The midst of a battle is no time to discuss moral implications or political niceties. Joab lives in a world of simple moral choices and decisions. He does not weigh and vacillate and second guess. Instead, Joab does that at which he has always excelled: He acts!" Brueggemann, *First and Second Samuel*, 320.

59. There is no reference to Absalom's body ever being transferred back to Jerusalem and reburied in the family tomb, as was the case with Saul and his sons, Abner, and Ishbosheth. Absalom's body would never lie next to that of his hated brother Amnon, a sad epitaph to a sad story.

60. Perhaps a portion of the Kidron Valley adjacent to the ancient City of David.

61. Today, an elegant monument in the Kidron Valley is called Absalom's Pillar. Actually, it dates to the Hellenistic period, much later than Absalom. The original monument has disappeared or been reused in later construction. During the medieval period, the so-called Absalom's Pillar was understood to be authentic and Jewish fathers were in the habit of encouraging their children to throw rocks at the monument as an object lesson never to rebel against the authority of their fathers!

62. Cf. Josh 7:26; 8:29.

63. See Eccl 1:2, following the KJV translation. TNIV has, "Utterly meaningless! Everything is meaningless."

MESSENGERS ON THE RUN

Like the battle itself, the account of the two couriers requires geographical explanation. Assuming that the heights of Qala'lat Er Rabad (ca. 3,376 ft elevation) near the modern city of Ajlun was the site of the initial engagement, I can plot with some plausibility the respective routes taken by Ahimaaz and the Cushite.[64]

Before describing the race, however, the dialogue between Ahimaaz and Joab requires comment. Having already delivered vital intel to David concerning Absalom's intentions, Ahimaaz now seized upon another opportunity to render service for his king. He wanted to be the messenger of victory: "Let me run and take the news to the king that the LORD has vindicated him by delivering him from the hand of his enemies" (2 Sam 18:19). Joab brusquely denied his request and dispatched a Cushite runner instead. Joab wasn't trying to be a kill joy; he just didn't want Ahimaaz to walk into a highly charged situation in which the king might lash out in fury at the messenger; after all, a direct, repeated order had been disregarded, and we remember how David dealt with the assassins of Ishbosheth.[65] Ahimaaz, however, wouldn't be put off. Twice he pleaded with Joab to let him be a courier: "Come what may, I want to run" (18:23). Joab relented and off ran Ahimaaz.

The Cushite probably served as a royal courier and possessed great endurance and speed. His homeland of Cush (Nubia [modern Sudan] or Ethiopia) was famous for its swift runners, a tradition that continues to this very day. Ethiopian distance runners (both men and women) have had great success on the international scene, sporting many Olympic and World Championship medals.

Which begs an obvious question: How did Ahimaaz beat him? The first century AD Jewish historian Josephus explained it this way. "Now he [Ahimaaz] took a nearer road than the former did, for nobody knew it but himself, and he came before Cushi" (*Ant.* 7.247). Possibly, but not likely. How could Ahimaaz, a Jerusalemite, know about a short cut route in Transjordan? Furthermore, if one studies a detailed topographical map of the region, a more plausible scenario emerges. Second Samuel 18:23 points us to the answer. Although Ahimaaz started out "after the Cushite," he "ran by way of the Plain [*kikkar*]," that is, the Jordan Valley. The Cushite opted to run as the bee flies, a more or less direct path, but one involving two deep wadis (canyons), the first of which (Wadi Rajib) had to be traversed.

64. For more details, see Helyer, "Come What May."
65. 2 Sam 4:9–12.

The climb out of this steep wadi (ca. 500 ft), followed by a difficult descent (ca. 1,980 ft) into the second, the Wadi Zarqa (Jabbok), was a killer and slowed the Cushite's pace considerably, enabling Ahimaaz to arrive several minutes earlier.[66] As the wise teacher Qoheleth said, "the race is not to the swift" (Eccl 9:11). Nor, in this case, is the race always to the one who runs the shorter distance—Ahimaaz actually ran a longer distance (one to two miles) but he reached Mahanaim first because his route was easier—for the most part being either downhill or relatively flat—and thus his overall pace was quicker.

Our narrator provides a memorable account of the arrival of the two couriers. A watchman on the wall was keeping sharp lookout. When he caught sight of a lone runner and reported to the king, David concluded it must be good news.[67] Then a second runner was spotted, and David took this as confirmation. As the first runner came closer the watchman recognized the distinctive running style of Ahimaaz. To this David responded: "He's a good man . . . He comes with good news" (2 Sam 18:27).[68] Ahimaaz did indeed bring good news: "Praise be to the LORD your God! He has delivered up those who lifted their hands against my lord the king" (18:28). But the king's first question to Ahimaaz and the one that mattered most to him as a father was: "Is the young man Absalom safe?" (18:29). Ahimaaz feigned ignorance—he just couldn't tell the king the truth.[69] That thankless task fell to the foreigner, the Cushite. After confirming the news of a resounding victory, the Cushite was asked the same question. He didn't hold back: "May the enemies of my lord the king and all who rise up to harm you be like that young man" (18:32). The king was devastated.[70]

66. One is reminded of the infamous "Heartbreak Hill" at the twentieth mile of the Boston Marathon where many runners run out of gas!

67. In other words, an army in flight would have many soldiers running for the relative safety of the fortress. A lone runner presaged a victory announcement to be followed by a more orderly return of the troops to the city.

68. "This moment is quite exceptional, and striking, in representing the arrival of the two messengers visually, from the perspective of the lookout on the wall reporting to David down below in the gate plaza. David's troubles with all his sons, it should be remembered, began when he himself looked down from the roof and saw a woman bathing." Alter, *David Story*, 308.

69. Ahimaaz knew Absalom's fate—news like that would have spread like wildfire among the troops. But face to face with the king, Joab's warning was probably ringing in his ears: "The king's son is dead . . . you don't have any news that will bring you a reward" (2 Sam 18:22).

70. One recalls the shock and subsequent death of Eli when he received word of the death of his two sons and the capture of the ark (1 Sam 4:17–18).

MOURNING IN THE GATE

David's grief over his son Absalom is one of the most heart-rending episodes in the Bible.[71] "O my son Absalom! My son, my son Absalom! If only I had died instead of you—O Absalom, my son, my son!" (2 Sam 18:33). Mary, the mother of Jesus, also had a "my son, my son" moment. She at least had an intimation it was coming. Already at Jesus' dedication in the temple courts, the aged Simeon prophesied: "This child is destined to cause the falling and rising of many in Israel, and to be a sign that will be spoken against . . . a sword will pierce your own soul too" (Luke 2:35). The moment of piercing occurred as she stood near the cross of her dying firstborn son at Golgotha and heard his agonizing cry: "My God, my God, why have you forsaken me?" (Mark 15:34).

The king's inconsolable grief was like a wet blanket. Instead of grand celebration and feasting the atmosphere felt more like a wake. Stunned and embarrassed the troops quietly "stole into the city" (2 Sam 19:3). Joab "the fixer" would have none of it. Always alert to political cross currents, he confronted the king in no uncertain terms: "Today you have humiliated all your men, who have just saved your life . . . " (19:5) and sternly warned him that if he wanted to maintain his throne, he'd better snap out of it and go down to his loyal followers and let them know how deeply grateful he was for their heroic measures to preserve his crown and family.[72] "If you don't, . . . not a man will be left with you by nightfall" (19:7). David knew Joab was right. "So the king got up and took his seat in the gateway" and all his men "came before him" (19:8).

David survived the most serious crisis of his career—and one of the most emotionally devastating.[73] For much of his life, David's cup overflowed (Ps 23:5). Now he drank the bitter dregs from a cup of sorrow. "Be merciful to me, LORD, for I am in distress; my eyes grow weak with sorrow, my soul

71. "These have got to be among the saddest, most heart-rending words ever spoken—words wrenched out of David's gut when the report was brought to him that his son had been murdered in the forest of Ephraim." Peterson, *Leap Over a Wall*, 193.

72. Gordon is undoubtedly correct when he notes, "David and the rest of the royal family might have paid with their lives, for there is no reason to suppose that Absalom would have behaved any differently from later usurpers like Baasha (1 Kgs 15:27–30), Zimri (1 Kgs 16:11–12), or Jehu (2 Kgs 10:6–11)." Gordon, *I & II Samuel*, 287–88. A somewhat analogous situation occurred in the British royal family following Princess Diana's tragic death. Tony Blair the Prime Minister, told the queen that if she didn't come back to London and participate in the public mourning, the future of the royal family tradition would be at risk.

73. Perhaps only the sneak attack upon Ziklag was of the same magnitude (1 Sam 30).

and body with grief" (Ps 31:9). About a thousand years later, David's greater son, Jesus of Nazareth, pleaded with Abba, his heavenly Father: "Take this cup from me." But then he added this all-important qualification: "Yet not what I will, but what you will" (Mark 14:36). Like his ancestor, Jesus drank from the cup of sorrow—not *because* of his sins, however, but *as a sacrifice for* the sins of the world (1 John 2:2). Like an echo from the past, as Jesus was dying, he prayed David's prayer: "Father, into your hands I commit my spirit" (Luke 23:46; cf. Ps 31:5).

Absalom was dead and his army scattered, but aftershocks followed his abortive coup. Although there will be happy days again for the House of David, things will never be quite the same. More troubles like storm clouds lay on the horizon. And the all-important question of succession must yet be settled. That's our focus in the next chapter.

13

MORE TROUBLES FOR THE HOUSE OF DAVID

Why, LORD, do you stand far off? Why do you hide yourself in times of trouble?

—PSALM 10:1

THE FIRST ORDER OF business was returning the exiled king to Jerusalem and repairing the damage done to national unity. The return, though not without conflict, was much easier than the repair. In fact, even during the golden age of Solomon, sores of discontent still festered, accounting for the secession of the northern tribes shortly after his death in 930 BC.

RETURN OF THE KING

Controversy and Consensus

Absalom's death and the flight of his army back to the west bank precipitated a national debate. A majority of Israelites (northern tribes) argued that the exiled king should be recalled (2 Sam 19:9–10).[1] This sentiment came to David's attention at Mahanaim. Troubled by a corresponding lack of

1. From English history we have a comparable situation after Cromwell's death and the collapse of the Commonwealth (1649–53), leading eventually to the recall of Charles II from exile in the Netherlands (1660).

enthusiasm on the part of his fellow tribesmen, he asked the two high priests to advocate on his behalf and shame the men of Judah into action: "Why should you be the last to bring the king back to his palace" (2 Sam 19:11).

David also issued an executive order with far-reaching consequences. He appointed Amasa as the new commander in chief in place of Joab. Even though Amasa was David's nephew, this appointment was quite unexpected because Amasa had served in that capacity for the usurper Absalom.[2] Perhaps David was trying to win over both Israelite and Judahite discontents and display a spirit of conciliation by this choice, but I think his primary motive was deep-seated anger directed at Joab. No doubt David had heard through the grapevine about Joab's role in his son's death and, even though he preserved David's throne, disobeying a direct order to spare his son reinforced the bad blood already existing between these two.[3] Joab, ever the resilient and resourceful one, accepted his demotion and bided his time. But not for long.

Cameos: Two Supplicants and a Supporter

Once again, our narrator zooms in on several key actors in the restoration drama. The men of Judah enthusiastically reaffirmed their allegiance to David and went down to Gilgal to await the king's arrival at the ford of the Jordan River.[4] They were joined by a thousand Benjamites, two of whom our narrator singles out for special mention. Recall that when David fled Jerusalem, he encountered two Benjamites, one supportive and the other hostile.[5] Now, in reverse order, these same two individuals rushed down to the ford and crossed over to assist the king and his retinue with their crossing.

2. 2 Sam 19:13; 1 Chr 2:17; 2 Sam 17:25.

3. As long as Absalom lived, he would pose a constant threat to David's reign. Joab reckoned that no one else would dare eliminate Absalom, least of all the king himself. So, he characteristically took matters into his own hands.

4. Gilgal was a prominent landmark in Israelite history. It was the site of the Israelites' first encampment in the land of promise (Josh 4:19) and the place where the new generation was circumcised and observed their first Passover (Josh 5:2–12). From Gilgal Joshua lead the Israelites in a successful invasion and settlement of the land. It was also one of the sites where Samuel held court and decided cases for the Israelites (1 Sam 7:16). Of great significance for the David story, at Gilgal Samuel both declared Saul as the first king of Israel (1 Sam 11:14–15) and then, in Yahweh's name, rejected him as king (1 Sam 13:8–15; 15:12–35).

5. 2 Sam 16:1–13

Shimei Pleads for Pardon

Shimei is desperate; he knows his life hangs in the balance and his only hope lies in David's mercy. He pushes forward and prostrates himself before the king. Openly acknowledging his offense, he pleads for clemency and appeals to the fact that he was the first to meet the king. Implied in his plea is a pledge of complete loyalty from that moment on.

Quite in character, Abishai took a dim view of Shimei's groveling before the king and he reminded David of the seriousness of the offense. Cursing Yahweh's anointed violated the law of Sinai and, in Abishai's opinion, was tantamount to high treason, a capital offense deserving death.[6] David had no stomach for it, nor did he have a stomach for the constant provocations incited by the sons of Zeruiah! Far too many young men had already died. The issue had been decided on the battlefield; now he decided to be magnanimous in victory. David gave his word to Shimei—he would be spared. As we later learn, however, Shimei's royal pardon lasted only as long as David lived.[7]

Ziba Seeks to Defend Himself

Ziba, our second person of interest, was one of the first arrivals at the crossing. He and his fifteen sons [!] and twenty servants spared no effort providing assistance to the king and retinue as they prepared to cross the Jordan. Ziba's zeal was prompted by a guilty conscience and he sought to indemnify himself against Mephibosheth's anticipated accusations against him.

Mephibosheth Pleads His Innocence

Indeed, crippled Mephibosheth was on the scene and granted an audience. He must have enlisted his servants' help to make the arduous descent to the Jordan and the river crossing. Hobbling into the king's presence, he looked awful. Disheveled and dirty, he gave every appearance of having been in mourning for an extended period. He came right to the point: "Ziba my servant betrayed me. And he has slandered your servant to my lord the king" (2 Sam 19:26). Like Shimei, he cast himself on the king's mercy and sagacity: "My lord the king is like an angel of God" (19:27). Declaring himself ready to accept whatever verdict the king handed down, he gratefully acknowledged that he owed the king his very life and livelihood.

6. Exod 22:28.

7. 1 Kgs 2:7–9, 36–46.

David was forced to render a verdict on the spot because there was no time for careful cross examination: "Why say more?" (2 Sam 19:29). Deeply grateful for the timely assistance provided by Ziba, he decided to split the estate in half. In my opinion, Ziba got away with lying, slander and grand theft.[8] Sometimes human justice falls short of the ideal. "There is something else meaningless that occurs on earth: the righteous who get what the wicked deserve, and the wicked who get what the righteous deserve" (Eccl 8:14). The divine tribunal, however, will eventually set the record straight: "For God will bring every deed into judgment, including every hidden thing, whether it is good or evil" (Eccl 12:14).[9]

Before leaving the episode of Mephibosheth's restoration to favor, I think it worthwhile to draw attention to the typological features of his life story, which illustrate God's marvelous plan of redemption. Like the crippled Mephibosheth, we all like sheep have gone astray and by our sins have become spiritual cripples. God comes to us like an orthopedic surgeon of the soul and restores us to health and wholeness. Although deserving death, by grace through faith in Christ we have been pardoned and privileged to sit at the kings' table as members of his family. Amazing grace, how sweet the sound!

Barzillai Provides a Proxy

Our octogenarian, Barzillai the Gileadite, made his way down to the crossing to say his goodbyes. David sought to reward him for his service above and beyond the call of duty by bringing him up to Jerusalem to finish out his days as a guest of the royal court. Barzillai's polite demurral is a studied piece of court etiquette. Reminiscent of the classic essay on aging in Ecclesiastes ("[when] the days of trouble come and the years approach when you will say, 'I find no pleasure in them'" (Eccl 12:1), Barzillai reminded the monarch that he wouldn't be able to enjoy the culinary and cultural delights of the royal court. And since death was on the horizon, he wanted to die and be buried in the family tomb in his home town.[10]

To further soften his turning down the royal invitation, Barzillai provided a proxy, his son (or perhaps relative) Kimham, who would serve at the pleasure of the king. Not to be outdone in generosity, David replied, "I will do for him whatever you wish. And anything you desire from me I will do

---

8. "This compromise is hardly to David's credit." Mackay, *1–2 Samuel*, 435.

9. Cf. Eccl 3:17; Rom 2:16; 1 Cor 4:5.

10. "At his advanced stage in life, Barzillai was far more interested in a dignified death than a dynamic life." Bergen, *1, 2 Samuel*, 432.

for you" (2 Sam 19:38).[11] Barzillai's curtain call is short and sweet: "The king kissed Barzillai and bid him farewell, and Barzillai returned to his home" (19:39). The contrast to Ahithophel's grim return home to commit suicide is striking.[12]

Crisis at the Crossing

Just when it seemed the David express was back on track, a new crisis erupted. Here's what happened. A large contingent of Israelite troops finally arrived at the crossing. When they saw that the king and his entourage had already crossed, they were incensed: "Why did our brothers, the men of Judah, steal the king away and bring him and his household across the Jordan, together with all his men?" (19:41). This sparked a furious exchange between the Judahites and Israelites. Claims and counterclaims flew back and forth, dredging up a litany of alleged grievances from the confederation days.[13] Our narrator breaks off the dispute with this observation: "the men of Judah responded even more harshly than the men of Israel" (19:43). This state of inter-tribal belligerency did not bode well for national unity.[14]

REBELLION OF SHEBA

Seizing the moment, another Benjamite, Sheba son of Bikri, exploited the tribal confrontation by calling for immediate secession: "We have no share in David, no part in Jesse's son! Everyone to your tents, Israel!" (20:1). In a stunning reversal, demonstrating the fragility of the united kingdom, "all the men of Israel deserted David to follow Sheba son of Bikri" (20:2). Out of the frying pan into the fire! David was now faced with a crisis potentially more serious than that of Absalom.

---

11. In Jer 41:17, we learn that in the days of Jeremiah there was a place called Geruth Kimham near Bethlehem. The name means "lodging place of Kimham" and may refer to a royal bestowal of property for Kimham's faithful service.

12. 1 Sam 18:23.

13. As in the days of Gideon (Judg 8:1–3) and Jephthah (Judg 12:1–6).

14. "The dispute between Judah and Israel is unsettled and has ominous reverberations. The events around Absalom have not created the breach. The division was there all along, covered over only by pious talk, grand political claims, and the power of David's person. The civil war has given new power, vitality, visibility, and credence to the old separatism. The united kingdom of David is exceedingly tenuous." Brueggemann, *First and Second Samuel*, 328.

Joab Murders Amasa

Meanwhile, "David returned to his palace in Jerusalem" (2 Sam 20:2). Two urgent matters had to be resolved. First, David must decide what to do with the ten concubines Absalom slept with. There's no denying it; the fate of these women was unjust and unpalatable. Though provided for, they were confined to their quarters and consigned to widowhood the rest of their days.

Living as chattel is not what God intended. Thankfully, this cultural pattern no longer prevails in modern, western society, though it still persists in some third world and Islamic cultures, in cults operating in the dark corners, and in a few churches still enslaved by a hyper-fundamentalist mentality.[15] When God's kingdom finally comes, and his will is done on earth as it is in heaven, you can be sure his original plan for men and women will be fully realized.[16]

The second, more politically pressing issue concerned Sheba's revolt and the threatened secession of the north. This must be nipped in the bud; delay would be fatal for any hopes of national unity. To this end, David summoned Amasa, his new chief of staff, and ordered him to mobilize the army of Judah and suppress the secessionists. Time was of the essence: "Come to me within three days, and be here yourself" (20:4). For unstated reasons, Amasa failed to meet the deadline, so David turned to Abishai, his other go-to guy, and commissioned him to deal quickly with Sheba because he "will do us more harm than Absalom did" (20:6). Abishai *and Joab* set out with the elite royal guards in hot pursuit of Sheba.

As the troops headed north, they took a break at the great rock in Gibeon and Amasa, with Judahite regulars, caught up with them. Ironically, this is where Abner and Joab's forces collided during the David-Ishbosheth civil war and Abner thrust his spear into the belly of Joab's brother Asahel (2 Sam 2:12–23). Joab once again took matters into his own hands. Under the guise of a friendly greeting, he caught Amasa off guard and stabbed him in the belly. Without waiting around, Joab and Abishai took off after Sheba. There's no disputing who was now in charge of the operation. Joab resumed the role of commander in chief and never relinquished it until his execution

---

15. "In certain middle eastern societies, women (and women in some Orthodox Jewish cultures) are still considered chattel having no legal existence outside their husbands, fathers, sons, and brothers. A husband owns his wife and any children of the marriage. In some areas, that chattel status is modified to only include sexual and reproductive rights that are owned by husbands." See "What Is the Historical Meaning?"

16. Matt 6:10; cf. Gen 1:27–31; Gal 3:28–29; Rev 21:4–5.

for treason at the end of his career.[17] One of Joab's men stood beside the body of Amasa as the soldiers resumed their forced march. When they saw his corpse in a pool of blood they stopped out of respect for his office. Joab's aid laid it out clear and simple: "Whoever favors Joab, and whoever is for David, let him follow Joab!" (2 Sam 20:11). He then dragged the body to the side of the road and covered it. "Everyone went on with Joab to pursue Sheba son of Bikri" (20:13).

Joab and a Wise Woman End Sheba's Revolt

Sheba made his way northward, probably trying to enlist support for secession. Apparently only Sheba's clan of Bikrites joined the movement in significant numbers. That forced Sheba to hole up in the northern city of Abel Beth Maacah. Joab promptly laid siege, building a siege ramp and battering ram to breach the wall. The outcome was not in doubt—Joab's troops would inevitably break through and wreak havoc on the citizens.

For the second time in the stories of David's troubles, a wise woman, in collaboration with Joab, steps into the breach and saves the day.[18] She requests a parley with Joab in which she appeals to his better angels. Why should he destroy a city with a long tradition of providing answers to perplexing questions, living in peace, and remaining loyal to the crown?[19] In fact, she reminded Joab that her city was reckoned "a mother in Israel" (20:19). To destroy it would be unthinkable. Joab agreed and explained that the king wanted just one man, the traitor Sheba ben Bikri. In short, if he were handed over, the city would be spared. She quickly agreed to his terms and promised: "His head will be thrown to you from the wall" (20:21). She persuaded the city fathers to act in their best interests and Sheba's head, like a football, soon sailed over the wall to Joab. Just as quickly, the troops broke off the siege, withdrew, and returned home. Mission accomplished, "Joab went back to the king in Jerusalem" (20:22). I would have loved to be a fly on the wall when Joab reported back to David! Once again, Joab the hard-nosed political realist kept the ship of state afloat.

17. 2 Kgs 2:28–34.

18. See 2 Sam 14:2–23.

19. Panitz-Cohen and Yahalom-Mack marshal evidence that both Abel Beth Maacah and Tel Dan were ancient cultic centers renowned for their oracular wisdom. See Panitz-Cohen and Yahalom-Mack, "Wise Woman," 26–33.

RECAP OF THE KING'S OFFICIALS

The narrator breaks off the story with another brief summary of David's offi-cials. Structurally, the two lists of David's cabinet members in 2 Sam 8:15–18 and 2 Sam 20:23–26 frame the narratives of David and his family.[20] Given what just happened at Abel Beth Maacah, it's no surprise to learn that "Joab was over Israel's entire army" (20:23). Several differences appear in the two lists, the first probably dating from the beginning of David's reign and the second from near the end. There are two minor differences or discrepancies between the names of one of the priests (Ahimelek and Abiathar) and the office of secretary (Seraiah and Sheva).[21] Of more importance, the first list mentioned David's sons as priests, a departure from the Law of Moses.[22] The second makes no mention of royal sons serving as priests. The second list, however, specifically mentions a certain Ira the Jairite who served as David's personal priest. This appears to have been a royal appointment in-stituted by David. His job description is not given, but he probably served as a personal chaplain and confidant. Given the numerous troubles that beset David's reign after the Bathsheba Affair, this is understandable. The most striking difference in the second list, however, concerns another new office. "Adoniram was in charge of forced labor" (20:24). Conquests of neighboring countries brought an influx of foreign slaves into the united kingdom and by their back-breaking labor and sweat much of the infrastructure necessary for an expanding empire was constructed. As we later learn, the extension of this labor force under Solomon to include native Israelites became a bone of contention and leading cause for the northern tribes' secession.[23]

Finally, there is a glaring omission in the second list. The glowing in-troduction to the first list is gone. "David reigned over all Israel, *doing what was just and right for all his people*" (8:15). Alas, a lot of water had passed under the bridge and the rosy prospects of the early years had paled. The Teacher of Ecclesiastes describes a scenario similar to David's rise to power from poverty only to be followed in his later years by his subject's dissatis-faction. "Those who came later were not pleased with the successor" (Eccl 4:16; cf. 4:13–15). David's best years were in the rear-view mirror.

---

20. Brueggemann, *First and Second Samuel*, 332. In fact, 2 Samuel 21–24 displays an internal unity as may be seen by the manner in which it is concentrically arranged. For a helpful way of visualizing this compositional technique, see Arnold, *1 & 2 Samuel*, loc. 12500.

21. These may be accounted for by textual corruption, death, retirement, or removal from office. See commentaries for more discussion.

22. Exod 40:15.

23. 1 Kgs 12:4–16.

THE GIBEONITE AFFAIR

At some unspecified time during David's reign, for three consecutive years, a severe famine gripped the land, the result of a significant shortfall in the amount of precipitation during the rainy season (Oct–Apr).[24] David sought Yahweh for intervention, who responded with a disturbing pronouncement, presumably through one of his prophets, Gad or Nathan: "It is on account of Saul and his blood-stained house; it is because he put the Gibeonites to death" (2 Sam 21:1). Apparently, Saul had annulled Joshua's vow of protection and "in his zeal for Judah and Israel had tried to annihilate them" (21:2).[25] Saul probably viewed a non-Israelite enclave located so close to his capital as militarily and politically untenable.[26] The number killed must have been considerable, and the survivors fled from their homes.

David summoned the surviving Gibeonites and asked them what he could do to make atonement for this atrocity. Uppermost in David's mind was restoration of Yahweh's blessing, with its attendant bountiful rainfall. The Gibeonites recognized their limited civil rights in Israel: they couldn't demand monetary compensation nor the right to exact personal vengeance.[27] When pressed by David, they requested that he hand over seven male descendants of Saul and authorize their execution at Gibeah, Saul's capital city. What is especially noteworthy is their description of Saul as "the LORD's chosen one" (21:6). By this expression, they were affirming their allegiance as loyal subjects of the kingdom of Israel. David consented to their request.

He was now faced with an excruciating decision. Whom should he choose to suffer the extreme penalty for Saul's outrage? Two sons of Rizpah and five sons of Merab were selected.[28] Excluded from the list was Me-

24. It should be noted that periodic droughts occur in the region both in biblical (Gen 12:10; Ruth 1:1 et al) and post-biblical times. Just recently, a seven-year period of below average rainfall seriously lowered the water levels in the Sea of Galilee and underground aquifers. Thankfully, the winter of 2018–2019 saw significantly higher than normal rainfall and snow, raising water levels above the so-called "black line." A deficit, however, still exists and several more years of above average rainfall are needed to achieve normal levels.

25. See Josh 9:1–27.

26. Recall that one of David's first acts as king of all Israel was the elimination of Jerusalemite as a Jebusite enclave in the heartland of his kingdom (1 Sam 5:6–10).

27. In the modern State of Israel, Arab citizens continue to experience discrimination despite being formally recognized as equals by Israeli law.

28. There is a textual problem with regard to the name of this mother. See TNIV footnote on 1 Sam 21:8. Merab is almost certainly original. Decisive in this question is the fact that Michal was not married to Adriel. Furthermore, after David and Michal had a falling out, "Michal daughter of Saul had no children to the day of her death" (1

phibosheth, son of Jonathan, "because of the oath before the Lord between David and Jonathan son of Saul" (2 Sam 21:17). And so, in April ("the barley harvest was beginning" [21:9]), seven Saulides were executed and their bodies exposed "on a hill before the LORD" (21:9).

This episode shocks modern readers.[29] Collective punishment imposed on the offspring of those convicted of capital offenses violates our sense of human decency and justice—to say nothing of contravening the penal code of virtually all modern nations. As a matter of fact, it even fails to pass muster with the Mosaic law code. "Parents are not to be put to death for their children, nor children put to death for their parents; each of you will die for your own sin" (Deut 24:16).[30]

So, how could David have allowed this to happen? "In accepting the Gibeonites' petition, David implements contemporary cultural norms associated with blood feuds that contravene divine law."[31] While he *may* have believed the sentence was justified, the text doesn't say he sought the will of Yahweh with regard to the *nature* of the penalty. Nor does it say Yahweh sanctioned the sentence; rather, David allowed the Gibeonites to exact their revenge.[32] Some sort of reparation was required, but not the sentence imposed on the Saulides.

Something happened that smote David's conscience. Rizpah's heroic and tragic vigil lasting from barley harvest till the autumn rains (about six months) stirred him to provide a proper burial for the victims.[33] Their bones were interred, along with the exhumed bones of Saul and his sons from Jabesh Gilead, in the family tomb of Kish at Zela in Benjamin. Following that, we read that "God answered prayer in behalf of the land" (2 Sam 22:14). One gets the impression that Rizpah's vigil and David's compassionate response and fervent prayer of intercession was what brought an end to the drought rather than the execution of Saul's descendants.[34]

Sam 6:23).

29. Payne calls it "strange and repellent." Payne, *I and II Samuel*, 259. Edersheim says, "there is not a more harrowing narrative in Holy Scripture than that connected with the famine which for three years desolated Palestine." Edersheim, *Bible History*, 38.

30. Bergen's attempt to justify David's action fails. None of the Pentateuchal texts he cites have to do with punishing the descendants of those guilty of homicide. Nor, tellingly, does he mention Deut 24:16. See Bergen, *1, 2 Samuel*, 445.

31. Mackay, *1–2 Samuel*, 453.

32. Peterson takes a similar tack: "Curiously, though he does start out to pray, he does not ask God what to do . . . Human sacrifice was not Israel's way of doing things. But David did what they asked." Peterson, *First and Second Samuel*, loc. 5235, 5249.

33. 2 Sam 21:10–14.

34. "Rizpah brought David to his theological senses, demonstrating that it is not sacrifice that God wants, but mercy; it is not by taking life that we expiate sin, but by

This appalling episode demonstrates the tragic consequences that inevitably follow in the wake of unjust and wicked actions perpetrated by rulers and the governments that support them. Saul's genocide against the Gibeonites was hardly the first and certainly not the last instance of state-sanctioned genocide.[35] In fact, who knows the number of similar atrocities "zealously" perpetrated down through the ages? The Third Reich and the Holocaust will forever serve as one of the most horrifying examples.[36]

After WWII, the allies tried twenty-four leading Nazis guilty of war crimes at the Nuremberg Trials. Twelve of the accused were sentenced to death (one, Hermann Göring, committed suicide in his cell), seven received prison sentences (ranging from ten years to life), three were acquitted, and two were not charged. Many other Nazis and those who cooperated with them were eventually brought to trial and sentenced. In no case, however, were their offspring punished for the crimes committed. Reparations, however, were imposed on Germany for allowing the Nazi government to plunge the world into a world-wide war costing about fifty-five million lives and to carry out the systematic murder of six-million Jewish men, women, and children. In addition, approximately six-million people of various ethnicities and alleged crimes and defects were also exterminated in the death camps. The very few Holocaust survivors still living today continue to receive payments from Germany.[37]

I conclude with this observation. Old Testament narratives are not primarily prescriptive and occasionally confront us with cultural practices superseded by the NT and modernity, the latter of which has been changed for the better by the impact of Christian teaching.[38] We still have a long way

---

honoring it, not by inhuman cruelties, but by human compassion (see Mic 6:7–8)." Peterson, *First and Second Samuel*, loc. 5266, ch. 21.

35. Of course, the most obvious instance of genocide in the OT is that of the Canaanites in the days of the conquest. According to Scripture, Yahweh did sanction this extreme judgment but only for a limited place and time. See Exod 23:32–33; 34:11–16; Deut 2:34; 3:6; 20:16–18; Ps 106:34–42. The topic requires a much more in-depth treatment than I can devote to it in this book. For some direction see Hess, *Joshua*, 46–51; Kaiser, *Hard Sayings*, 206–207; Madvig, "Joshua," 3:246–47.

36. In the twentieth century alone, 1.5 million Armenians were either massacred or expelled by the Turkish government. Dictators like Stalin (Russia), Mao-Tse Tung (China), and Pol Pot (Cambodia) liquidated literally millions of their own citizens. Hafez Al-Assad (Syria) massacred tens of thousands of Syrian citizens and Serbs in Bosnia murdered one-hundred thousand Muslims. Many more such atrocities have been perpetrated in "civilized society."

37. Until 1989 Germany paid about 14 billion dollars to Israel in reparations. For a number of years Germany supplied the State of Israel with Mercedes Benz tour buses.

38. "Unfortunately, failure to understand both the reason for and the character of Hebrew narrative has caused many Christians in the past to read the Old Testament

to go before we arrive at the New Jerusalem, and sometimes the Dark Lord and fallen human nature conspire to unleash unimaginable evil. In such times, the people of God must hold tightly to this hope: God's messiah "will reign on David's throne and over his kingdom, establishing and upholding it *with justice and righteousness from that time on and forever. The* zeal of the Lord Almighty will accomplish this" (Isa 9:7). May his kingdom come speedily and in our day![39]

THE CENSUS CRISIS

Another crisis engulfed David's kingdom near the end of his career. Once again considerable mystery surrounds this episode and I can only offer some suggestions as to the nature of the offense.

Pride Precipitates a Plague

What immediately strikes the reader of this text is the puzzling reference to the anger of Yahweh against Israel and his inciting David against them by taking a census. Our perplexity only increases when we read the later account of this story by the Chronicler. He attributes the instigation to Satan who in turn incited David to take the census (1 Chr 21:1). So, what are we to make of this story?

The primary question to be answered has to do with the nature of the offense. Why was a military census wrong in the first place? Wouldn't this be helpful information for the king and his generals? Our surprise increases when we read the intensity of David's confession: "David was conscience-stricken after he had counted the fighting men, and he said to the LORD, 'I have sinned greatly in what I have done. Now LORD, I beg you, take away the guilt of your servant. I have done a very foolish thing'" (2 Sam 24:10). But why was it sinful and foolish?

Some suggest David failed to follow the requirement of Exodus 30:12: "When you take a census of the Israelites to count them, each one must pay the LORD a ransom for his life at the time he is counted. Then no plague will

---

story very poorly . . . in our experience, people force incorrect interpretations and applications on narrative portions of the bible as much as or more than they do on any other parts." Fee and Stuart, *How to Read the Bible*, 89. See their full discussion in ch. 5, 89–106. On the impact of Christianity on modern society see Hill, *What Has Christianity Ever Done?*

39. Echoing the Jewish Kaddish prayer recited daily during the shiva (seven-day period of mourning) for a deceased loved one.

come on them when you number them. Each one . . . is to give a half shekel . . . This half shekel is an offering to the LORD."[40] But if that were the case, surely the sacred historian would have so stated; furthermore, the penalty far exceeds the offense. The answer more likely lies in a violation of the divine ideal for Hebrew kingship as defined in the book of Deuteronomy. In a section dealing with qualifications and guidelines for kings, seven stipulations are spelled out:[41]

1. He must be Yahweh's choice.

2. He must be a Hebrew.

3. He must not acquire great numbers of horses.

4. He must not take many wives.

5. He must not accumulate personal wealth.

6. He must have a personal copy of the law and read it regularly.

7. He must not consider himself better than his subjects.

At first glance, none of these seem relevant to the situation at hand. Perhaps, however, a closer look at stipulation three provides an answer. At face value, one wonders why it should be considered sinful for a Hebrew king to acquire large numbers of horses. As one who grew up on a cattle ranch in Oregon with many saddle horses, I can't imagine there could be something inherently wrong with owning these magnificent animals! What is striking, however, is the absence of horses in the Hebrew army during the days of the conquest under Joshua. They were exclusively for infantrymen. Furthermore, they hamstrung those they captured in battle.[42] This practice continued even during the days of David.[43] Only in the halcyon days of Solomon and later during the divided monarchy do we read of large numbers of horses.[44] But note carefully, it isn't just a matter of owning and riding horses; it really refers to acquiring chariot horses.

Chariots were the equivalent of battle tanks. Powerful Israelite kings like Ahab marshalled large chariot corps in their battles with enemy states.[45]

40. Andrews and Bergen, *I & II Samuel*, 367.

41. Deut 17:14–20.

42. They severed the tendon at the back of the hock, rendering them unable to function effectively (Josh 11:6, 9).

43. David spared only one-hundred horses from Hadadezer's chariot corps (2 Sam 8:4).

44. 1 Kgs 4:26–28; 10:28; 18:5; 22:14; 2 Kgs 3:7.

45. In fact, at the battle of Karkar (853 BC), Ahab headed a coalition of western states against Assyria in which he fielded the largest contingent of chariots (2,000). See

The principle appears to be this: a truly theocratic kingdom must rely on Yahweh, not military manpower or technology, to overcome its enemies. A Davidic psalm expresses this conviction: "The LORD gives victory to his anointed. He answers from his heavenly sanctuary with the victorious power of his right hand. Some trust in chariots and some in horses, but we trust in the name of the LORD our God" (Ps 20:6–7).[46]

To take the argument one step further, the real nub of David's sinful action was his desire to glory in his military might. No neighboring state could rival him or stand toe to toe against him in battle. He reveled in that and wanted to have a permanent record of the military strength he possessed. Even though Joab tried his best to talk David out of it, he was overruled and the census went forward.[47] At the end of nine months and twenty days, the survey team led by Joab and his officers returned to the capital.[48] The total number of fighting men was impressive for such a relatively small kingdom, 1,300,000.[49] In Yahweh's eyes, however, the undertaking was reprehensible. Militarism flowing from misplaced national and personal pride was the bottom line.[50] David may even have intended to enlarge the empire through military aggression against neighboring states.[51]

For his egregious transgression, a grievous punishment was decreed. Given three options, three years of famine, three months of defeat at the hands of enemies, or three days of plague, David chose to cast himself on Yahweh: "Let us fall into the hands of the LORD, for his mercy is great, but do not let me fall into human hands" (2 Sam 24:14). Note that the entire nation fell under this divine judgment because its king succumbed to personal ambition and pride. History is littered with instances in which a people suffer on account of the folly of their leader.[52] Corporate solidarity is an

---

Oppenheim, "Fight Against the Aramean Coalition," 278–79.

46. See also Pss 21; 33:17; 147:10.

47. How telling that unscrupulous Joab pushed back against the king's directive!

48. Alter observes that nine months and twenty days is the normal gestation period for humans. Ironically and tragically, the census-taking period ends not in life but in the death of some seventy-thousand Israelites. Alter, *David Story*, 354.

49. In Chronicles, Joab reported the number at 1,570,000 (1 Chr 21:5), although he left out of reckoning the Levites and Benjamites "because the king's command was repulsive to him" (2 Sam 21:6).

50. "It was despicable because it put nationalism ahead of zeal for the Lord, the kingdom of Israel ahead of the kingdom of God." Bergen, *1, 2 Samuel*, 444. American Christian nationalism commits the same folly. See Helyer, *Life and Witness*, 50–56.

51. Dillard, "David's Census," 106.

52. E.g., Germany experienced massive death and destruction as a consequence of Hitler's obsession with Aryan supremacy, hatred of the Jewish people, and territorial expansion for the "Fatherland." His demonic agenda was shared by the Nazi party and

inescapable fact of human existence. Sometimes the many suffer because of the sin(s) of the one (or few). In this case, however, the people of Israel were probably not without fault. In fact, I think it likely many shared in the misguided nationalism of their monarch.[53]

A plague of unspecified but supernatural origin swept through the land. The toll was terrible: "seventy thousand of the people from Dan to Beersheba died" (2 Sam 24:15).[54] However, as the angel of the LORD "stretched out his hand to destroy Jerusalem the LORD relented concerning the disaster" (24:16)—an eleventh-hour stay of execution.[55] When David saw (in a vision?) the destroying angel, he confessed his sin and claimed responsibility for the plague: "I, the shepherd, have done wrong." He then cried out for the penalty to "fall on me and my family" (24:17). The shepherd of Israel was willing to give his life for his sheep—a singular attitude unparalleled in the royal succession.[56] In this case, however, the sheep too must bear the brunt of deserved punishment.

A brief digression is in order. Almost half a millennium later, the "terrible swift sword"[57] of Yahweh's anger was not stayed but unleashed against Jerusalem—when Nebuchadnezzar besieged and destroyed Jerusalem in 586 BC. Ezekiel the prophet, in a resettlement camp in Babylon (Iraq), prophesied this dreadful moment: "I will draw my sword from its sheath and cut off from you both the righteous and the wicked . . . Then all people will know that I the Lord have drawn my sword from its sheath; it will not return again" (Ezek 21:3–4).[58] This imagery returns in the Apocalypse of John. In this case, however, King Jesus wields his sharp sword against the

---

many non-party citizens.

53. "It must be such a punishment as the people must have a large share in, *for God's anger was kindled against Israel*, v. 1. Though it was David's sin that immediately opened the sluice, the sins of the people all contributed to the deluge." Henry, *Commentary*, 478.

54. The account reminds us of the tenth plague on the Egyptians, the death of the firstborn (Exod 11).

55. The reader may recall that in the days of Hezekiah, a similar, last minute reprieve spared Jerusalem from massacre at the hands of Sennacherib, king of Assyria. The angel of Yahweh was also the agent of deliverance by putting to death 185,000 Assyrian troops in one night (2 Kgs 19:35–36).

56. "This is one of the nobler actions of the covenant king, as he prioritizes the well-being of his subjects." Mackay, *1–2 Samuel*, 487.

57. From Julia War Howe's "Battle Hymn of the Republic" (1852).

58. The entire chapter of Ezek 21 should be read in order to grasp its graphic imagery. Ezekiel's contemporary, Jeremiah, also employed the imagery of Yahweh's sword to convey the fate of Jerusalem at the hands of Nebuchadnezzar (Jer 12:12; 19:7; 25:29; 47:6).

rebellious nations of the world under the leadership of the Beast (antichrist) and the Dragon (Satan). Their defeat ushers in the New Jerusalem in all its splendor. This too was glimpsed in visions vouchsafed to his prophets, most memorably in Isaiah: "In that day, the Lord will punish with his sword—his fierce, great and powerful sword—Leviathan the gliding serpent, Leviathan the coiling serpent; he will slay the monster of the sea" (Is 27:1).[59]

Pardon Points to the Temple

The location of the divine reprieve in David's day will thereafter play a prominent role in redemptive history. The angel of Yahweh hovered over the summit of Mount Moriah, the location of Araunah the Jebusite's threshing floor. But on that very day, the prophet Gad came to the king with a word from Yahweh. "Go up and build an altar to the LORD on the threshing floor of Araunah the Jebusite" (2 Sam 24:18).[60] David ascended the summit and, in a scene reminiscent of Abram's purchase of a burial site from Ephron the Hittite, he bought Arunah's threshing floor and oxen for fifty shekels.[61] "David built an altar to the Lord there and sacrificed burnt offerings and fellowship offerings. Then the Lord answered his prayer in behalf to the land, and the plague on Israel was stopped" (24:25).

This was a major milestone in the history of Israel. Why? Because on the site where the angel of death hovered, the Cherubim would hover above the footstool of Yahweh.[62] David was privileged to purchase the site and prepare the plans for Yahweh's House, the First Temple. The Chronicler goes into great detail concerning David's plans for the temple, which in turn, were passed on to his son, Solomon.[63] In addition, David gave directives concerning the ministry of the priests and Levites, and his psalms served

59. Leviathan is a mythological beast symbolically portraying Satan (cf. Gen 3:1). For background see Helyer, *Yesterday*, 40–44.

60. It is significant that Araunah the Jebusite not only lives in Jerusalem, he owns property there. In contrast to Saul, David did not ethnically cleanse Jerusalem of the Jebusites when he conquered the city. They continued to live there and some, like Arunah, may even have embraced the faith of Israel. See 2 Samuel 24:23.

61. Abram paid four-hundred shekels for the field and burial cave of Ephron the Hittite (Gen 23:16). It's hard to know whether the price Abram paid was exorbitant or whether the price paid by David was below market value. The amount of land involved and the valuation of the shekel makes a direct comparison problematic. About a thousand years separates the two episodes.

62. 1 Sam 4:4; 2 Sam 6:2; 1 Kgs 6:25–28; 2 Kgs 19:15; 1 Chr 28:2; 2 Chr 3:1–2; Pss 99:5; 132:7.

63. 1 Chr 28:1—29:9.

as the core of Israel's national hymnbook. I take up David's contribution to Israel's faith and worship in our concluding chapter.

Before leaving this episode, however, I want to probe further its theological significance. In David's willingness as the shepherd of Israel to lay down his life for his sheep, one hears echoes of another shepherd, a good shepherd who did "[lay] down his life for the sheep" (John 10:11). The reader recalls that the threshing floor of Araunah was the probable location of Abraham's near sacrifice of Isaac. At the critical moment when Abraham stretched out his hand to kill his beloved son Isaac, "the angel of the LORD called out to him from heaven, "Abraham, Abraham! . . . Do not lay a hand on the boy" (Gen 22:11–12). In David's vision, Yahweh said to the angel, "Enough! Withdraw your hand" (2 Sam 24:16). The echo is unmistakable. The angel of Yahweh was present at both events. There is more going on here than meets the eye.

Fast forward a millennium later. During an intense theological debate with the religious leaders of Jerusalem, Jesus intimated that he had been present at the near-sacrifice of Isaac. Indeed, he even claimed to pre-exist Abraham: "Before Abraham was born, I am!" (John 8:58). Not surprisingly, they picked up stones to stone him for blasphemy. Not long afterward, following another tense encounter, they again tried again to stone him "because [he], a mere man, claim[ed] to be God" (John 10:13). When Scripture is read as one grand, overarching narrative composed of many complementary narratives, one can't help noticing that this mysterious angel of Yahweh is sometimes identified as Yahweh himself in disguise.[64] In my view, the angel of Yahweh at Moriah was none other than the pre-incarnate Christ.

Let's take this one step further. Although Jesus did not die on the Temple Mount, he was executed a short distance away at Golgotha.[65] Prior to his death, in the Garden of Gethsemane, Jesus petitioned his heavenly Father: "Take this cup from me. Yet not I will, but what you will" (Mark 14:36). At three in the afternoon of the next day (traditional time for the evening sacrifice at the temple), as Jesus was dying on the cross, he cried out, "My God, my God, why have you forsaken me?" (Mark 15:34). This time God did not intervene. Instead, his wrath against sin was poured out on his beloved son

64. As already noted in the case of Jacob at Mahanaim (Gen 32:30). But see also the account of Manoah the father of Samson who equates the angel of Yahweh with God himself (Judg 13:21–22). In the story of the three visitors to Abram and Sarah, the narrative identifies one of the visitors as Yahweh (Gen 18).

65. It's only about five-hundred yards away. The place where Abraham was going to sacrifice Isaac is actually identified as "the region of Moriah" (Gen 22:2). Golgotha may well be considered part of that region. As it turns out, the traditional site of Golgotha, the Church of the Holy Sepulchre, is slightly higher in elevation than the Temple Mount.

who bore it in his body. "Yet it was the LORD's will to crush him and cause him to suffer, and though the LORD makes his life an offering for sin, he will see his offspring and prolong his days, and the will of the LORD will prosper in his hand" (Is 53:10).[66]

This is the best news ever: "For God so loved the world that he gave his one and only Son, that whoever believes in him shall not perish but have eternal life" (John 3:16). Isaac the beloved son was spared on Mount Moriah; the firstborn sons of the Hebrews in Egypt were spared from the tenth plague; Jerusalem was spared from a plague in David's day on Mount Moriah. Each were unique previews of the greatest story ever told when a Father *did not spare his beloved Son*: "He who did not spare his own Son, but gave him up for us all—how will he not also, along with him, graciously give us all things" (Rom 8:32).

The central mystery of Christianity is the incarnation.[67] The mysterious angel of the Lord who could take on the appearance of a man, actually became a man! The writer to the Hebrews spells it out in all its splendor: "We . . . see Jesus, who was made lower than the angels for a little while, now crowned with glory and honor because he suffered death, so that by the grace of God he might taste death for everyone . . . he too shared in their humanity . . . he had to be made like his brothers and sisters in every way" (Heb 2:9, 14, 17).[68] The Apostle Paul's chimes in with his magnificent confession in praise of Christ, "Who being in very nature God, did not consider equality with God something to be used to his own advantage; rather, he made himself nothing by taking the very nature of a servant, being made in human likeness. And being found in appearance as a human being, he humbled himself by becoming obedient to death—even death on a cross! (Phil 2:5–8). A Charles Wesley hymn captures the response of every believing heart:

> And can it be that I should gain
> an interest in the Saviour's blood?
> Died he for me, who caused his pain?
> For me, who him to death pursued?
> Amazing love! How can it be
> that thou, my God, shouldst die for me?
>
> 'Tis mystery all: the Immortal dies!
> Who can explore his strange design?

66. See Rom 5:6–11; 1 Pet 3:18; Col 1:22.

67. 1 Tim 3:16.

68. The entire section Heb 2:5–18 needs to be carefully read and pondered.

In vain the first-born seraph tries
to sound the depths of love divine.
'Tis mercy all! Let earth adore.

THE ADONIJAH AFFAIR

There is one more piece of unfinished business. David's successor must be determined. This, too, was not accomplished without serious jeopardy. Two brothers jostled for the crown. The loser lost his life.

Adonijah's Abortive Coup

Adonijah makes a bold preemptive move. In so doing, he has significant backing. Two towering figures, Joab, the celebrated commander in chief and Abiathar, one of the high priests, both of whom had been with David from the very beginning of his career, throw their support behind Adonijah. His bid for the throne looks promising.

Let's back up a moment and set the stage. Adonijah's attempt to seize power came as King David was nearing the end of his life and suffering from the infirmities of old age. One affliction was particularly distressing: his inability to keep warm "even when they put covers over him" (1 Kgs 1:1).[69] David's attendants came up with a solution. They sought out a beautiful young virgin to serve as a heating pad![70] Her name was Abishag, and she unwittingly played a role in the ensuing power struggle.

Adonijah is another Absalom. Taking a page out of Absalom's playbook, he launched a publicity blitz complete with an entourage of chariots and runners. He too was handsome and, most importantly, next in line for

---

69. I sympathize with David. At this point in my senior years, from November to May, my feet, nose, ears, and hands are regularly cold. I go about my house with heavy socks and heating pad for my feet and a sock cap because I refuse to turn up the thermostat higher than 72 degrees. Years ago, my wife and I spent several months in Jerusalem during the winter in rooms that did not have central heating. Believe me, it can be cold and damp in stone buildings. One soon discovers that several layers of clothing and a sock cap are required for any degree of comfort.

70. Actually, the precise capacity in which Abishag served the king is uncertain. If the object were to provide bodily heat, she was more like a nurse. This in fact is the interpretation of Josephus (*Ant.* 7.343 [XIV. 43]). It may be, however, that she served as a test of the king's virility and thus, in accordance with ancient near eastern culture, his capacity to govern. In any case, she entered David's chambers as either a concubine and member of his harem, or as a queen. More likely, she had the status of concubine.

the crown by birth order.[71] Fueling his ambition was the assumption that a majority of Israelites viewed him as the legitimate successor of his father. In his own words, "the kingdom was mine" (1 Kgs 2:15).

The narrator, however, inserts some disquieting information: David never criticized or disciplined him. Alas, another unruly son cast his eyes on the crown. We've already called attention to David's delinquency in this regard; his failure to discipline Amnon, Absalom, and Adonijah played a role in each of their tragic deaths. This is not to absolve them of their guilt and misbehavior and place it all on David. But David should have provided fatherly admonition and correction, regardless of past moral failures.

So, what should David have done in regard to the question of succession? He should have formally and publicly announced his successor. That would have prevented much of the sibling rivalry inevitably generated in a polygamous household.[72] Unfortunately, David has shriveled from the charismatic, forceful leader of his earlier days into an ailing old man who leaves to others the pressing matters of state—just the kind of environment that invites ambitious politicians like Adonijah to take matters into their own hands.

Adonijah doesn't have the audacity to stride into the royal palace and there proclaim himself king. Like Absalom, he left the city, had himself proclaimed king by his supporters, and then planned a triumphal return and splendid coronation ceremony. Unlike Absalom, however, he did not go to Hebron; instead he chose a nearby landmark just south of the royal city, "the Stone of Zoheleth near En Rogel"(1 Kgs 1:9).[73] Adonijah invited all his brothers, except Solomon, and all the officials of Judah, except Nathan the prophet. Conspicuously omitted from the guest list were Benaiah, captain of the guard, and the high priest Zakok. Like his elder brother Absalom, Adonijah overestimated his support and underestimated his opposition. Another "pride goes before destruction" story was about to play itself out.

71. 2 Sam 3:4.

72. In the seventh century BC, after Sennacherib King of Assyria was assassinated by his sons Adrammelek and Sharezer (2 Kgs 19:37), a power struggle broke out between Esarhaddon and his brothers. When he emerged victorious after a brutal six-month civil war, he executed the assassins. Later, while still living and in good health, Esarhaddon publicly proclaimed his successor the crown prince Ashurbanipal in order to prevent another power struggle. See Wiseman, *ANET*, 535–41.

73. Modern *Bir Ayyub* [Job's Well]. So, why did Adonijah choose En Rogel for his acclamation party? I wonder if the notion of entering the city from the south and ascending up its streets to the palace on the summit of Ophel ridge appealed to his sense of pageantry and showmanship? At any rate, "it was ideally located for Adonijah's purpose of presenting David with a *fait accompli*, counting on David's illness to render him incapable of overturning Adonijah's plans." Patterson and Austel, *1, 2 Kings*, 428.

David's Countermove

Nathan springs into action. He knows all too well what will happen if Adonijah is successful in his bid for the throne. None of Solomon's supporters (himself included) would escape banishment or death, least of all Solomon and probably his mother Bathsheba. Nathan must prepare for another dramatic and tense encounter with David. A lot of lives depend on his success. First, he coaches Bathsheba on what to say and then arranges to arrive during her plea to add his support.[74] This is Nathan's Hushai moment!

Bathsheba is the key player in turning the situation around. She must be granted an audience and alert the king to the deadly peril about to befall her and her son. Furthermore, she must remind him to keep his promise concerning Solomon. Not to be missed in this scene is the location where it unfolds: David is confined to his bed in his bedroom. In calling attention to this detail, the narrator very subtly alludes to the circumstances in which David's troubles first began: "One evening David got up from his bed" (2 Sam 11:2).[75] Ironically, Bathsheba now appears before the king in his bedroom to plead for her life and that of her son.

The case to be made was straightforward: David had sworn an oath in the name of Yahweh that Solomon would succeed him on the throne. Although this is the first time we read about David's promise and oath, there's no reason to doubt that he had previously given it. Yahweh promised David: "I will raise up your offspring to succeed you, who will come from your own body, and I will establish his kingdom" (2 Sam 7:12). After David's first child by Bathsheba died in infancy, she gave birth to Solomon, whom Yahweh loved and named Jedidiah ["loved by the Lord"].[76] Presumably it was then that David promised Bathsheba that Solomon would be his successor.

By preemptively proclaiming himself the new king, Adonijah had precipitated a national crisis. This unsanctioned move raised the all-important question: Will Adonijah be allowed to annul the king's promise to Solomon? Unspoken but understood was another: Will Adonijah be allowed to banish or, more likely, kill Bathsheba and her son Solomon?

Suddenly, as if stimulated by a massive shot of adrenaline, David snapped out of his lethargy and seized the reins of power. The old warrior began barking out orders like he did in former times:

First, Bathsheba was summoned to appear before him again and he reassured her that he would keep his promise. Then Zadok, Nathan, and

---

74. Recall the similar coaching Joab gave to the wise woman of Tekoa (2 Sam 14).

75. See Alter, *David Story*, 364.

76. 2 Sam 12:24–25.

Benaiah were ordered to anoint Solomon as the next king of Israel. They first mounted Solomon on the king's mule and escorted him down to the Gihon spring, in the Kidron Valley. Appropriately, the spring that provided King David access to the Jebusite city now provided a fitting venue to anoint a new king in Jerusalem, King Solomon. There Nathan the prophet and Zadok the high priest anointed him with oil. Then with trumpet blasts and loud acclamations he was publicly proclaimed king over all Israel. "Long live King Solomon!" (1 Kgs 1:34). Finally, in joyful procession, the royal retinue accompanied Solomon as he ascended to the palace where he was installed on the throne of David as "ruler over Israel and Judah" (1 Kgs 1:35).

Adonijah's party not only got crashed, it got crushed! The tumult of Solomon's acclamation ceremony, only about a half mile up the Wadi Kidron from En Rogel, was so loud "the ground shook" (1 Kgs 1:40). Joab, the commander in chief, was especially alarmed by the sound of the trumpet. He knew that meant one of two things: "either a call to arms or the proclamation of a king."[77] Given the circumstances, it could only be the latter. At that very moment, Jonathan, son of Abiathar, arrived. In a scene of high drama and dark humor, Adonijah warmly invited him in: "A worthy man like you must be bringing good news" (1:42).[78] Jonathan's reply was devastating: "Not at all!" (1:43). He quickly informed the group what had happened and just as quickly it was every man for himself. Adonijah made a beeline for the tent where the ark of the covenant was housed. He took hold of the horns of the altar and refused to budge. His action was the equivalent of seeking sanctuary. It was his only hope for survival.

Absalom and Adonijah were like two peas in a pod; both puffed up with pride. As the bitter consequence of pride, Absalom hung suspended by his hair at the mercy of Joab, and Adonijah clung to the horns of the altar at the mercy of Solomon. Adonijah was fortunate—Solomon showed mercy, albeit a provisional mercy. "If he shows himself to be worthy, not a hair of his head will fall to the ground; but if evil is found in him, he will die" (1:52). Note that Solomon addresses his remarks not directly to Adonijah but to his royal court. Adonijah was placed on probation and his status made a matter of public record. Adonijah, who just hours earlier envisioned himself residing in the king's house in a state of regal splendor, was now sent to his own house in a state of limbo—once again mirroring what happened to Absalom.

---

77. Alter, *David Story*, 371.

78. One recalls David's confidence that the two runners spotted approaching Mahanaim were bearers of good news (2 Sam 18:25–26). Ahimaaz, son of Zadok, was welcomed by David as "a good man . . . who comes with good news" (2 Sam 18:27).

David's Charge to Solomon

David's last days drew near. It was *Con te partirò* ["time to say goodbye"] and he shared his final words with his son and successor. His speech continues the Hebrew tradition of revered figures delivering their last words. The final speeches of Jacob,[79] Moses,[80] Joshua,[81] and Samuel[82] all assume programmatic importance in the unfolding of redemptive history. David's swan song falls into two parts:

1. Solomon's relationship with Yahweh

2. Solomon's relationship with three individuals

The first part is crucial. The vertical relationship with Yahweh always assumes highest priority. Reminiscent of Moses' final words to Joshua, David exhorts Solomon to be courageous and obedient. The specifics of that obedience are spelled out in the Law of Moses. Compliance with these two exhortations will assuredly result in blessing, both personal and national. If Solomon obeys Yahweh, all he does will prosper. If the people of Israel continue to obey Yahweh, the House of David will always have "a successor on the throne of Israel" (2 Kgs 2:4).

Then David charged Solomon to settle accounts with three individuals. For two of them it was a day of reckoning. For the third it was a day of recognition. The first person to be dealt with was the most difficult. Joab was a national hero and arguably the one person most responsible for the longevity of David's reign. Two reasons account for this unexpected sentence: Joab murdered Abner and Amasa in cold blood, both of them respected military leaders (but also rivals), and he got away with it. As David saw it, justice must be served and the Law of Moses demanded the death penalty. Though not explicitly stated, Joab burned his bridge to a royal pardon by disobeying direct orders and killing Absalom and then supporting Adonijah.

This unpleasantness was followed by a lovely gesture—recompense for faithful service. Because of Barzillai's generous support of David in his hour of need, all his sons were given an open invitation to dine at the royal table with Solomon. As mentioned earlier, Barzillai's son, Kimham, was also granted a royal bequest in Judah.

One more troublemaker must be dealt with. Shimei the Benjamite escaped death when he threw himself on the mercy of David down at the

79. Gen 49.
80. Deut 32–33.
81. Josh 24.
82. 1 Sam 12.

crossing of the Jordan. Now, as David lay dying peacefully, he instructed Solomon to make sure Shimei didn't die peacefully. The Benjamite fire-brand's actions and words were treasonous. Solomon must find a shrewd way to settle the score—and eliminate a potential troublemaker.

The narrator inserts a note that "Solomon sat on the throne of his fa-ther David, and his rule was firmly established" (1 Kgs 2:12). Seemingly, equilibrium had been achieved and the House of David could move on to bigger and better things. The reader, of course, is waiting in anticipation for the other sandal to drop. Right on cue, Adonijah dropped the other sandal.

Adonijah's Last Hurrah

Adonijah, like Absalom, couldn't abide living in limbo. So, he decided to risk all on one throw of the dice—what did he have to lose? As it turns out, his life! He decided to ask permission to marry Abishag, David's concubine. With brazen chutzpah, he requested Bathsheba to intercede with the king on his behalf. Really? Whatever in the world possessed him to make such a request? Was he woefully ignorant of dynastic politics?[83] Or was he hope-lessly in lust, like his brother Ammon, with this beautiful virgin? Or, throw-ing caution to the wind, was he playing his last card in a desperate gambit to seize the throne? It's impossible to say for sure, but I think Adonijah was still confident he had the backing of the military and many in the priesthood—he may even have been secretly encouraged by Joab and Abiathar to take this audacious step. Adonijah and his supporters reckoned that Solomon was still vulnerable. They reckoned dead wrong!

In any case, what is quite unexpected is Bathsheba's cooperation. How could she be so naïve? Or was her motherly compassion stirred by the crushing setback Adonijah had suffered and she wanted to cushion the blow by providing some consolation? She was, after all, familiar with loss and emotional pain.

Dynastic politics accords no room for sentiment. Solomon sees right through the ploy and immediately issues an executive order. "Adonijah shall be put to death today!" (1 Kgs 2:24). Benaiah, captain of the guard, wielded his "terrible swift sword" and the question of succession was settled once and for all. But not all old scores were settled—yet.[84]

83. Recall that when Abner was "strengthening his own position in the house of Saul" (2 Sam 3:6), he slept with Saul's concubine Rizpah. Ishbosheth immediately called him to account, but was afraid to take action. Likewise, Absalom's sleeping with David's concubines signaled a new regime.

84. "This was the first in a bloody trilogy of executions." Smith, *Books of History*, n.

Abiathar Banished to Anathoth

The first co-conspirator to pay the price was Abiathar the high priest. He was summarily summoned and sentenced. Abiathar, who survived Saul's pogrom at Nob, fled to David for safety, served him faithfully as priest and keeper of the ephod, participated in his coronation, and supported him throughout his reign, even during the dark days of Absalom's rebellion, finally stubbed his toe. He must have known about David's oath to Bathsheba concerning Solomon, but for whatever reasons, he supported Adonijah. Solomon doesn't mince words: "You deserve to die" (2:26). In contrast to Saul's maniacal acts of retribution, Solomon exercised restraint. Abiathar was dismissed and banished to his hometown of Anathoth.[85]

Justice Catches Up with Joab

Joab didn't need to read the tea leaves. He knew the jig was up. Like Adonijah, he fled to the horns of the altar and stoically took his stand beside the altar. Solomon ordered Benaiah to enter the sanctuary and kill him.

Pause and put yourself in Benaiah's sandals. This was a very difficult moment for him. He wasn't afraid of Joab; after all, Benaiah was a ferocious warrior whose exploits were legendary—including facing a lion in a pit on a snowy day and emerging victorious.[86] But killing Joab was an animal of a very different kind!

Benaiah had served alongside and under the command of Joab for some years. These two men shared a history that only fellow soldiers who have fought together can fully appreciate. Above all else, Joab was a celebrated war hero, a national icon. But now it all came down to this—a disgraceful death for a mighty defender of Israel. Intensifying his emotional turmoil over a thankless task, Benaiah didn't want to kill Joab in the sacred tent beside the holy altar—it didn't seem right. Speaking on behalf of the king, he ordered Joab to come out. Joab refused. "No, I will die here" (1 Kgs 2:30).

Benaiah delayed and reported Joab's refusal to Solomon. I think Benaiah held out hope that a last-minute deal could be brokered similar to the original one with Adonijah. But Solomon was adamant. "Do as he says. Strike him down and bury him" (2:31). Now Benaiah's loyalty and future

---

p. 1 Kgs 2:23–25.

85. Anathoth, located about three miles from Jerusalem, was the residence of a number of priestly families. For a striking parallel to the career of Jeremiah the prophet, see Helyer, *Life and Witness*, 2.

86. 2 Sam 23:20–23.

career were at stake. As distasteful as it was, he entered and dispatched Joab. "How the mighty have fallen!" (2 Sam 1:27).

Benaiah buried Joab "at his home out in the country" (1 Kgs 2:34). At long last, Joab's many sins had found him out and now there was a new commander in chief over all Israel, Benaiah ben Jehoiada.

Shimei Pays for His Wrongdoing

Shimei was summoned before Solomon. Without bothering to rehearse his shameful and treasonous behavior, Solomon placed him under virtual city arrest. Under no circumstances may he leave. Even crossing the Kidron Valley immediately east of Jerusalem constituted a violation of parole and would issue in an automatic death sentence.

In a revealing vignette, we learn what led to Shimei's day of reckoning. Three years later, two of his slaves ran off to seek sanctuary with Achish king of Gath. Shimei left Jerusalem, went down to Gath, and recovered his slaves. This suggests two things about Shimei: he was a harsh master and willing to risk all to protect his investments.

A geographic note clarifies the situation. Shimei's home in Bahurim was just a couple of miles to the east of Jerusalem, across the Kidron and on the other side of the Mount of Olives. But Shimei didn't need to cross the Kidron in order to go down to Gath because it lay on the west, down on the coastal plain. He successfully recovered his slaves, but he couldn't cover his tracks. His movements were detected and reported to the king.

Shimei probably tried to justify his violation of parole by appealing to a technicality—he hadn't crossed the Kidron. Solomon wasn't swayed by semantic quibbles. Shimei's trial was swift. Solomon read out the verdict: "You know in your heart all the wrong you did to my father David. Now the LORD will repay you for your wrongdoing" (2:44). His execution was just as swift. Benaiah's "terrible swift sword" dispatched the last of the recreants.

The Succession Narrative has run its course. The last line ties a bow around the story: "The kingdom was now established in Solomon's hands" (1 Kgs 2:46). Long live the king! He did. Like his father, he reigned forty years over all Israel.

DEATH NOTICE OF KING DAVID

I backtrack and conclude with David's obituary: "he rested with his ancestors" (2:10). Short and simple. No mention of a period of national mourning, no grand requiem recounting his many accomplishments, no building of a magnificent monument.[87] Just the bare facts. He was buried in the City of David and "reigned forty years over Israel—seven years in Hebron and thirty-three in Jerusalem" (2:11).[88] But what a story! It's time to pay tribute to his lasting legacy.

87. David's obituary is quite short in comparison to that of Jacob or Moses (Gen 49:33—50:14; Deut 34). Samuel's obituary, however, is abbreviated like David's (1 Sam 25:1).

88. The location of his burial was a departure from standard Israelite practice. Because of the ritual purity laws, corpses were buried in caves outside the city. Although it is still disputed, I think David's tomb has been discovered on the lower portion of the ancient city of David (i.e., the eastern hill). See Shanks, "King David's Tomb?" 64; and Kenyon, *Archaeology*, 333. Be that as it may, most scholars agree that the medieval and modern Orthodox Jewish tradition that David's tomb is on the western hill (modern Mount Zion) beneath the traditional Christian site of the Upper Room is mistaken. See Murphy-O'Connor, *Holy Land*, 115–18.

14

LEGACY OF DAVID

The man who was raised on high, the anointed by the God of Jacob, the sweet psalmist of Israel.

—2 SAMUEL 23:1 [ESV][1]

David King of Israel yet lives and endures.

—*ROSH HASHANAH* 25A

So, HOW DOES ONE do justice to a bigger-than-life character like David? The short answer is, not easily! But one must at least try because he was by any reckoning a superstar personality who left a lasting legacy that far transcended the Early Iron Age of Israel. Just one small measure of his greatness lies in the amount of OT text devoted to his life and reign—sixty-six chapters with his name appearing more than one-thousand times! No other figure so dominates Israel's history like David and all succeeding kings were

---

1. The NIV has "the hero of Israel's songs," but I prefer the translation in the ESV, similar to that of the REB, HCSB, KJV, NASB, and NLT. See also Clines, *Dictionary of Classical Hebrew*, V:704.

evaluated by the standard he set.[2] Furthermore, the prophets who followed anticipated a future Davidic king who would raise the bar to an entirely new level: "He will reign on David's throne and over his kingdom, establishing it and upholding it with justice and righteousness from that time on and forever" (Isa 9:7). So, however inadequate, here is my attempt to say something about why David's life and witness remains so important for God's people in all places and times, not least our own.

The Military and Political David

One of the great disappointments of David's career was Yahweh's denial of his request to build the temple because he had shed much blood. The narratives about David underscore a grim reality that he personally had to confront—the neighboring states did not take kindly to his ascension to power and, consequently, regional wars dominated much of his early career. David was amazingly successful on the battlefield; in fact, he never lost a military engagement in his entire career! Following his felling of Goliath, all his enemies fell beneath his feet. "People I did not know now serve me, foreigners cower before me; as soon as they hear of me, they obey me. They all lose heart; they come trembling from their strongholds" (2 Sam 22:44–45). David had a ready answer for his military mastery in his song of praise.

> The Lord thundered from heaven . . . He shot his arrows and scattered the enemy . . . He reached down from on high and took hold of me . . . He rescued me from my powerful enemy, from my foes, who were too strong for me . . . With your help I can advance against a troop; with my God I can scale a wall . . . He trains my hands for battle; my arms can bend a bow of bronze. You make your saving help my shield; your help has made me great . . . You armed me with strength for battle; you humbled my adversaries before me. You made my enemies turn their backs in flight, and I destroyed my foes . . . You have delivered me from the attacks of the peoples; you have preserved me as the head of nations . . . He gives his king great victories. (2 Sam 22:14–51)

No other explanation suffices to explain his spectacular success. He was Yahweh's chosen one raised up to accomplish Yahweh's purpose for his people Israel and ultimately for the entire world. At every point in the narrative, his divine destiny shines through. The result was breathtaking.

---

2. 1 Kgs 3:14; 9:4; 14:8; 15:3, 5, 11; 2 Kgs 14:3; 16:2; 18:3; 22:2.

A weak confederation of tribes was united under a charismatic king who then dominated the land bridge between Asia, Europe, and Africa. It was an unparalleled time in the history of Israel.

The resulting military and political dominance in the Levant led to a dramatic rise in the standard of living, international commerce and diplomacy, and the enhancement and flowering of Hebrew culture.[3] It was in many ways the beginning of a golden age, climaxed by the reign of David's heir and successor, Solomon. It was also a preview of another unparalleled golden age when a scion of the House of David will one day rule over the entire world.[4]

David possessed remarkable leadership ability. Men followed him, fought alongside him, and fell in battle for him. The narrator of Second Samuel records a list of some of the outstanding warriors who were instrumental in bringing about the Israelite empire.[5] Some of these men rivalled the exploits of Greek heroes like Achilles, Ajax, Hector, and Odysseus.[6] David's great Hall of Heroes showcased "the Thirty." Standing at the apex of these celebrated champions were three extraordinary military men whose achievements elevated them to the top of the class. Reading and pondering the exploits of Josheb-Basshebeth, Eleazar ben Dodai, and Shammah ben Agee, one marvels at their courage and skill as fighters. They were nothing if not ferocious! Not surprisingly, these mighty men accomplished their daring deeds in combat with Philistine warriors, among the most feared and respected soldiers in the Levant.

A subgroup within the Thirty consists of three soldiers who earned the equivalent of the Medal of Honor. They did so by exhibiting bravery above and beyond the call of duty. During a campaign in which the Philistines invaded the Valley of Rephaim and even occupied Bethlehem, David expressed a wistful longing "for a drink of water from the well near the gate of Bethlehem!" (2 Sam 23:15). Three men immediately volunteered and, like genies in a bottle, basically said, "Your wish is our command." Off they went, risking life and limb to break through the Philistine lines, draw water from the well, and deliver it to David. When they offered it to him, he refused to

3. An early version of the Pentateuch, Joshua, Judges, many of the Psalms, and some of the wise sayings of the sages, now included in the book of Proverbs, may have been written during this period of classical Hebrew language and literature.

4. See Isa 2:1–5; 9:6–7; 11:1–9; 32:1–3.

5. 2 Sam 23:8–39.

6. The events of the *Illiad* are not far removed in time from those of the books of Judges and 1–2 Samuel. Cyrus Gordon called attention to the many biblical parallels and attributed them to common roots in the east Mediterranean world. See Gordon, *Common Background*.

drink it; instead, he poured it out before Yahweh as a drink offering. "Far be it from me, LORD, to do this! . . . Is it not the blood of men who went at the risk of their lives?" (2 Sam 23:12). With men who would go to such extraordinary lengths in the service of their sovereign, it's no wonder neighboring states could not prevail against "all the king's men." David had that special something that both attracted valiant men into his service and motivated them to render, if required, "the final measure of devotion."[7]

As extraordinary as the achievements of the Three were, two other warriors outshone them and were appointed senior officers. The first, Abishai, was David's nephew. Raised to the rank of chief of the Three because of his amazing exploits in battle, he was "held in greater honor than the Three" (23:19). Credited with killing three-hundred men with his spear, Abishai typically commanded one of the two wings (or divisions) of David's army, his brother Joab commanding the other.

Then there was Benaiah ben Jehoiada, who played a leading role in Solomon's ascent to the throne. Benaiah appears to have been a Philistine convert to Yahweh who loyally served King David throughout his military career. His exploits were the stuff of legends: Two of Moab's mightiest warriors, a lion trapped in a pit on a snowy day, and an Egyptian champion of gigantic proportions, proved no match for this fierce fighter. As famous as the Three, though not one of their number, he was held in higher honor than any of the Thirty and David appointed him captain of the guard—this man had David's back![8]

A few general comments are required about the Thirty whose names probably graced a special hall in David's cedar paneled palace. Because their names were written down in Scripture, their celebrated role in Israelite history has been preserved for all generations. As the writer of Hebrews puts it, "[they] became powerful in battle and routed foreign armies" (Heb 11:34).

Significant for his absence from the Thirty is the man who played such a crucial role in David's rise to power and career as king over all Israel. Even though Joab is mentioned three times in the list of names,[9] and despite a distinguished career as commander in chief, he was never inducted into the Military Hall of Fame. A bold and innovative general with extraordinary military instincts, he was also a ruthless practitioner of realpolitik and never let kinship or sentiment get in the way of political and personal power. As mentioned earlier, probably no human being was more responsible for David's success than Joab, but he lacked David's spiritual sensitivity

7. From Abraham Lincoln's eulogy for those who fell at the Battle of Gettysburg.

8. 2 Sam 23:20–23.

9. 2 Sam 23:18, 24, 37.

and allowed his political agenda to run roughshod over mercy and moral integrity. Joab never abased himself; that would have been demeaning and beneath his dignity. This proud warrior died as he had lived—by the sword.

When one surveys the list of names and their tribal affiliations and ethnicity, it's no surprise that Judahites predominate. Nonetheless, in addition to the Philistine Benaiah, there were other non-Hebrews—such as Uriah the Hittite, Igal ben Nathan from Zobah (Aram/Syria), Zelek the Ammonite, and Ithmah the Moabite—who attained to this select company of thirty-seven.[10]

The last name in the list, Uriah the Hittite, evokes sadness because it reminds us of David's monumental moral failure. How tragic that a convert to Yahweh should suffer such a disgraceful death arranged by the one he loyally served. We wish the story could have ended on a better note than that. But such is life lived east of Eden.

The Lyrical and Musical David

David's legacy reaches far beyond his military and political accomplishments; the Spirit of Yahweh bestowed upon him remarkable lyrical and musical abilities. As noted at the outset of David's career, he began his service in the House of Saul as a therapeutic musician employed to soothe the troubled monarch when an evil spirit came upon him. Skilled as an instrumentalist playing the harp and lyre—"Awake, harp and lyre! I will awaken the dawn" (Ps 57:7)—he also excelled as a vocalist, as witnessed at Abner's state funeral ("The king sang this lament for Abner" [2 Sam 3:33]). The impact on the listeners was intense: "all of Joab's men wept over him [Abner] again" (2 Sam 3:34).

Second Samuel incorporates four lyrical compositions of David. The first, discussed earlier, was a moving elegy, "The Lament of the Bow," composed after the death of Saul and Jonathan and commissioned as a national song of lament.[11] The second, as just mentioned above, was a lament for Abner. The third was a lengthy song of praise that parallels almost verbatim Psalm 18 and celebrates Yahweh's deliverance of David from his enemies. The narrator apparently inserted it, with minor alterations, as a fitting tribute to David's remarkable achievements, all attributed to Yahweh the rock,

---

10. Ithmah the Moabite is included in the parallel list in 1 Chr 11:46. The "Thirty" was apparently augmented by several others whose names simply couldn't be excluded because of their valor and achievements. The original title, however, continued to designate this group of military heroes.

11. 2 Sam 1:19–27.

fortress, deliverer, refuge, shield, horn, stronghold, and savior of David and his people Israel.[12] The fourth composition, a didactic poem, sums up David's unique vocation to be Yahweh's exalted and anointed man.[13]

David's lyrical legacy, of course, exists in a much more extensive corpus than these four pieces. Of the one-hundred fifty canonical Psalms in the Hebrew Bible, seventy-three are attributed to David in the superscriptions.[14] In addition, the NT identifies Psalms 2 and 95 as Davidic.[15] These devotional and liturgical masterpieces have lifted the spirits and consoled the brokenhearted of countless generations of believers (and even unbelievers). To take just one example, no piece of world literature is as universally recognized as the matchless twenty-third Psalm. The lasting legacy of the Book of Psalms can scarcely be overstated.[16]

The Book of Psalms, the national hymnbook of Israel, showcases David's lyrical genius and spiritual sensitivity. The Hebrew title of Psalms, *tĕhillîm*, means, "(songs of) praises." Though apt as a description for many of the compositions, one who has spent time reading and meditating on them knows that in fact a wide spectrum of human emotions come to expression, reflecting varied responses to various circumstances and occasions in the form of complaints, laments, petitions, sage observations about life, testimony, and even imprecations on enemies.[17]

Yahweh is the central character and his characteristics are celebrated. Reigning high and lifted up "enthroned between the cherubim" (Ps 99:1), he also "looks down and sees all humankind" (Ps 33:13) as a father who "has compassion on his children" (Ps 103:13). He thus hears "the desire of the afflicted . . . encourage[s] them, and . . . listen[s] to their cry, defending the fatherless and the oppressed" (Ps 10:16–18). David never tires of praising Yahweh for "all his benefits" (Ps 103:2), but pride of place is accorded his mercy and forgiveness, especially highlighted in Psalms 32 and 51. Psalm 103:11–12 gives voice to the testimony of all the redeemed of all ages: "For

12. 2 Sam 22:2–51.

13. 2 Sam 23:1–7.

14. Pss 3–9; 11–32; 34–41; 51–65; 68–70; 86; 101; 103; 108–10; 122; 124; 131; 138–45. The LXX lists 84 and the Vg. 86. Although some modern scholars dismiss the ascriptions as historically worthless, a good case can be marshalled for their essential reliability. See Thomson and Kidner, "Psalms," 985.

15. Ps 2 in Acts 4:25 and Ps 95 in Heb 4:7.

16. "It would be difficult to overestimate the significance, for Jew and Gentile, of the book of Psalms." Thomson and Kidner, "Psalms," 981.

17. "Nowhere else in the Scriptures is found such a varied collection of religious poetry, with 150 psalms in the Hebrew text and 151 psalms in the LXX." Brown, "Psalms, Book of," 661.

as high as the heavens are above the earth, so great is his love for those who fear him; as far as the east is from the west, so far has he removed our transgression from us" (Ps 103:11–12).

The Chronicler highlights David's major contribution to the worship of Israel in the First Temple,[18] a lasting legacy living on in the worship of the Second Temple and still re-echoing in the synagogue liturgy of modern times. Of course, the national hymnbook of Israel has also played a major role in Christian worship throughout the centuries. Even contemporary Christian worship songs reflect indebtedness to the book of Psalms. Besides providing the materials for the temple's construction, he organized the Levites, numbering thirty-eight-thousand men above the age of thirty, into four categories:[19]

Number	Task
24,000	Overseers of workmen
6,000	Officials and judges
4,000	Gate keepers
4,000	Musicians

Think of it—four-thousand specially trained musicians dedicated to the praises of Yahweh. These instruments included lyres, harps, cymbals, trumpets, horns, and probably also flutes and tambourines.[20] One can only imagine the glorious sounds that filled the temple courtyards during the morning and evening services, Sabbaths, New Moon, and the appointed festivals. If only those ancient psalms set to music and performed live before packed audiences could have been recorded for posterity—an echo of the angelic choirs and a foretaste of the New Jerusalem![21]

King David set apart three ministers of music to supervise and train 288 Levitical musicians, perhaps the size of the Levitical choir and orchestra when at full strength—there could scarcely have been room in the inner temple courtyard for four-thousand musicians and singers. The names of these musical maestros—Asaph, Heman, and Jeduthun—appear in several Psalm superscriptions, much like our modern hymnbooks that mention the authors of the lyrics and the musicians who set them to music.[22]

18. 1 Chr 23:2–5; 25:1–31.

19. According to 1 Chr 23:1–3, among David's last instructions was a directive that all Levitical males twenty and older were enlisted for temple service.

20. 1 Sam 10:5 and Isa 5:12 mention pipes.

21. See Rev 4:8–11.

22. For Asaph, see Pss 73–76; 78–83; for Jeduthan see Pss 39, 62, 77; for Heman see

The varied repertoire of the national hymnbook reflects a wide range of human emotions in response to the vicissitudes of life. Scholars have classified these compositions into various literary types as listed below in chart form:[23]

Type	Life-setting	Examples
Individual Song of Thanksgiving	Formal act of worship in order to give thanks for a specific blessing	29, 33, 104, 111, 113
Individual Lament	Most common in the Psalter; reflects personal crises of various kinds (illness, enemies, affliction)	6, 13, 31, 39
Communal Lament	Formal act of worship; some external crisis threatening the nation	12, 44, 74, 79
Royal Psalms	More of a functional than a literary designation; aspects of kingship	2, 20, 21, 45, 72, 110
Hymns	Regular worship or festivals in the temple	8, 29, 33, 104, 111, 113
Wisdom Psalms	Reflects the wisdom tradition; didactic in character	1, 37, 49, 73, 119
Songs of Trust	Expressions of confidence in Yahweh's care and guidance of the faithful	23–28

From these various types I select a few excerpts from those attributed to David.

Psalm Type	Passage/s
Individual Psalm of Thanksgiving	"Sing joyfully to the LORD . . . it is fitting for the upright to praise him" (Ps 33:1); "Praise the LORD, my soul" (Ps 104:1).

Ps 88. Interestingly, Heman was a grandson of the prophet Samuel (1 Chr 6:33). Ethan in Ps 89 may be a variant name for Jeduthan. The sons of Korah are credited with Pss 84–85, 87–88.

23. Adapted from Helyer, *Yesterday*, 393.

Individual Lament	"My soul is in deep anguish. How long, LORD, how long?" (Ps 6:3); "How long LORD? Will you forget me forever? How long will you hide your face from me?" (Ps 13:1).
Communal Lament	"Help LORD, for no one is faithful anymore . . . You, LORD, will keep the needy safe and will protect us forever from the wicked" (Ps 12:1, 7).
Royal Psalm	"He said to me, 'You are my son, today I have become your father. Ask me, and I will make the nations your inheritance, the ends of the earth your possession'" (Ps 2:7–8).
Hymn	"LORD, our Lord, how majestic is your name in all the earth!" (Ps 8:1).
Wisdom Psalm	"Take delight in the LORD and he will give you the desires of your heart. Commit your way to the LORD; trust in him and he will do this: He will make your righteous reward shine like the dawn, your vindication like the noonday sun" (Ps 37:4–6).
Song of Trust	"The LORD is my shepherd, I lack nothing . . . Surely goodness and love will follow me all the days of my life, and I will dwell in the house of the LORD forever" (Ps 23:1, 6).

A helpful exercise in this regard is to thumb through a modern hymnal and note its contents, organization, and categories of sacred songs.[24] These are useful analogies to what we observe in Psalms. Indeed, the Christian hymnal is a direct descendant of the liturgical traditions of ancient Israel. If the church was born with a canon in its hands, it was also born with hymns on its lips—and those songs bear the unmistakable impress of a Hebraic legacy.[25]

In these devotional and liturgical masterpieces, we hear the voice of the "sweet singer of Israel," a voice revealing a soul sold out to Yahweh to a degree rarely matched among mortals. "I say to the LORD, 'You are my Lord; apart from you I have no good thing'" (Ps 16:2). "One thing I ask from the

24. I lament the widespread replacement of hymnals by contemporary lyrics projected onto a screen and performed (mostly) by praise bands. May there be a return to the rich heritage of Christian hymnody!

25. Helyer, *Yesterday*, 392.

LORD, this only do I seek: that I may dwell in the house of the LORD all the days of my life, to gaze on the beauty of the LORD and to seek him in his temple" (Ps 27:4). "I will extol the LORD at all times; his praise will always be on my lips" (Ps 34:1). A Levitical lyricist captures David's desire for Yahweh in these memorable lines: "As the deer pants for streams of water, so my soul pants for you, my God.[26] My soul thirsts for God, for the living God. When can I go and meet with God?" (Ps 42:1–2).

David's prayers and praises spring from his heart and so should ours. Reading Psalms reminds us that any time is prime time for prayer. As the Apostle Paul aptly puts it "rejoice always, pray continually, giving thanks in all circumstances; for this is God's will for you in Christ Jesus" (1 Thess 5:16–17). And speaking of Christ Jesus, the Gospel of Luke especially emphasizes Jesus as a man of prayer, in fact, his disciples were so impressed by his prayer life they famously requested that he teach them to pray (Luke 11:1). He bequeathed to all his followers a model prayer, traditionally called the Lord's Prayer but better described as the Disciples' Prayer (Matt 6:9–13).

When reading the Gospels, one realizes just how important the Psalms were for Jesus both devotionally and theologically. Passages and prayers from the Psalter were often on the Master's lips, whether in theological debate, public preaching, or private devotion. Especially significant is the fact that as he suffered on the cross, the passion narratives record him fulfilling passages from the psalms[27] and reciting passages from a psalm of lament[28] and a wisdom psalm.[29] If King David described himself as "a man of prayer" (Ps 109:4), how much more was the greater Son of David who often "spent the night praying to God" (Luke 6:12).[30]

THE THEOLOGICAL DAVID

Linked with David's legacy of praise and prayer is his theological contribution. From the narratives recording his rise and reign and from his inspired songs, one has available a rich resource of theological reflection upon the matchless name of Yahweh: "LORD, our Lord, how majestic is your name in all the earth!" (Ps 8:9). Here are a few observations on Davidic theology.

---

26. Above the facade of the Church of All Nations (the traditional site of the Garden of Gethsemane), one sees two deer, recalling Ps 42.

27. Ps 22:18; cf. John 19:24.

28. Ps 22:1; cf. Matt 27:46.

29. Ps 31:5; cf. Luke 23:36.

30. See Mark 9:29; Matt 21:22; Luke 10:21; 22:45.

When David is first introduced into the story of Israel, we are immediately struck by his unwavering loyalty to and complete confidence in Yahweh, the living God who possesses all power, "the LORD Almighty" (1 Sam 17:45). Hearing Goliath defy the armies of the living God of Israel deeply offended him. Because this all-powerful God desired for "the whole world [to] know that there is a God in Israel" (1 Sam 17:46) and because "those who trust him wholly, find him wholly true,"[31] David exhibited extraordinary courage, confident Yahweh would enable him to defeat Goliath. This introductory episode contains the core convictions of Davidic theology—his subsequent career elaborates on these truths.

The Davidic psalms, in fact, amplify the narrative theology of the books of Samuel. For example, the David stories depict Yahweh as the all-powerful one who graciously comes to the aid of his anointed and chosen one. A quick perusal of Psalms 3, 5, 7, 8, 9, and 20–21, to mention but a few, celebrate this truth with exquisite librettos. Yahweh's choice of young David is accompanied by the all-important gift of Yahweh's Spirit. After Samuel anoints David with oil, the narrator adds this significant comment, "and from that day on the Spirit of the LORD came on David *in power*" (1 Sam 16:13). The narrator includes among David's last words this key affirmation: "The Spirit of the Lord spoke through me; his word is on my tongue" (2 Sam 23:2). The Davidic psalms testify to their ultimate source—poetic utterances bearing the imprint of the Holy Spirit.

Consider how David's description of Yahweh as the Almighty One re-echoes in Davidic hymnody. For example, two classic examples of a hymn—Psalm 8 and Psalm 19:1–6—celebrate Yahweh's power over and in all creation. The heavens and heavenly bodies are "the work of your fingers" (Ps 8:3), which "declare the glory of God . . . proclaim the work of his hands" and "display knowledge" (Ps 19:1–2). Human beings are "crowned with . . . glory and honor" (Ps 19:5) and placed over the rest of the created beings on the planet. Psalm 139, a wisdom psalm, portrays in matchless poetry the sovereign, omnipotent, and omniscient Yahweh who knows everything about human beings because he made and monitors them. Yahweh's knowledge is infinitely superior to that claimed in the TV commercial by Farmers Insurance: "We know a thing or two, because we've seen a thing or two." Yahweh knows everything, because he's foreseen everything! David breaks out in rapturous praise to Yahweh "because I am fearfully and wonderfully made . . . How precious to me are your thoughts, God! How vast is the sum of them" (Ps 139:14, 17).

---

31. From the hymn "Like a River Glorious" by Frances R. Havergal.

I pause briefly to point out how David's view of Yahweh as the creator and controller of all things stands in stark contrast to the theology of Israel's neighbors and reflects David's indebtedness of the revelation on Mount Sinai.[32] The polytheistic paganism of the ancient Near East with its pantheon of deities who exercise limited control over various aspects of the created order finds no counterpart in David's worldview. Yahweh, and Yahweh alone, exists, creates, governs, and judges his creation. Goliath's curses on David in the names of his so-called gods is nothing but empty prate, an exercise in futility, because there is only one true and living God: "For who is God besides the LORD? And who is the Rock except our God?" (Ps 18:31).

The Davidic Psalms frequently recall and reflect upon events in his life, passages that reveal his unwavering trust in Yahweh.[33] No matter what the occasion, he sensed Yahweh's hand upon his life and rested in this certainty: In the words of a well-known hymn, "Not a doubt nor a fear, / Not a sigh nor a tear, / Can abide while we trust and obey."[34] Here in chart form are a few examples to illustrate the point:

Saul's men surround David's room in an assassination attempt (1 Sam 19:11).	"I am in the midst of lions . . . They spread a net for my feet . . . " (Ps 59:4, 6); "My heart, O God, is steadfast . . . I will sing and make music . . . For great is your love, reaching to the heavens; your faithfulness reaches to the skies" (Ps 59:7, 10).
When David flees to Achish, he fears for his life and pretends to be insane (1 Sam 21:10–15).	"When I am afraid, I put my trust in you. In God, whose word I praise—In God I trust and am not afraid. What can mere mortals do to me?" (Ps 56:3–4); "This poor man called, and the LORD heard him; he saved him out of all his troubles" (Ps 34:6).
David escapes from Achish and seeks refuge in a cave in Adullam (1 Sam 22:1).	"I will take refuge in the shadow of your wings until the disaster has passed" (Ps 57:1).
Doeg the Edomite informs on Ahimelek the priest (1 Sam 22:9–10).	"Why do you boast of evil, you mighty hero? Why do you boast all day long, you who are a disgrace in the eyes of God?" (Ps 52:1); "Surely God will bring you down to everlasting ruin" (Ps 52:5).

---

32. See, e.g., Exod 20:4–5, 11.

33. My list is adapted from Mackay, *1–2 Samuel*, 28.

34. From the hymn "Trust and Obey," lyrics by John H. Sammis.

David was in danger of being trapped and besieged by Saul and his forces (1 Sam 23:7–13).	"Keep me free from the trap that is set for me, for you are my refuge. Into your hands I commit my spirit; redeem me, LORD, my faithful God" (Ps 31:4–5).
David stays in the wilderness strong-holds and in the hills of the Desert of Ziph. Day after day Saul searches for him, but God does not give David into his hands (1 Sam 23:14).	"I thirst for you, my whole being longs for you, in a dry and parched land where there is no water" (Ps 63:1); "Because you are my help, I sing in the shadow of your wings. I cling to you; your right hand upholds me. Those who seek my life will be destroyed; they will go down to the depths of the earth" (Ps 63:7–9).
The men of Ziph betray David's hideout (1 Sam 23:19).	"Arrogant foes are attacking me; ruth-less people seek my life—people with-out regard for God. Surely God is my help; the LORD is the one who sustains me" (Ps 54:3–4).
David brings the ark of the covenant to Jerusalem (1 Sam 6).	"I will allow no sleep to my eyes or slumber to my eyelids, till I find a place for the LORD, a dwelling for the Mighty One of Jacob" (Ps 132:4–5).
David successfully wages war against the surrounding nations (2 Sam 8:1–14).	"Give us aid against the enemy, for human help is worthless. With God we will gain the victory, and he will tram-ple down our enemies" (Ps 60:11–12).
David commits adultery with Bath-sheba and arranges the murder of her husband Uriah (2 Sam 11).	"When I kept silent, my bones wasted away through my groaning all day long . . . Then I acknowledged my sin to you and did not cover up my iniquity. I said, 'I will confess my transgression to the LORD.' And you forgave the guilt of my sin" (Ps 32:3, 5); "Have mercy on me, O God . . . according to your great compassion blot out my transgres-sions. Wash away all my iniquity and cleanse me from my sin. For I know my transgressions, and my sin is always before me. Against you, you only have I sinned and done what is evil in your sight . . . Create in me a pure heart, O God, and renew a steadfast spirit within me. My sacrifice, O God, is a broken spirit; a broken and contrite heart you, O God, will not despise" (Ps 51:1–4, 10, 17).

Absalom leads a revolt and forces David to flee (2 Sam 15–17).	"Many are saying of me, 'God will not deliver him.' But you, Lord, are a shield around me, my glory, the one who lifts my head high. I call out to the Lord, and he answers me from is holy mountain" (Ps 3:1–3); "I will not fear though tens of thousands assail me on every side" (Ps 3:1–3, 6).
Ahithophel, David's adviser, joins Absalom's revolt (2 Sam 15:31).	"Even my close friend, someone I trusted, one who shared my bread, has lifted up his heel against me. But may you have mercy on me, Lord; raise me up, that I may repay them" (Ps 41:9–10).

These selections reveal the spirit of a man after God's heart, a spiritual sensitivity almost totally lacking in Saul and rarely equaled in Israel's history. David knew Yahweh experientially and intimately. His personal communion with God was such that David knew it wouldn't end with death. In fact, he was persuaded that after passing through the "darkest valley," a metaphor depicting death (Ps 23:4), he would "dwell in the house of the Lord forever" where he would experience "joy in [his] presence, with eternal pleasures at [his] right hand" (Ps 16:6, 11).

Concluding Observations: David and His Greater Son

Psalm 132 puts a bow on the life and witness of David. This "orphan" psalm, occurring in the songs of ascent section between two psalms attributed to David, is classified as a royal psalm on the basis of its content. It may be from David's own hand but more likely by a contemporary such as Asaph or Jeduthun. At any rate, the Psalm captures three outstanding facts about David that I leave with the reader.

First, David moved the ark of the covenant from Kiriath Jearim to Jerusalem and thereby transformed Jerusalem into the religious and spiritual center of the nation.[35] Verses 6–9 probably refer to this important moment. There Solomon built a magnificent temple and focal point of spiritual devotion. The site of the First and Second Temples still serves as a magnet for Jewish and Christian pilgrims from literally all over the world, partially fulfilling Isaiah's grand vision:

35. For Mount Zion and Jerusalem as metaphors and symbols see Helyer, *Mountaintop Theology*, 133–37.

> In the last days the mountain of the LORD's temple will be estab-
> lished as the highest of the mountains; it will be exalted above
> the hills, and all nations will stream to it. Many peoples will
> come and say, "Come, let us go up to the mountain of the LORD,
> to the house of the God of Jacob." (Isa 2:2–3)

Transposed into a higher key, Jerusalem the City of David becomes
the Holy City, the heavenly city of all the redeemed: "But you have come
to Mount Zion, to the city of the living God, the heavenly Jerusalem" (Heb
12:22), "the Jerusalem that is above" (Gal 4:25). The redeemed wait with
eager anticipation for the fulfillment of the Apostle John's vision: "I saw
the Holy City, the new Jerusalem, coming down out of heaven from God,
prepared as a bride beautifully dressed for her husband. And I heard a loud
voice from the throne saying, "Look! God's dwelling place is now among
the people, and he will dwell with them. They will be his people, and God
himself will be with them and be their God" (Rev 21:2–3).

Secondly, Psalm 132 centers on the Davidic covenant in which Yahweh
promises David that one of his descendants will sit on his throne. Solomon
fulfilled that pledge. But Yahweh also promised that if David's descendants
would keep the Sinai covenant, they too would "sit on [David's] throne forever and ever" (Ps 132:12). Alas, the condition was not met and the house of
David ceased when the last Davidic king, Zechariah, was exiled to Babylon.
Nonetheless, Yahweh promised:

> For the LORD has chosen Zion, he has desired it for his dwelling,
> saying, "This is my resting place for ever and ever; here I will sit
> enthroned, for I have desired it . . . Here I will make a horn grow
> for David and set up a lamp for my anointed one. I will clothe
> his enemies with shame, but his head will be adorned with a
> resplendent crown." (132:13–17)

The NT explicitly proclaims that the horned and anointed one is none other
than the Lord Jesus Christ, the Son of David.[36] In the eighth century BC, the
peerless prophet Isaiah had already prophesied the good news:

> For to us a child is born, to us a son is given, and the government
> will be on his shoulders. And he will be called Wonderful Coun-
> selor, Mighty God, Everlasting Father, Prince of Peace. Of the
> increase of his government and peace there will be no end. He
> will reign on David's throne and over his kingdom, establishing
> and upholding it with justice and righteousness from that time

36. Among others see Acts 2:22–36; 3:17–26; 4:25–30; 13:22–41; 15:15–18; Rom
1:1–6.

on and forever. The zeal of the LORD Almighty will accomplish
this. (Isa 9:6–7)

The third feature of Psalm 132 that stands out in bold relief is David's
steadfast love [*hesed*] for Yahweh. He began his career defending Yahweh's
honor; he continued his career in Jerusalem as the king over all Israel by
making it his top priority to uphold Yahweh's honor. To achieve this end,
he denied himself physical comfort and rest in order to ensure that Yahweh
would be honored and worshiped at the very center of his kingdom.[37] Here
is the true measure of the man. His ambition to rule was subordinated to his
ambition to exalt Yahweh. And herein lies the open secret to spiritual power
and a paradigm for leadership in all places and times.

Saul and his daughter Michal failed to get it. David himself stumbled
badly. His son Solomon started well but faltered. Solomon's successors and
the kings of Israel for the most part failed miserably, elevating political power and personal pleasure above prostration before the true King of Israel.
The good news is that David's greater Son did not falter or fail. When offered
a choice of unlimited power and splendor if he would worship and serve the
devil, he opted to "worship the Lord . . . and serve him only" (Matt 4:10).

Finally, I conclude with a word of explanation to the reader. This book
has fourteen chapters. That's deliberate. I wanted to present David's life in
fourteen chapters because it seemed fitting to do so. My reasoning is based
on a Jewish technique of interpretation called *gematria*.[38] In *gematria*, the
letters of a word are assigned a numerical value according to their order in
the alphabet. Thus, the first letter in the Hebrew alphabet is *aleph* [A] and
is assigned the value of one and so on through the alphabet of twenty-two
letters.

Matthew's Gospel, considered the most self-consciously Jewish Gospel, employs *gematria* in its genealogy of Christ. A distinctive feature of
Matthew's genealogy is its division into three sections: Abraham to David,
David to Jeconiah, and Jeconiah to Jesus the Messiah. Each segment is said
to be fourteen generations.[39] What is not obvious to the English reader is the
fact that David's name, in Hebrew, when assigned numerical value based on
the letters, equals fourteen. The breakdown is as follows: D=4, V=6, D=4
for a total of fourteen.[40] So, Matthew artificially arranged the genealogy into

37. Ps 132:2–5.

38. See Helyer, "*Gematria.*"

39. A close reading of the OT genealogies shows that there were in fact more than
forty-two generations from Abraham to Jesus.

40. The original Hebrew texts consisted only of the consonants. Readers just knew
how to vocalize the words. Vowels were indicated later in the Masoretic text (the

a fourteen-generation scheme whereby David son of Jesse is placed at the mid-point of the genealogy. Matthew's intention is to demonstrate that Jesus fulfills both the Abrahamic and Davidic covenants and that, as King David's direct descendant, Jesus of Nazareth is the true King of Israel.[41] Matthew's Jewish Christian readers would have recognized and appreciated the subtle use of *gematria* to make an important theological point.

A major christological focus in Matthew is the Davidic sonship of Jesus of Nazareth.[42] Jesus not only fulfills the Davidic Covenant; he transcends and elevates it to a level only possible if he is truly the unique Son of God. Sure enough, right at the center of Matthew's Gospel, at Caesarea Philippi, Peter makes his great confession: "You are the Messiah, the Son of the living God" (Matt 16:16). Jesus pronounces a blessing on Peter and attributes his confession to "my Father in heaven" who revealed it (16:17).

The Apostle Paul chimes in when writing to the Roman Church: "Paul, a servant of Christ Jesus . . . who as to his earthly life was a descendant of David, and who through the Spirit of Holiness was appointed the Son of God in power by his resurrection from the dead: Jesus Christ our Lord" (Rom 1:1, 3–4).

The Apostle John completes the trio of major NT witnesses: "The Word became flesh and made his dwelling among us" (John 1:14). "We have seen his glory, the glory of the one and only Son, who came from the Father, full of grace and truth" (John 1:14). "Everyone who believes that Jesus is the Messiah is born of God" (1 John 5:1). "See, the Lion of the tribe of Judah, the Root of David, has triumphed" (Rev 5:5).

In God's redemptive program, the life of David was a pivotal moment, and at several key moments within this moment, the "one who was raised on high and . . . anointed by the God of Jacob" (2 Sam 23:1) foreshadows his Greater Son. David the man after God's own heart was chosen, empowered, and protected to prepare the way for the eventual triumph of his great descendant the "King of Kings and Lord of Lords" (Rev 19:16). "Come, Lord Jesus" (Rev 22:20).

---

authorized text of the Hebrew Bible) with signs called vowel points. Modern Hebrew books and newspapers, however, are unvocalized (except for foreign words or cases where there could be ambiguity in pronunciation). Children simply learn how to vocalize the text. One can even do this in English. For example, Cn y rd ths?

41. See. Matt 27:37, 42.

42. Matt 1:20; 9:27; 12:23; 15:22; 20:31; 21:9, 15; 22:42–45.

BIBLIOGRAPHY

Aharoni, Yohanan. *The Archaeology of the Land of Israel*. Translated by A. F. Rainey. Philadelphia: Westminster John Knox, 1982.

Alter, Robert. *The David Story: A Translation with Commentary of 1 and 2 Samuel*. New York: Norton, 1999.

———. "Introduction to the Old Testament." In *The Literary Guide to the Bible*, edited by R. Alter and F. Kermode. Cambridge: Belknap, 1987.

Anderson, A. A. *2 Samuel*. Word Biblical Commentary 11. Nashville: Thomas Nelson, 1989.

Andrews, Stephen J., and Robert D. Bergen. *I & II Samuel*. Holman Old Testament Commentary 6. Nashville: B & H, 2009.

Arnold, Bill T. *1 & 2 Samuel*. NIV Application Commentary. Grand Rapids: Zondervan, 2003. Logos Library System Version 7.19.2019.

Baldwin, Joyce G. *1 and 2 Samuel*. Tyndale Old Testament Commentaries 8. Downers Grove, IL: InterVarsity, 1988.

Baly, Denis. *The Geography of the Bible*. Rev. ed. New York: Harper & Row, 1974.

Beitzel, Barry J. *The Moody Atlas of the Bible*. Chicago: Moody, 2009.

Ben-Dov, Meir. *Historical Atlas of Jerusalem*. New York: Bloomsbury Academic, 2002.

Ben-Yosef, Erez. "Archaeological Views." *Biblical Archaeology Review* 45:6 (Nov/Dec 2019) 54–55, 63.

Bergen, Robert D. *1, 2 Samuel*. Expository Commentary 3. Wheaton, IL: Crossway, 2019.

Biran, Abraham, and Joseph Naveh. "The Tel Dan Inscription: A New Fragment." *Israel Exploration Journal* 45 (1995) 1–18.

Blomberg, Craig. *Jesus and the Gospels: An Introduction and Survey*. 2nd ed. Nashville: B & H Academic, 2009.

Borschel-Dan, Amanda. "Colossal Ancient Structures Found at Gath May Explain Origin of Story of Goliath." *Times of Israel*, July 26, 2019. https://www.timesofisrael.com/colossal-ancient-structures-found-at-gath-may-explain-origin-of-story-of-goliath/.

Bright, John. *A History of Israel*. 4th ed. Louisville: Westminster John Knox. 2000.

Brown, William P. "Psalms, Book of." In *The New Interpreter's Dictionary of the Bible*, edited by Katharine Doob Sakenfeldm et al., 4:4661–68. Nashville: Abingdon, 2009.

Brueggemann, Walter. *David's Truth in Israel's Imagination and Memory*. 2nd ed. Minneapolis: Fortress, 2002.

————. *First and Second Samuel: Interpretation: A Bible Commentary for Teaching and Preaching.* Louisville: John Knox, 2012.

Bush, Frederick W. *Ruth, Esther.* Word Biblical Commentary 9. Dallas: Word, 1996.

Childs, Brevard S. *Biblical Theology: A Proposal.* Minneapolis: Fortress, 2002.

Clines, David J. A., ed. *The Dictionary of Classical Hebrew.* 8 vols. Sheffield: Sheffield Academic, 1993–2011.

Davies, Philip. *In Search of Ancient Israel.* London: T & T Clark, 1992.

Dempster, Stephen G. "Shobi." In *Anchor Bible Dictionary,* edited by David Noel Freedman, 5:1224–25. Yale: Yale University Press, 1992.

Dillard, Raymond. "David's Census: Perspective on 2 Samuel 24 and 1 Chronicles 21." In *Through Christ's Word: A Festschrift for Dr. Philip E. Hughes,* edited by W. R. Godfrey and J. L. Boyd, 94–107. Phillipsburg, NJ: Presbyterian & Reformed, 1985.

Edersheim, Alfred. *Bible History: Old Testament.* London: Religious Tract Society, 1887.

Fee, Gordon P., and Douglas Stuart. *How to Read the Bible for All Its Worth.* 3rd ed. Grand Rapids: Zondervan, 2003.

Finkelstein, Israel, and Alexander Fantalkin. "Khirbet Qeiyafa: An Unsensational Archaeological and Historical Interpretation." *Tel Aviv* 39 (2012) 38–63.

Finkelstein, Israel, and Neil Asher Silberman. *The Bible Unearthed: Archaeology's New Vision of Ancient Israel and the Origin of Its Sacred Texts.* New York: Touchstone, 2001.

France, R. T. *Matthew.* Tyndale New Testament Commentary 1. Downers Grove, IL: InterVarsity, 1985.

Fretz, Mark Ju, and Raphael I. Panitz. "Caleb." In *Anchor Bible Dictionary,* edited by David Noel Freedman, 1:809–11. Yale: Yale University Press, 1992.

Garfinkel, Yosef, and Hoo-Goo Kang. "The Relative and Absolute Chronology of Khirbet Qeiyafa: Very Late Iron Age I or Very Early Iron Age IIA?" *Israel Exploration Journal* 61 (2011) 171–83.

Garfinkel, Yosef, Saar Ganor, and Michael G. Hasel. *In the Footsteps of King David: Revelations from an Ancient Biblical City.* New York: Thames & Hudson, 2018.

Goetze, Albrecht. "Plague Prayer of Mursilis II." *Ancient Near Eastern Texts,* edited by James B. Prichard, 394–96. Princeton: Princeton University Press, 1969.

Goldingay, John. *1 and 2 Samuel for Everyone.* Louisville: Westminster John Knox, 2011.

Gordon, Cyrus. *Common Background of Greek and Hebrew Civilizations.* New York: Norton, 1965.

Gordon, Robert P. *I & II Samuel: A Commentary.* Grand Rapids: Zondervan, 1988.

Hasel, G. F. "Caleb." *International Standard Bible Enyclopedia,* edited by James Orr et al., 1:573–74. Rev. ed. Grand Rapids: Eerdmans, 1988.

Hays, Richard. *The Moral Vision of the New Testament: A Contemporary Introduction to New Testament Ethics.* New York: HarperCollins, 1996.

Helyer, Larry R. "Come What May, I Want to Run!" *Near East Archaeological Society Bulletin* 48 (2003) 1–12.

————. *Exploring Jewish Literature of the Second Temple Period: A Guide for New Testament Students.* Christian Classics Bible Studies. Downers Grove, IL: InterVarsity, 2002.

————. "Gematria." In *T & T Clark Encyclopedia of Second Temple Judaism,* Vol. I–II, edited by Loren T. Stuckenbruck and Daniel M. Gurtner, 284–85. London: T & T Clark, 2019.

———. *The Life and Witness of Jeremiah: A Prophet for Today*. Eugene, OR: Cascade, 2019.

———. *Mountaintop Theology: Panoramic Perspectives of Redemptive History*. Eugene, OR: Cascade, 2016.

———. "'Proclaim It Not in the Streets of Ashkelon' (2 Samuel 1:20)." *Near East Archaeological Society Bulletin* 54 (2009) 11–21.

———. *Yesterday, Today and Forever: The Continuing Relevance of the Old Testament*. 2d ed. Salem, WI: Sheffield, 2004.

Henry, Matthew. *Matthew Henry's Commentary on the Whole Bible: Complete and Unabridged in One Volume*. Peabody, MA: Hendrickson, 1994.

Hess, Richard. *Joshua: An Introduction and Commentary*. Tyndale Old Testament Commentaries 6. Downers Grove, IL: InterVarsity, 2008.

———. "Reading and Writing in Ancient Israel." *Bulletin for Biblical Research* 19 (2009) 1–9.

Hill, Jonathan. *What Has Christianity Ever Done for Us? How It Shaped the Modern World*. Downers Grove, IL: InterVarsity, 2005.

Hoffmeier, James. "The Aftermath of David's Triumph over Goliath." *Archaeology in the Biblical World* 1.1 (1991) 18–23.

Hoffmeier, James K., and Alan R. Millard, eds. *The Future of Biblical Archaeology: Reassessing Methodologies and Assumptions*. Grand Rapids: Eerdmans, 2004.

Howard, David M., Jr. "Amnon." *Anchor Bible Dictionary*, edited by David Noel Freedman, 1:196–97. Yale: Yale University Press, 1992.

James, Carolyn Custis. *The Gospel of Ruth*. Grand Rapids: Zondervan, 2008.

Jones, Preston. "Living with War: A Job-like Wondering Met with Silence." *Critique* 1 (2019) 2–4.

Kaiser, Walter C., Jr. *Hard Sayings of the Old Testament*. Downers Grove, IL: InterVarsity, 1996.

Kaiser, Walter, and Paul Wegner. *A History of Israel from the Bronze Age through the Jewish Wars*. Rev. ed. Nashville: B & H Academic, 2016.

Kalas, J. Ellesworth. *A Faith of Her Own: Women of the Old Testament*. Nashville: Abingdon, 2012.

Katz, Hayah, and Avraham Faust. "The Chronology of the Iron Age IIA in Judah in the Light of Tel 'Eton Tomb C3.'" *Bulletin of the American Schools of Oriental Research* 371 (2014) 103–27.

Keener, Craig S. *Christobiography: Memory, History, and the Reliability of the Gospels*. Grand Rapids: Eerdmans, 2019.

Kenyon, Kathleen. *Archaeology in the Holy Land*. 5th ed. Nashville: Nelson, 1985.

Kirsch, Jonathan. *King David: The Real Life of the Man Who Ruled Israel*. New York: Ballantine, 2001.

Kitchen, Kenneth A. "How We Know When Solomon Ruled." *Biblical Archaeology Review* 27:5 (Sept/Oct 2001) 32–37, 58.

Klein, Ralph W. *1 Samuel*. Word Biblical Commentary 10. Waco, TX: Word, 1983.

Kobayashi, Yoshitaka. "Methegh-Ammah." *Anchor Bible Dictionary*, edited by David Noel Freedman, 8:800. Yale: Yale University Press, 1992.

Lemche, N. P. "David's Rise." *Journal for the Study of the Old Testament* 10 (1978) 2–25.

Lucker, Lamonte M. "Ephrathah (person) and Ephrathah (place)." *Anchor Bible Dictionary*, edited by David Noel Freedman, 2:557–58. Yale: Yale University Press, 1992.

Luther, Martin. *Table Talk.* Lexington, KY: Beloved, 2014.

Mackay, John L. *1–2 Samuel.* Expository Commentary 3. Wheaton, IL: Crossway, 2019.

Madvig, Donald H. "Joshua." In *Expositor's Bible Commentary,* Vol. 3: *Deuteronomy, Joshua, Judges, Ruth, 1 & 2 Samuel,* edited by Frank E. Gaebelein, 239–374. Grand Rapids: Zondervan, 1992.

Mare, W. Harold. "Zion." *Anchor Bible Dictionary,* edited by David Noel Freedman, 6:1896–97. New York: Doubleday, 1992.

Matthewson, Steven D. "An Exegetical Study of Genesis 38." *BibSac* 146 (1990) 373–92.

Mazar, Eilat. "Did I Find David's Palace?" *Biblical Archaeology Review* 32:1 (2006) 16–27, 70.

———. *Preliminary Report on the City of David Excavations 2005 at the Visitors Center Area.* Jerusalem: Shalem, 2007.

McCarter, P. K., Jr. *II Samuel: A New Translation with Introduction, Notes, and Commentary.* Anchor Yale Bible 8. Garden City: Doubleday, 1980.

Merrill, E. H. *Kingdom of Priests: A History of Old Testament Israel.* Grand Rapids: Baker, 1987.

Monson, James M. *Geobasics in the Land of the Bible.* Rockford, IL: Biblical Backgrounds, 2008.

Monson, James M., with Steven P. Lancaster. *Regions on the Run: Introductory Map Studies in the Land of the Bible.* Rockford, IL: Biblical Backgrounds, 1998, 2006, 2009.

Murphy-O'Connor, Jerome. *The Holy Land: An Oxford Archaeological Guide from Earliest Times to 1700.* 5th ed. Oxford: Oxford University Press, 2008.

Oppenheim, A. Leo. "The Fight Against the Aramean Coalition." *Ancient Near Eastern Texts: Relating to the Old Testaments,* edited by James B. Pritchard, 276–79. Princeton: Princeton University Press, 1969.

Panitz-Cohen, Nava, and Naama Yahalom-Mack. "The Wise Woman of Abel Beth Maacah." *Biblical Archaeology Review* 45 (2019) 26–33.

Patterson, Richard D., and Herman J. Austel. 1 *Samuel–2 Kings.* Rev. ed. Grand Rapids: Zondervan, 2009.

Payne, D. F. *I and II Samuel.* Daily Study Bible. Philadelphia: Westminster, 1982.

Peterson, Eugene H. *First and Second Samuel.* Westminster Bible Companion. Louisville: Westminster John Knox. 1999.

———. *Leap Over a Wall: Earthy Spirituality for Everyday Christians.* New York: HarperOne, 1998.

Pinker, Steven. *The Better Angels of Our Nature: Why Violence Has Declined.* New York: Viking, 2011.

Provan, Iain, V. Philips Long, and Tremper Longman III. *A Biblical History of Israel.* 2nd ed. Louisville: Westminster John Knox, 2015.

Rasmussen, Carl G. *Zondervan NIV Atlas of the Bible.* Grand Rapids: Zondervan, 1989.

Rainey, Anson F., and R. Steven Notley. *The Sacred Bridge: Carta's Atlas of the Biblical World.* Jerusalem: Carta, 2006.

Razzall, Katie, and Yasminara Khan. "Male 'Honour' Cases Underreported." *BBC News,* April 11, 2017. https://www.bbc.com/news/uk-39485348.

Reich, Ronny. *Excavating the City of David: Where Jerusalem's History Began.* Jerusalem: Israel Exploration Society and Biblical Archaeological Society, 2011.

Romey, Kristin. "Ancient DNA May Reveal Origin of the Philistines." *National Geographic*, July 3, 2019. https://www.nationalgeographic.com/culture/2019/07/ancient-dna-reveal-philistine-origins/.

Schuster, Ruth. "Israeli Soldiers, Archaeologists Dig Up Watchtower from King Hezekiah's Time in Their Firing Zone." *Haaretz*, June 19, 2019. https://www.haaretz.com/archaeology/.premium.MAGAZINE-israeli-soldiers-dig-up-watchtower-from-king-hezekiah-s-time-in-their-firing-zone-1.7394256.

Shanks, Herschel. "Is This King David's Tomb?" *Biblical Archaeology Review* 21:1 (1995) 63–65, 67.

Sites, Kevin. "The Unforgiven." *Aeon Magazine*, April 9, 2014. https://aeon.co/essays/how-do-soldiers-live-with-their-feelings-of-guilt.

Smedes, Lewis B. *Sex for Christians: The Limits and Liberties of Sexual Living*. Rev. ed. Grand Rapids: Eerdmans, 1994

Smith, James E. *The Books of History*. Old Testament Survey Series. Joplin, MO: College Press, 1995.

Strong, Justin David. "From Pets to Physicians: Dogs in the Biblical World." *Biblical Archaeology Review* 45:3 (May/June 2019) 46–50.

Stuhlmacher, Peter. *How to Do Biblical Theology*. Princeton Theological Monograph Series 38. Eugene, OR: Wipf and Stock, 1995.

Thompson, John A. "Gibeon, Gibeonites." *Baker Encyclopedia of the Bible*, edited by Walter A. Elwell, 1:863–64. Grand Rapids: Baker, 1988.

Trible, Phyllis. "A Human Comedy." In *God and the Rhetoric of Sexuality*, by Phyllis Trible, 166–200. Philadelphia: Fortress, 1978.

Vannoy, J. Robert. "2 Samuel." *Today's New International Version Study Bible*, edited by Kenneth L. Barker et al., 462. Grand Rapids: Zondervan, 2006.

"Violence Against Women." *Human Rights Watch*. https://www.hrw.org/legacy/wr2k1/women/women2.html.

Weisfeld, I. H. *David the King*. New York: Bloch, 1983.

Wesley, John. *The Complete Sermons*. Scotts Valley, CA: CreateSpace, 2013.

"What Is the Historical Meaning of Chattel and Chattel Law?" Answers.com, June 23, 2010. https://www.answers.com/Q/What_is_the_historical_meaning_of_chattel_and_chattel_law.

Wright, Paul H. *Greatness, Grace, and Glory*. Jerusalem: Carta, 2008.

———. *Understanding Great People of the Bible: An Introduction Atlas of Biblical Biography*. Jerusalem: Carta, 2016.

Yamauchi, Edwin M. *The Stones and the Scriptures*. Downers Grove, IL: InterVarsity, 1973.

Yamauchi, Edwin M., and Donald J. Wiseman. *Archaeology and the Bible*. Grand Rapids: Zondervan, 1979.

Youngblood, Ronald F. *1 & 2 Samuel*. Expositor's Bible Commentary 3. Grand Rapids: Zondervan, 1992.